# Being a Priest Today

Christopher Cocksworth is Principal of Ridley Hall, Cambridge, having been Director of the Southern Theological Education and Training Scheme. He is the author of a number of books including *Evangelical Eucharistic Thought in the Church of England* (Cambridge University Press, 1993) and *Holy, Holy, Holy: Worshipping the Trinitarian God* (Darton, Longman & Todd, 1997). Christopher is married with five children.

Rosalind Brown is a residentiary canon at Durham Cathedral. Prior to this she taught on two ordination training schemes in Salisbury. She was ordained in the United States where she lived for several years and was a member of an Episcopal Religious Community. Rosalind is the author of several prize winning hymns, some of which are published in *Sing! New Words for Worship* (Sarum College Press, 2004), and of *Being a Deacon Today* (Canterbury Press, 2005).

# Being a Priest Today

Christopher Cocksworth
and Rosalind Brown

*Second Edition*

CANTERBURY
PRESS
Norwich

Text © Christopher Cocksworth and Rosalind Brown 2002, 2006

First published in 2002 by the Canterbury Press Norwich
(a publishing imprint of Hymns Ancient and Modern Limited,
a registered charity)
13–17 Long Lane, London
EC1A 9PN

Fourth impression 2004
Second Edition 2006
Second impression 2007

The authors assert their moral rights under the
Copyright, Design and Patents Act, 1988, to be identified as the
Authors of this Work

British Library Cataloguing in Publication data

A catalogue record for this book is available from the
British Library

ISBN 1-85311-729-3/978-1-85311-729-9

Typeset by Regent Typesetting, London
Printed and bound in Great Britain by
William Clowes, Beccles, Suffolk

# CONTENTS

# ACKNOWLEDGEMENTS

Material from *Common Worship: The Ordination of Priests, also called Presbyters*, copyright © The Archbishops' Council 2005, is reproduced by permission.

'Madam', by Micheal O'Siadhail is reproduced from *Our Double Time*, 1988, by permission of Bloodaxe Books, publishers.

'The Minister', 'The Belfry', 'The Bright Field', 'Waiting for It', 'In Church', by R. S. Thomas are reproduced by permission of J. M. Dent, publishers.

Unless otherwise indicated, the scripture quotations herein are from the New Revised Standard Version of the Bible, Anglicized edition, copyright © 1989, 1995 by the Division of Christian Education of the National Council of the Churches of Christ in the United States of America, and are used by permission. All rights reserved.

To all those whom we have helped
to prepare for ordained ministry at

The Southern Theological Education
and Training Scheme

Diocese of Salisbury Ordained Local Ministry Scheme

and

Ridley Hall, Cambridge

# Some Introductory Words

It just so happens that the day we are writing this introduction is the *Feast of Christ the King*, the last Sunday of the Church's year. This year, the Old Testament reading is from Jeremiah 23. It tells of God's judgement on the leaders of Israel, who had failed to serve God's people, and then speaks the promise of God:

> Then I myself will gather the remnant of my flock out of all the lands where I have driven them, and I will bring them back to their fold, and they shall be fruitful and multiply. I will raise up shepherds over them who will shepherd them. (Jeremiah 23:3–4)

The prophecy goes on to say that the way God will come to his people to lead them in his paths will be through the righteous one, the one who will reign over the people of God, embodying the presence and purposes of God among them.

This is a vision of the Church of Jesus Christ – a people gathered around the saving God, a people among whom God rules as the righteous one who gives himself for the life of the world. And it is a people among whom some are called to serve after the manner of this God, in the pattern of Jesus Christ, to care for God's people so that they become all that God longs for them to be – a community that bears fruit and multiplies.

The people of God are called to make music for the world. It is a music that sounds freedom in all the corners of the earth. It is the music of Jesus Christ – God's gift of life for the world. The pastors of God's people are called to help the Church enthral the world with the sound of Christ. Sometimes they are like the person who sweeps the floor making the place ready for the performance. Other times they are like the restorer, who skilfully repairs the instruments when they have been damaged. All of the time they are like the conductor whose overriding passion is to draw the best sound from each person, and to bring the sounds of each uniquely gifted person into an ordered whole, so that together, in time and in tune, the people of God can play the score of God's mercy, truth and goodness to a world battered by its own noise but starved of the sound of God.

And this will be the sort of music making where everybody plays, where there is scope for individuality and spontaneity within the rhythm of the whole. It will be an infectious and generative activity that will put a new song into the hearts of all who hear *and* place an instrument in their hands, inviting them to join in the music of the mystery and magnificence of God's love for the world.

This is a book about that sort of pastor. It a book for those who want to think more about the priestly ministry of leading and shaping, guiding and forming God's priestly people.

Over recent years there have been major changes in the ordained ministry. It was not long ago that those training for ordination were mainly young men destined to work in parishes as stipendiary clergy for the rest of their lives. Today things are very different. No longer are colleges filled exclusively with young men. Instead colleges, courses and schemes train men and women of all ages for a variety of priestly vocations in hospitals, prisons, schools, colleges, religious communities and the armed forces, as well as the familiar parishes, newer team ministries and pioneering situations. Large numbers of people have a vocation to self-supporting ministry, often as ministers in secular employment whose main focus of ministry is not the parish but the workplace. Ordained Local Ministers represent the understanding of stability of ministry in one place rather than deployability, life experience rather than youth is often the gift that they bring to their ministry. And so the list goes on. We have trained people from and for all these ways of ministry, and ourselves have backgrounds that are not limited to parish ministry. As we have tried to uncover the *roots* and *shape* and *fruit* of priestly ministry, we have found ourselves drawing heavily from the writings of previous generations, but we have in mind that the context today has changed from theirs and that new perspectives as well as tried and tested wisdom belong together.

When we were approached to write about *being a priest*, one of the first things we realized was how different we are from each other, and therefore how different our own living out of the priestly vocation has been. Our experiences of family life (with one of us single and the other married), education and work, church and vocation – not to mention gender – are all different. At the same time we share many things in common, not least that for some years we worked together in theological education on an ecumenical training scheme. As we say at the beginning of the first chapter, there is no one way of being a priest and we are ourselves living proof of this. Although we have written this book together, our distinctive voices come through at times and we have not hesitated to use some personal illustrations. Christopher is responsible for most of chapters 1–4 and 10, Rosalind for most of chapters 5–6 and 8–9, and we shared the writing of chapter 7. Since we are both ordained in the Anglican Church (one in England, the other in America), that is the context and focus of our writing, but we work in ecumenical situations and value deeply other church traditions. We quote from authors from many different traditions in the book and hope that it will have something to offer to God's people in the rich variety of church life, even if some of the details and language are noticeably Anglican.

We are grateful to those who have helped us: colleagues with whom we work and from whom we have learnt at STETS, Salisbury OLM Scheme and Ridley Hall (and especially Paul Weston for advice with Chapter 10), our other friends and our families for their generosity and support, Christine Smith and Anna Hardman of Canterbury Press for their encouragement and patience. Finally, our thanks must go to those we have helped to prepare for ordained ministry and who have done so much to inspire us. We are excited about the prospects for the Church by the quality of these people and to them we gladly dedicate this short book.

Christopher Cocksworth
Rosalind Brown

*The Feast of Christ the King*

# Preface to the Second Edition

Since we wrote this book the Church of England has continued to develop its understanding and expression of the ministry of all baptized people. There is a renewed emphasis on mission, and in the creative response that is necessary if the Church is to proclaim the gospel afresh in every generation. The Church of England has also approved a new Ordinal, only the third in the 450 years since the Reformation shaped the emerging fresh expressions of the Church in England. We have, therefore, taken the opportunity presented by these developments to add a further chapter to this book in which we consider some of the implications for those who are called to priestly ministry within the Church in the twenty-first century, as well as to update some sections of the original chapters.

We are greatly encouraged by the response to the book since its publication, and offer this second edition in the hope that it will continue to be of help and support to people called to be priests in God's Church.

Rosalind Brown
Christopher Cocksworth

*Feast of the Annunciation 2006*

# PART 1

# THE ROOT OF PRIESTLY LIFE

# I

## BEING CALLED

Go at the call of God,
the call to follow on,
to leave security behind
and go where Christ has gone.
Go in the name of God,
the name of Christ you bear;
take up the cross, its victim's love
with all the world to share.

Go in the love of God,
explore its depth and height.
Held fast by love that cares, that heals,
in love walk in the light.
Go in the strength of God,
in weakness prove God true.
The strength that dares to love and serve
God will pour out in you.

Go with the saints of God,
our common life upbuild,
that daily as we walk God's way
we may with love be filled.
O God, to you we come,
your love alone to know,
your name to own, your strength to prove,
and at your call to go.[1]

## Setting the scene

'There is no *one* way of being a priest'.[2] These words of Rowan
Williams are true. People are very different. Parishes and other
contexts for ministry are very different. Types of ministries are
very different. That is why this book is not primarily about
*ministry*. We are not trying to say to different people in different
contexts exercising different types of ministry *how* they should
minister. The matrix of possibilities for ministry is endless. They
depend on *who* you are (e.g. an extrovert or an introvert), *where*
you are (e.g. an urban or a rural environment, a parish or workplace context) and *what* other responsibilities you have in life
(e.g. a marriage, children, other employment). The permutations
are affected by any number of psychological, social, economic,
theological and cultural factors that renders futile any attempt to
offer a blueprint for ministry regardless of the particularities of
personality, place and position.

Nevertheless, as we have both sought to live out the ordained
life and as we have prepared men and women for stipendiary and
self-supporting ordained ministry in a range of different contexts, and as we have looked back over some of the 'pastoral
classics' written over the centuries – some of them at times of
massive cultural shifts comparable with our own day – we have
become convinced that that there are certain conditions, characteristics and consequences of an ordained life that stand in
common across the centuries, cultures and contexts.

We have chosen to use an organic model to express these. We
have thought in terms of a tree with its roots, shape and fruit.
There are certain *conditions* that determine the identity of the
priest, roots that go deep into the Church's life in God. There are
*characteristics* that define the life of the priest, features that give
it a recognizable shape. When the conditions are right and the
characteristics in place, there will be some *consequences*, some
outcomes of grace to the ministry of the priest, just as when all is
well with the roots and shape of a tree, good fruit is produced for
the good of all. The shape and fruit of the ordained life are the
subject of later chapters. We begin now with the roots. It is an

exploration that requires us to dig deeply into some historical and theological ground.

## Vocational identity

A lot of theological blood has been spilt over whether ordination is about what we do, a set of functions that activate our ordination, or about who we are, a way of being in the life of the Church that is indelibly marked upon us at ordination. More technically, is ordination *functional* or *ontological*? In John's Gospel Jesus cuts through these sorts of unnecessary distinctions with the help of his own organic analogy of the vine. He tells his disciples that they are his friends, friends who love each other. They are like the branches of a vine. They are connected to Christ as the vine and to each other as fellow branches. They have been chosen to be with Christ. Christian identity is fundamentally *relational*. It is a called identity, a vocational identity. This calling into Christ precedes what we do for Christ and even how we live for Christ, though at the same time it predetermines our doing and being as Christians.

Our calling into Christ is simultaneously a calling into Christ's messianic ministry, his service. Yet Jesus says that we are not slaves who are told what they have to do and who know that their obedience is required by their position in life. We are his friends, people who have been called to be with Christ and who, being with Christ, learn to love as he loves and to do as he does. Function is a modern mechanical concept, concerned with productivity. Ontology is a Greek philosophical concept, concerned with questions of being or existence. Both may betray a predilection for power – power that comes from effective control over sources and systems, or power that comes from a permanent, guaranteed existence in the scheme of things. But the only power that Jesus offers his disciples is the power of love. It is a love that we receive through being embedded into Christ and it is a love that we embody in the life of the Christian community. This dynamic, energetic, relational vitality is the sap of Christian life that propels us into Christian ministry as we live from the life of

Christ into which we have been called. All that we are in Christ
and all that we do for Christ arise from a vocation, a calling into
a certain sort of relation to him – a relationship of extraordinary
grace.

All this applies to our baptismal identity in Christ as we share
in his life and then begin to walk in his way. It also applies to the
particular identity of the ordained in a particular way. Christ has
called us to play our part in the life of the vine. We must now
consider what that part is.

## The priestly people of God

The first letter of Peter is a good guide for anyone wanting to
consider the place of the ordained in the life of the people of
God. The letter takes for granted the ministry of presbyters
(*presbuteroi* in Greek, often translated as 'elders' in English
versions of the Bible), but makes some of the strongest statements about the priestly identity of the whole people of God to
be found in the New Testament.

> Come to [Christ], a living stone, though rejected by mortals
> yet chosen and precious in God's sight, and like living stones,
> let yourselves be built into a spiritual house, to be a holy priest-
> hood, to offer spiritual sacrifices acceptable to God through
> Jesus Christ . . . you are a chosen race, a royal priesthood, a
> holy nation, God's own people, in order that you may pro-
> claim the mighty acts of him who called you out of darkness
> into his marvellous light. (1 Peter 2:4–5, 9)

We will come on to the ministry of those called to presbyteral
ministry in the life of the Church in the next section of this chapter, but it is worth noting at this stage that the definition of the
people of God as a priestly community, within which certain
members of that community are called to exercise different ministries, is not a New Testament invention. Indeed, 1 Peter is quoting a pastiche of Old Testament references which celebrate the
privilege of the covenant people to minister before Yahweh, the

God of Israel, and to proclaim his works to the nations. God's people have always been a 'royal priesthood' (Exodus 19:6) with certain people called from within the community to shape and to form its life so that it may witness to the world. Yet the priestly ministry of Christ adds a new dimension to the identity and activity of God's people in the new covenant. 1 Peter's architectural analogy of the building uses a similar structure to John's organic image of the vine. We are keyed into Christ and our lives and service operate from Christ's life and service. We are embedded into Christ and so we embody the characteristics of Christ.

Christ's life is lived before God and before the whole created order. Christ is the Son whose joy is to adore the Father. The tender scene of the boy Jesus absorbed in the life of the temple, saying to his parents 'Did you not know that I must be in my Father's house' (Luke 2:49) is a window into the eternal intimacy of God's Trinitarian life in which the Son, moved by the Spirit, serves the Father with irrepressible devotion. Christ is the eternal priest who lives with another for the praise of another.

Christ is also the mediator between God and the world. All things were made through him. He is God's communication with the world and the world's communication with God. He dwelt in the world, sharing our life (Hebrews 2:17), attracting people by his holiness, astounding them by his teaching and healing, amazing people with his humility, apprehending them even in his death and then astonishing people with his risen life. As Dietrich Bonhoeffer said, this was 'a man for others' – a human being who lived and died for the justification, reconciliation and sanctification of others. Christ is the eternal priest who lives with others for the blessing of others.

Dallas Willard is fond of saying that following Christ means doing the things that Jesus did and teaching the things that Jesus taught *in the manner that Jesus did and said them*.[3] It is a good summary of the calling of the Church. We are not just to announce the good news of God's coming rule and reign, we are to demonstrate the presence of God's kingdom breaking into our world and we are to do both in such a way as to express and embody the priestly mind and method of Christ. Robert

Moberly, in his seminal study of *Ministerial Priesthood*, described the Christlike orientation of the Church as an 'intense "for-other-ness"'. It is manifested both in the Church's self-giving to God and in its self-giving to the world.

> The Church is priestly because from her proceeds the aroma of perpetual offering towards God. The Church is priestly because her arms are spread out perpetually to succour and intercede for those who need the sacrifice of love . . . Then the Church is God's priest in the world and for the world, alike as presenting to God on the world's behalf that homage which the world has not learned to present for itself, and a spending and suffering for God in service to the world.[4]

Moberly goes on to explain that this 'for-other-ness' is not merely a strategy for coping with humanity's present problems and limitations. It is not a case of some being in need and some trying to meet that need. This way of living is actually the fulfilment of God's design for humanity. It is, in the language of David Ford, a life lived facing God and others.[5] Made in the image of God, we are created as relational beings whose full human identity can be only realized through open and respectful relationships *with* others. This *with-other-ness* and *for-other-ness* is the sort of life that Jesus lived – a life lived before the face of God and before the face of others, open to all the possibilities of genuine encounter that come when we allow ourselves to look into the eyes and to be seen by the eyes of another.

Being *with* others so that we may be *for* others involves more than giving ourselves to others. It also requires us to receive from others. Jesus' devotion to God is not only the expression in the conditions of human life of the Son's eternal glorification of the Father, it is also the mirror of the Father's glorification of the Son and of the Son's reception of all that the Father gives. Even Jesus' ministry was not one-way traffic. His creation of a 'community of the face'[6] speaks of Jesus' natural enjoyment of others. The affection of the woman who anointed Jesus' feet with her oil and tears and then wiped them with her hair is received by Jesus.

Jesus' words from the cross to the penitent thief, 'Today you will be with me in paradise', are the poignant words of a person anticipating the future in the permanent company of others.

This sort of life – a life that loves the other – is the sort of priestly life lived with the other for the other that the Church is called to live. We can only live this life in the power of the Spirit who enthuses us with the love of Christ and forms within us the other-orientated life of Christ, the truly ecstatic life, the life that finds its joy in the other. In this way we participate in the priesthood of Christ. As we see in 1 Peter, when we 'offer spiritual sacrifices acceptable to God' we are exercising our priesthood through Christ and when we 'proclaim the mighty acts of God', Christ is exercising his priesthood through us. It is not that Christ has done his work which somehow qualifies us to do our work. It is rather that Christ's perfect priestly sacrifice for sin has allowed us to enter into the holy place of his presence before the Father so that we may participate in his priestly prayer for and proclamation to the world. There is only one Christian priesthood, and that is the priesthood of Christ, the priest into whose ministry we are gathered through baptism and by faith, and in whose life human identity is perfected.

## The presbyter among the priestly people of God

The insistence of 1 Peter on the priestly character and ministry of God's people is well stated in the Porvoo Agreement between the Church of England and the Nordic Churches.

> All the baptised . . . are called to offer their being as 'a living sacrifice' and to intercede for the Church and the salvation of the world. This is the corporate priesthood of the whole people of God and the calling to ministry and service.[7]

However, as we said earlier, 1 Peter maintains, in a very natural, matter-of-fact sort of way – showing there was nothing contentious in what he was saying – a dual reference to both the priestly character of the people of God and the particular ministry of those appointed presbyters in the early Christian communities.

I exhort the elders (*presbuteroi*) among you to tend the flock that is in your charge (*kleros*), exercising the oversight (*episcopē*), not under compulsion but willingly, as God would have you do it. (1 Peter 5:1–2)

Other New Testament documents, especially the book of Acts, indicate that the appointment of elders was part of the missionary strategy of the early Church. After churches had been planted in different areas presbyters were appointed to tend and nurture their new life. This certainly seems to be the pattern in the new churches of the Iconium region in what is now southern Turkey established during Paul's first missionary journey (Acts 14:21–23) and in Crete later in Paul's ministry (Titus 1:5). Elsewhere we are told that there were presbyters in Ephesus in western Turkey (Acts 20) and, according to 1 Peter, in a large number of other churches in western Turkey and in the north of the country as well (1 Peter 1:1). Clearly the Church in Rome, from where 1 Peter was written, also had its presbyters. We can see from the more established church life towards the end of the first century reflected in the letters of Timothy and James that presbyters played a prominent part in church life (1 Timothy 4:14, 5:15; James 5:17) and it is very clear that in the earliest Christian community – the Jerusalem church – presbyters were very evident, particularly in the decision-making processes of the Church (Acts 15). Elders were a familiar part of synagogue life and it seems that their office was transferred in a natural sort of way to the new Christian communities.

All this amounts to very clear evidence for the existence of presbyters in the embryonic life of the Church. But what did they do? It is clear that they provided leadership within the churches and they probably did so in a collegial way because it is likely that each church had more than one presbyter. However, it is worth saying that the images and verbs used in the New Testament to describe the work of the presbyters are more subtle and nuanced than most of our contemporary talk of 'church leaders', and that most of the explicit references to 'leaders' occur in only one chapter of the book of Hebrews. Leadership was undoubtedly a key role of the elders in the early Christian communities but perhaps the example of the self-effacing leadership of Christ, the experience of the guidance of the Spirit and the dynamics of Christian existence in one mutually dependent body, made the churches careful about how they defined the form of leadership consistent with the new life of the gospel. It is a caution reflected in the ordination prayers of the Christian tradition.

For one of the best indications of the part played by presbyters in the life of the New Testament communities we need to turn to Paul's farewell address to the Ephesian elders in Acts 20. Paul had spent about three years in Ephesus. He had used it as a base from which to reach much of western Turkey. His time there had been extraordinarily eventful. He had found Apollos there and other followers of Jesus whose understanding and experience of the faith was seriously limited. His ministry among them led to a Pentecost-type outpouring of the Spirit that was the beginning of the sort of ministry summarized in Dallas Willard's catchphrase. Paul taught as Jesus taught about God's kingdom to Jews and Gentiles and he did as Jesus did. People were healed and delivered, and the powerful exponents and authorities of Ephesian pagan and Jewish religion were challenged and undermined. As we shall see in a moment, Paul seems to have handled himself with great personal integrity, devotion to the work of God and deep love for the new community of Christ emerging around him.

In Acts 20 Paul is travelling near Ephesus. He sends word to the Ephesian elders that he would like to meet with them again, convinced that this will be his last time ever to see them. In a moving and emotional address in which Paul's affection for them and for the whole Ephesian church is very clear, he implores them:

Keep watch over yourselves and over all the flock, of which the Holy Spirit has made you overseers (*episcopoi*), to shepherd the Church of God that he obtained with the blood of his own Son. (Acts 20:28)

These are words that were to keep reappearing in the ordination prayers of the churches, so it is worth spending some time with them. The predominant image is pastoral – pastoral, that is, in the sense of the shepherding that was familiar to first-century people and which fills the biblical use of any pastoral metaphor: a demanding life dedicated more to developing health than maintaining comfort, more used to keeping them on the move than finding spuriously safe places to hide, committed to building up the life of the whole flock so that it is strong, energetic and generative, able to grow in quality and quantity. Paul would not have seen any opposition between the pastoral and the missionary. The Church of his day was missionary. The effectiveness of its mission required presbyters who could preserve its missionary character as a body in continual motion towards God's purposes. Presbyteral ministry therefore clearly involved oversight. Paul even calls the presbyters 'overseers' – *episcopoi* in Greek, often translated as 'bishops'. By the middle of the second century the ministry of the *episcopoi* became distinguished from the ministry of the *presbuteroi* but at this stage they appear to be two ways of describing the same ministry. In fact, for some time after the second century their ministries were closely identifiable and certainly much of the work of a bishop up to at least the fourth century was very similar to work of many parish priests today. Teaching was a key element in the presbyter-bishop's oversight of the life of the people. With a 'firm grasp of the word' (Titus 1:9) they were to 'labour in preaching and teaching' (1 Timothy 5:17). They were to keep watch over, look after, oversee the life of Christ's people, working with other ministries to ensure that the Church in that place is deeply rooted in the word and life of Christ, so that the body can 'build itself up in love' (Ephesians 4:16).

Paul knew from his own experience that 'keeping watch' involved protecting the people from danger, even the danger that might erupt from within (Acts 20:19–20) and supporting the weak, especially the poverty stricken (Acts 20:35). He commends the presbyters to follow his example. The ease with which Paul encourages them to look to his example signals another theme that consistently reoccurs not only through the biblical witness but also in the liturgies of the churches and other repositories of the Church's wisdom about its ordained ministries. As well as his compassion for the weak and his commitment to the health of the Church, there are at least three other features of Paul's style of ministry that deserve attention. The first is simply that his ministry was genuinely *ministry* or, in Greek *diakonia*, meaning service: 'You yourselves know how I lived among you ... *serving* the Lord with all humility' (Acts 20:19). His ministry was rooted in an incarnational identification with the people and demonstrated itself through faithful evangelistic preaching and catechetical teaching in the most difficult and life-threatening of circumstances. All ministry is diaconal, earthed in a consistent, committed care of the Church after the manner of Jesus, the homeless rabbi who redefined leadership in terms of service, made the towel a symbol of authority and lived as the servant who gave his life as a ransom for many. So intrinsic was *diakonia* to the identity of the Church that its first ordination service was for seven people, 'full of the Holy Spirit and of wisdom' appointed to serve the Jerusalem church by taking a particular responsibility for the care of its widows (Acts 6:1–6). And from the fourth century it became increasingly normal for presbyters to be first ordained deacons, underlining that *service* remains the basis of all ministry.

The second feature of Paul's time in Ephesus that is worth noting follows as a natural consequence of his dedicated *diakonia*: his tears. Paul had ministered with tears (Acts 20:19, 31). It had been painful to build the Church in Ephesus, there were dimensions of its culture that were deeply unaccommodating to the gospel. And after all they had been through together it was a painful process for Paul and the elders to bid their farewells to each other (Acts 20:37), intensified by the uncertainty that faced them all. Again the example of Jesus was the backdrop to their ministry. His self-depiction as a servant of others was a conscious adoption of the suffering servant motif in the Isaianic prophecies. Jesus knew that to serve the people in the messianic ministry of God's new order carried with it the mantle of suffering. Servanthood and suffering were yoked together as surely as motherhood and the pain of labour in the birth of God's kingdom.

When the Polish priest, Maximillian Kolbe, confessed to a crime he had not committed to save another person from death in a Nazi concentration camp, he was stepping into the footprints of Jesus, the suffering servant, and joining the many martyrs of every century who have been ready to follow the logic of Christian *diakonia*.

Third, Paul shows a radical dependence on the Holy Spirit. We saw earlier how his time in Ephesus was marked by dramatic activity of the Spirit. Now, in his farewell to the elders, he describes himself as 'captive to the Spirit' (Acts 20:23), hints at his attentiveness to the voice of the Spirit guiding and leading him to new opportunities for ministry and reminds them it is the Holy Spirit who has made them overseers in the Church. I remember speaking to John Wimber, another extraordinary church planter, about the dynamic of the Church's ministry. Describing the way that throughout the book of Acts the Spirit guides, enables and orders the life of the Church, he said, 'we need an ecclesiology that recognizes the Spirit as the true administrator of the Church'. Sitting in St Paul's Cathedral some years later while attending a consecration of a bishop, I was reminded of our conversation and his challenge when I heard the Archbishop of Canterbury quote from Acts 20:28 in the ordination liturgy as he handed the new bishop his pastoral staff: 'Keep watch over the whole flock in which the Holy Spirit has appointed you shepherd'. At its best, Anglican ecclesiology is profoundly pneumatological, and its liturgy prays what it once agreed in dialogue with the Eastern Orthodox Churches, 'the Church is that Community which lives by continually invoking the Holy Spirit'.[8] Only ministry that is empowered by the Spirit can claim to be sharing in the ministry of Jesus the *Christos*, the anointed one.

The exhortation in 1 Peter 5 to the presbyters in other churches in Turkey is remarkably similar to Paul's advice to the Ephesian elders. They are instructed to 'tend the flock in their charge (*kleros*)', to exercise 'the oversight' and to be 'examples' to those in their care. The mention of the *kleros* is interesting. It is the word from which we derive our word *clergy,* which is generally but quite unhelpfully used to distinguish the ordained from the laity. Of course, the presbyters were as much a part of the *laos* as every other member of the body of Christ. *Laos* simply means 'people' and strictly refers to all God's people, whatever their particular ministry. The *kleros* of the presbyters is not a right of privilege but a rite of responsibility. Within the *laos,* the people of God, the presbyters are given a particular *kleros,* a charge or responsibility, literally a 'lot'. As Acts 20:28 reminds us, it is a charge of immense value, it is the care of 'the Church of God that he obtained with the blood of his own Son'. Presbyters are not a caste outside the *laos,* they are a category within the *laos.* They are members of the *laos* who are placed in a particular pastoral relation to other members of the *laos.* It is not a position that gives them any right to 'lord it over the people' (1 Peter 5:3), rather it places on them the pattern of the 'chief shepherd' (1 Peter 5:4) Christ's servanthood. The spirit of 1 Peter 5 and Acts 20 is well expressed in the bishop's words to those about to be ordained priest in the Anglican Ordinal (1550/1662):

> Have always therefore printed in your remembrance, how great a treasure is committed to your charge. For they are the sheep of Christ, which he bought with his death, and for whom he shed his blood. The Church and Congregation whom you must serve, is his Spouse, and his Body.[9]

We said at the beginning of the chapter that Christian identity is fundamentally relational. We concentrated on the believer's relation to Christ and on the calling to follow him in ministry. The place of the presbyters in the people of God helps us to see the interrelationality between all the members of the body and its different ministries. Presbyters are defined by their relationship to other members of the *laos.* Their calling by Christ and their appointment by the Holy Spirit into this ministry among the people is an ecclesial event. It happens as the Church recognizes its need and discerns the call of God upon these people. Their ministry is given to them and received from them by the Church. Within this overall context of calling, consent and collaboration, presbyters are related to other specific ministries in the life of the Church. In the New Testament communities they have a derivative relation to the apostles. This is not to say that every elder was appointed by an apostle, though some were. It is rather a case of the ministry of presbyters being part of the apostles' plan for preserving the integrity of the newly planted communities and for propagating their life. The future of the delicate shoots of new life depended on the dynamics of grace by which they were founded. The apostolic gospel holds within it the genetic information for the health and growth of the churches. The presbyters were to serve these generative capacities of the apostolic faith in the way gardeners work to ensure that what is sown is allowed to grow with its natural energies (Titus 1:9).

In some church communities there were deacons – Philip in Jerusalem, Phoebe in Rome and those referred to in the letter to Timothy probably in a number of churches in Turkey. Several other distinctive ministries can be observed in various New Testament communities, such as prophets and evangelists, and all sorts of other giftings such as healing and hospitality, compassionate care and generous giving, operated among the people in a common experience of life in Christ's body. Presbyters fitted into this network of ministry, each ministry finding its place in relation to the other. 'A fundamental principle of Christianity is that of social dependence,' said Charles Gore.[10] Each person, though uniquely gifted and equally privileged to stand and serve in God's presence, is dependent on the ministries of others, not only to give to God but to receive from God. The co-inherence of one ministry in another is a profound manifestation of the recovery of God's image in Christian existence. It is evidence of our participation in the Trinitarian life of God in which each divine person lives *in* and *through* the other, *for* the other in the ultimate pattern of priestly identity.

No doubt there were differences in structure of ministry from church to church in the New Testament period and it is quite possible that presbyters appeared on the church scene earlier in some places than in others. Probably there was some tension between the more spontaneous giftings and ministries of the Spirit discovered by Christians as they worshipped and witnessed together and their more formally designated office. We are not attempting a watertight historical case or trying to prove a pattern of ministry established in the early life of the Church that can just be lifted out of that time and transplanted into our time. The New Testament is far too interesting and complex for that sort of treatment, and the history of the Church is littered with too many failed attempts to do so. Certainly a brief survey like this needs to be nuanced and refined in all sorts of ways. But it does seem difficult to deny that the first century of the Church's life was generally familiar with the ministry of presbyters in its interconnected life. And they were most definitely part of the warp and weave of the second-century Church and beyond.

The relationship between presbyters and other members of the people of God is one of the most significant aspects of the ordination liturgies of the Church.[11] Our earliest example comes from the *Apostolic Tradition of Hippolytus*, an influential manual of church order probably originating from Rome in the third century. The ordination liturgy of the *Apostolic Tradition*, and other early sources show a carefully balanced *ecology* between presbyter and people. Ordinations are ecclesial events in which the interdependence between presbyter and people is expressed at a number of points, not least in the basic requirement that each presbyter is ordained to a particular Christian community. This is the origin of the 'title parish' to which Anglicans are ordained today. There is no such thing as an 'absolute ordination', a conferral of position in the Church abstracted from the realities of service within a local community of Christians.

The two critical moments in the early rites were the election of the presbyter and the equipping of the presbyter with the needful gifts for ministry through prayer and the laying on of hands. The election was not a modern democratic process but it was a formal recognition by the people that the candidate for ordination had been called by God and would be received by them. The fourth-century *Canons of Hippolytus* invite the people to declare

'we choose him' and in the *Apostolic Constitutions*, the people
were asked three times whether they believed that the person was
worthy to be ordained. *'Axios'*, 'He is worthy', would have been
their reply, though we know that when Demophilos, a follower
of Arius' teaching, was appointed bishop of Constantinople in
370 AD some of the people cried out *'Anaxios'*, 'He is not
worthy!' In Rome things were more restrained. A statement was
read to the people on the Wednesday and Thursday before the
ordinations and then by the pope at the ordination itself inviting
them to declare any objection to the ordinations – a sort of
publishing the banns of ordination – and if silence was kept the
ordination could go ahead.

Although it was the bishop who prayed the ordination prayer
and who, accompanied by other presbyters, laid hands on the
candidates, the action was seen very much as the work of the
Church. It was preceded by the prayers of the people in which
they called upon God to equip the candidate with the particular
gifts needed for this new ministry, and the bishop was seen to be
speaking on behalf of the Church when he prayed:

> God and Father of our Lord Jesus Christ, look upon this your
> servant, and impart the Spirit of grace and counsel of the
> presbyterate, that he may help and govern your people with a
> pure heart . . .[12]

These words from the *Apostolic Tradition* reappear in several
other ordination prayers through the centuries. Helping and
governing God's people with the grace and counsel of the Spirit
and with a pure heart is the calling of the presbyters. They are to
'shepherd the people blamelessly' (*Canons of Hippolytus*) and to
be their steward (*Sacramentary of Serapion*) as 'an instrument of
the Holy Spirit always having and bearing the cross of [God's]
only begotten Son' (*Testamentum Domini*). These various
images from a number of fourth-century ordination prayers and
the relationship they envisage between the presbyter and other
members of God's people are succinctly gathered together in the
*Apostolic Constitutions*:

O God . . . now look upon your holy Church and increase it, and multiply those who preside in it and give them strength that they may labour in word and deed for the building up of your people.[13]

Presbyters are to preside over the priestly people of God and to labour (as later eastern prayers put it) for 'the edification and perfecting of [the] saints'. Very much in the spirit of these ordination prayers, John Chrysostom, the brilliant fourth-century preacher and author of *On the Priesthood*, one of the pastoral treasures of the theological tradition, said that priests 'must consider one end only, the edification of the Church':

For the Church is Christ's own body . . . and [those] who are entrusted with the task of developing it into health and beauty should look round at every point, lest there be a spot or wrinkle, or any other blemish, marring its bloom and comeliness, and in short should make it worthy, so far as lies within human power, of the pure and blessed Head which it possesses.[14]

John likens the priest to a parent bringing life to birth or to a navigator of a ship guiding 'a ship to safety in the midst of a stormy sea' and makes much of the image in Matthew 24:25 of the 'faithful and wise slave, whom his master put in charge of his household' to protect and prosper them.[15] We will return to these and other images of presbyteral ministry in the next chapter.

The early ordination liturgies, and the accompanying voices of the fourth century, give some precision to the interdependence between presbyter and people that we see in the New Testament. The presbyter needs the people to be a presbyter. The people need a presbyter to be the people of God. The one, as Daniel Hardy puts it, interanimates the other. This is not to fall into a crudely functional notion of ordination, as though people are only ordained to the extent that they are performing presbyteral activities. Neither is it to imply a clericalized understanding of the Church in which the Church can only be present and active

when authenticated by the ordained. But it is to say that presbyters are ordained to serve the 'health and beauty' of the
Church and that the 'bloom and comeliness' of the Church
requires the sort of presiding ministry that presbyters are called
to exercise. The particular pastoral responsibility laid upon the
presbyter is to see that the Church grows into its natural form –
the priestly body of Christ, a community embodying and demon-
strating the *with-other-ness* and *for-other-ness* of God's life of
love.

We will think more about the presiding ministry of the
presbyters and their animation of the people of God in the next
chapter. At the close of this one, there are three further points
worth noting from the early ordination liturgies. The first is that
the ministry of presbyters is closely related to the ministry of
deacons and bishops. The early western ordination prayers are
the most explicit about the relationship between bishops and
presbyters, even to the point of unhelpfully calling presbyters a
'lesser order' and 'secondary preachers', but all the early liturgies
assume a closely connected ministry between the two orders. The
ministry of deacons is also assumed in the liturgies and two eastern ordination prayers refer to the complementary ministry of
prophets and teachers who also share in the building up of the
Church. Second, the prayers, especially the eastern ones, have a
strong emphasis on the work of the Spirit not only in the ordination service but throughout the ministry of the ordained. 'Ordain
. . . Lord, by the coming of your Holy Spirit', one prayer
implores; several others ask for 'the great gift of your Holy
Spirit'. The prayers recognize that the Spirit is not only the source
of the presbyter's gifts for ministry but is also the gift that will be
imparted through the presbyter's ministry. The Spirit is invoked
as the people gather around the bishop to ordain the presbyter in
the ordination liturgy so that the presbyter can invoke the Spirit
on the people in other liturgies of the Church:

> May [your servant] be worthy and meet to call down your
> Holy Spirit from heaven for the spiritual quickening of those
> who are born over again in the luminous font.[16]

In similar language John Chrysostom compared presbyters at the Eucharist to Elijah on Mount Carmel and concluded that they 'stand bringing down not fire, but the Holy Spirit . . . [to] kindle the souls of all, and make them appear brighter than silver refined by fire'.[17]

The third consistent feature of the ordination prayers, eastern and western, is the calling on the presbyter to live a holy life that will be an example to the Church. This is an expectation that we saw in 1 Peter 5 and Acts 20 and which is never far away from any mention of the designated ministries in the New Testament. The ordination prayers continue the theme, and the *Canons of Hippolytus* ask God to make the life of the presbyter 'higher than that of all his people, without dispute' and 'envied by reason of his virtue by everyone'. The bishop's charge in the contemporary Roman rite puts it more positively: 'Let the holiness of your lives be a delight to Christ's faithful, so that by word and example you may build up the house which is God's Church.' Later the bishop prays, in words almost identical to those found in our most ancient version of the Roman rite's ordination prayer dating from the eighth century, that God will 'renew within them the Spirit of holiness'.[18]

# Being for the Other

You laid aside your rightful reputation
And gave no heed to what the world might say;
Served as a slave and laid aside your garments
To wash the feet of those who walked your way.

You touched the leper, ate with those rejected,
Received the worship of a woman's tears:
You shed the pride that keeps us from the freedom
To love our neighbour, laying down our fears.

Help us to follow, Jesus, where you lead us,
To love, to serve, our own lives laying down;
To walk your way of humble, costly service,
A cross its end, a ring of thorns its crown.

Draw us to you and with your love transform us:
The love we've seen, the love we've touched and known;
Enlarge our hearts and with compassion fill us
To love, to serve, to follow you alone.[1]

## The priestly ministry of the presbyter

So far we have talked quite a lot about the *presbyters*. We are, of course, in very good company. Even John Henry Newman in the first of his famous Tracts, said, 'I am but one of yourselves – a presbyter'. But, you may well ask, when are we going to talk about *priests*? Well, it is no bad thing to remind ourselves that in its earliest centuries the Church was very reticent about describing individual Christians as priests. *Hierus*, the Greek word for priest, was reserved for Christ, the true priest of the Church, and for the Church itself which, as a body, shared in the priesthood of its head. The ministry of the priests, the *hiereis* of the Old Testament, had been fulfilled in Christ and was now being enacted corporately through the new covenant community. In the Roman Catholic Church, where Latin remains the official language, this care over language has often been preserved in its more technical statements, such as the Second Vatican Council's *Decree on the Ministry and Life of Presbyters* and the liturgy it inspired, 'The Ordination of *Presbyters*'. And yet we know that in the Roman and in several other traditions, Anglicanism included, presbyters are usually called priests and that this way of describing them goes back to at least the third century.

Some Christians find this embarrassing and prefer to speak about ministers, pastors, parsons or are more comfortable with more occupational descriptions like vicar, rector or chaplain. Others justify calling some ministers *priests* on linguistic grounds, making the point that when *sacred*, the old English word used for *hierus* in Greek and its Latin equivalent *sacerdos*, went out of use, *préost* (like the old French *prestre*) became the everyday word for *presbyter* and *sacerdos*. Hence, it is argued, our '*priest*', derived from '*préost*', means nothing more than the original Greek *presbuteros*. And there have certainly been many who, like Richard Hooker in the late sixteenth century, have believed that it was a mistake to continue with this apparent semantic confusion and that we should revert to the more ancient term of presbyter. For our part we do not think that it is so easy to dismiss the nomenclature as a semantic mistake precisely because the presbyter's ministry among the priestly people of God takes on certain priestly characteristics. Our task in the first part of the chapter is to explore those characteristics in order to see whether by a *graceful analogy*, as Ronald Knox put it in a famous university sermon, *presbyters* can be also called *priests*.

In the previous chapter we said that the presbyter is called to be an example to the people of God and to preside over its priestly life. This is an extraordinarily high calling. The people we serve, as the Anglican Ordinal impresses upon us, are 'a great treasure', they are Christ's spouse and body, a 'royal priesthood' appointed and anointed 'to proclaim the might acts of God' (1 Peter 2:9) before the world. We saw that the calling to be an example to Christ's priestly people is intricately entwined in scripture and the tradition of the Church. Timothy is told to 'set the believers an example in speech and conduct, in love, in faith, in purity' (1 Timothy 4:13). The ancient Armenian liturgy of the Eastern Church prays that the presbyter will live 'in righteousness and by . . . example, teaching those who believe . . . [and so] may truly shepherd the people'.[2] In the ordination prayer in the new Roman Catholic Ordinal the bishop prays, in words that are among the few lines singled out as the central and necessary validating element in the rite: 'may they be examples of right conduct'. The same emphasis is repeated in the Church of England at almost every available point. The Canons and the Ordinal require priests to be 'wholesome examples and patterns to the flock of Christ' and the 'capacity to offer an example of faith and discipleship' is one of the stated criteria for selection of those offering for the ordained ministry.

All of this, of course, can sound very insular and moralistic, as if the ordained are just to be rather rarefied objects of virtuous living that the small Christian minority in our culture would do well to imitate. Have we been called simply to be good for the good of the Church? Well, in one sense, yes we have – and being good is no easy thing, for 'only God is good' (Luke 18:19), and the Church is no small thing in the purposes of God. But the calling to be good has a particular quality (an indicative and active quality, as we shall see later) about it, and is a far more dynamic business than the immediate images conjured up by exhortations to exemplary behaviour. Being examples to Christ's people involves being an example *of* Christ's people. It is a calling to *indicate* the identity of the Church by embodying the characteristics of the Church. It is a calling to live out the way of being to which  the Church is called. The Church is called to be a holy priesthood. The presbyter is called to signify this priestly calling. In more sacramental language, the presbyter is a *sign* of the priestly life of the Church.

There was a fascinating and very important debate in the late nineteenth century about priesthood between J. B. Lightfoot, the Cambridge New Testament scholar and R. C. Moberly the Oxford professor of Pastoral Theology. It was a quintessentially Anglican exchange. They were passionate but polite, committed both to reformation principles and to the catholic inheritance, showing a detailed attention to scripture and to the application of scripture in the tradition of the Church. Although they differed about quite a lot, including the origin and role of bishops in the Church, they found themselves agreeing – in Lightfoot's words, quoted approvingly by Moberly – that:

> Hitherto [in the early centuries of the Church] the sacerdotal view of the Christian ministry has not been held apart from a distinct recognition of the sacerdotal functions of the whole Christian body. The minister is thus regarded as a priest, because he is the mouthpiece, the representative of the priestly race . . . So long as this important aspect is kept in view, so long as the priesthood of the ministry is regarded as springing from the priesthood of the whole body, the teaching of the Apostles has not been directly violated.[3]

Moberly went on to say that 'The ordained priests are priests only because it is the Church's prerogative to be priestly' and that they are always, in their 'own spiritual attitude and effort – to Godward for man, to manward for God – called to realize, and (as it were) to personify, the characteristic priestliness of the Church'.[4]

In the late twentieth century, very much in the style of Lightfoot and Moberly, the House of Bishops of the Church of England claimed that the priest is called to embody the four classic marks of the Church – oneness, holiness, catholicity and apostolicity.[5] There is richness in this idea that is worth pursuing. We are to be *one*, integrated, at peace with ourselves, body, mind and spirit, able to live authentically with ourselves and with

integrity with others, respecting difference but enjoying togeth-
erness. We are to be *holy*, icons of a new way of living, fully alive
in our humanity, gladly receiving all that our creaturely human
life offers and allowing it to be infused with faith, hope and love.
We are to be *catholic*, connected to the *holos*, the whole, faithfully living life with others. We are to be *apostolic*, people sent to
save, thrust out with the same generative energy that we see in
those who first gave birth to the Church. This is part of what it
means to be appointed to a representative ministry. The Church
is saying 'We want to be able to look at you and be reminded of
what we have been called to be. And remember, that as we place
you in this relation to us, so the world will look to you to read
us.' Presbyters, therefore, may be called *priests* because they *indicate* or signify the *priestly* identity of the people of God.

While very content with the representative calling of the presbyter, Lightfoot and Moberly were quite clear that this was not a
vicarial ministry in the sense of doing something in place of the
people of God. There was no question in their minds that we are
to be holy to exempt the Church from being holy. Our priestly
calling does not erase the priestly calling of the people of God. It
exemplifies it and, as we shall see, empowers the people of God to
realize their true identity as the priestly people of God. 'For-other-
ness' cannot do otherwise. Its inspiration is caught in Irenaeus'
catchphrase – ' the glory of God is a human person fully alive and
the life of humanity is to see God'. Priestly ministry longs for
human beings to live with the vibrancy and joy, trustfulness and
confidence, individuality and sociality for which God destined us
and which glorifies God because it demonstrates that God is the
creator whose purposes are for the good of the other.

Before we move on to look more closely at the *activating* calling of the priest, it is worth spending some more time consider-
ing the depth of the Church's calling. Ephesians 4, one of the
most inspiring chapters in the New Testament about the calling
of the Church, urges the people of God to come 'to maturity, to
the measure of the full stature of Christ' (4:13). The true calling
of the Church is to express and to enact the life of Christ in the
world. Christ's life is the life that is *one* with the Father and the

Spirit. Christ's is the life that is given to the world to bring all things into communion with God. Christ's life is the life that is *holy*, brought to birth by the Holy Spirit, the life that ministered in the Spirit and was offered to the Father through the Spirit and raised to life by the Spirit. Christ's is the life that is *catholic*, related to all God has made, embracing all the world in out-stretched arms on the cross. Christ's is the life that is *apostolic*, perpetually sent by the Father in the breath of the Spirit to bring God's purposes to completion. Some more words from Irenaeus catch something of the priestly heart of Christ: 'The Word of God, Jesus Christ our Lord: who for his immense love's sake was made that which we are, in order that he might perfect us to be what he is'.[6] The stature of the Church is nothing less than the stature of the life of Christ.

The priestly identity of the Church that presbyters are called to *indicate* and to *signify*, is nothing less than the priestly identity of Christ. Therefore, although 'priesthood in the presbyteral order'[7] arises from the priesthood of the whole people of God, its ulti-mate source is the person of Christ. Priests are to 'set the example of the Good Shepherd always before them as the pattern of their calling', declares the bishop in the Anglican rite. 'Know what you do, imitate what you celebrate and conform your life to the mys-tery of the Lord's cross', the bishop says to the newly ordained in the Roman Catholic rite as the bread and the chalice to be used in the Eucharist that follows their ordination are placed into their hands. It is good advice for those called to preside among the priestly people of God and to minister to God's people with a pure heart – 'imitate what you celebrate'. Let the pattern of Christ's living, dying and rising be yours.

John Chrysostom was quite clear on the personal qualities needed for this priestly life. John attempts to explain to his very dear friend Basil why he felt utterly unable to join him in being ordained. John and Basil were both monks. They knew that the Church wanted to ordain them but John was sure that he was not ready to serve the Church in this way, at least at this time. The problem was that he could not bring himself to tell Basil. Convinced that his hesitation would undermine Basil's sense of vocation, John pretends to go along with the plan to be ordained but when members of the local church come to collect them he makes himself very scarce, leaving Basil to be ordained alone. Basil is heartbroken at the deceit but vows never to force John to justify himself. Nevertheless, John is keen to try to show Basil both why he could not go through with it and why he was sure that it was right for Basil to be ordained. '*Do you know the power of love?*', he asks Basil. 'Yes I do,' responded Basil. He knew that love worked, even if he also knew that he had 'not performed the half of it'. John tells him that 'this choice virtue, the badge of the disciples of Christ, which is higher than the spiritual gifts, was, I saw, nobly implanted in your spirit and laden with much fruit'.[8] John then goes on to recount a recent story of Basil standing by a friend who had been wrongfully accused and so exposing himself to great personal risk. Basil cannot deny the incident and confesses to John, 'I know no other form of love than to be willing to sacrifice my own life when one of my friends who is in danger needs to be saved'. This is enough to prove John's case. After reminding him of Jesus' saying, that 'No one has greater love than this, to lay down one's life for one's friends' (John 15:13), he says to Basil, 'If no greater love than this can be found, you have already reached the height of it, and both by your deeds and your words you have stood on love's summit'.[9]

The power of love is the essence of Jesus' priesthood and the fundamental calling of the Church. The marks of people's readiness to serve Christ in the presbyteral ministry are the depth of their desire to see the Church realize its calling and the consistency of their commitment to help it to do so by the power of love: 'I, therefore, a prisoner of the Lord, beg you to lead a life worthy of the calling to which you have been called' (Ephesians 4:1). This desire and commitment for the forming of Christ's life in his people lies at the heart of the presbyteral ministry. In the Anglican rite, the bishop says on behalf of the people, 'We trust that . . . you are fully determined, by the grace of God, to . . . grow up into [Christ's] likeness, and sanctify those with whom you have to do'. This expresses well the dynamic of the presbyter's calling to be an example to the people of God. Presbyters are called to be holy as every Christian is called to be holy but the particular quality of their calling has a priestly dimension. They are called to be holy so that others may be holy. They are to be enabling examples, *activators* as well as *indicators* of the Church's true being and life. In sacramental language, they are not just *signs* of the priestly identity of the Church but *effectual signs* of its priestly life, catalysts as well as paradigms. They are to effect what they signify, means of grace which God uses to form his people into that which Christ has initiated them: one, holy, catholic and apostolic royal priesthood declaring in word and deed, in praise and prayer, the mighty acts of God before the world (1 Peter 2:9). Presbyters are called to be *animators* of the priestly people of God, tools in the hand of Christ by which he draws his people more fully into his life and fashions his image in them:

> See that you never cease your labour, your care and diligence, until you have done all that lieth in you, according to your bounden duty, to bring all such are or shall be committed to your charge, unto that agreement in the faith and knowledge of God, to that ripeness and perfectness of age in Christ, that there be no place left among you, either for error in religion, or for viciousness in life.[10]

By placing the ordained in this particular relationship to other members of the people of God – a relationship of pastoral responsibility for the priestly fulfilment of the people of God – the Church is, at the same time, placing the ordained in a particular vocational relationship to Christ. This is not to deny Lightfoot's principle that 'the priesthood of the ministry springs from the priesthood of the whole body'. It is simply to say that one way the priesthood of the whole body acknowledges its dependence upon the discipling and training of Christ is by appointing some of its members to watch over the Church with the eyes of Christ and to see that it grows into what it is called to be. The vocation of presbyters is to 'to serve Christ the Teacher, Priest, and Shepherd in his ministry which is to make his own body, the Church, grow into the people of God, a holy temple'.[11]

*The concentrated priestly ministry of the presbyter*

The priestly ministry of presbyters finds its most intensive form in those focused moments when they are entrusted, as Lightfoot put it, with 'the performance of certain sacerdotal functions belonging properly to the whole congregation'.[12] Martin Luther, the great sixteenth-century reformer and passionate advocate of the priesthood of all believers, used to talk of the 'common priesthood' of all the faithful appointing the 'called priesthood' of the ordained to act in its name. This notion of the ordained priest being – as the catholic Anglicans, Charles Gore and Robert Moberly contended – organs of the priestly people, through whom the body operates at particular times and in particular ways, seems to run across the traditions. Richard Baxter, a leading Puritan of the seventeenth century and author of the pastoral classic *The Reformed Pastor*, told the clergy who gathered at his regular conferences that:

> Another part of our work is to guide our people, and be as their mouth in the public prayers of the Church, and the public praises of God: as also to bless them in the name of the Lord. This sacerdotal part of the work is not the least. A great part of God's service was wont in all ages to the Church to consist in public praises and eucharistical acts in Holy Communion.[13]

The Church agrees that for some purposes it will shape itself like an hour glass. It determines, for example, that in certain of its liturgical actions it will concentrate its priestly prerogative to mediate the forgiveness of God on to one person, who speaks this word of forgiveness so that the people can be freed to minister reconciliation in their relationships with each other and through their life in the world.

The danger, of course, with this image is that it could imply that the local congregation is the repository of the priesthood of the whole. In fact, the local church is a local manifestation of the one Church and part of the priest's role as a sign of the catholicity of the Church is to represent the priesthood of the whole Church. This is one reason why priests are ordained by bishops whose ministry of oversight over various congregations connects them with each other. Hence, the blessing a priest pronounces over a congregation is not part of a collusive circle of self-congratulation. Its authority is not derived from this particular congregation, even though the ministry of a priest in any one place requires a delicate ecology of care and consent between priest and people. The blessing is the voice of Christ spoken through the whole Church to the expression of the Church in this place. It is Christ, through one part of his body, speaking words of peace and strength to another.

This focused form of the 'priesthood of the presbyteral order' is keenly felt in one's ministry beyond the life of the immediate congregation. Although funerals, marriages and certainly baptisms are very much actions of the Church that properly involve more ministries than the priest's, it is possible as a priest to find the priestly calling of the Church to commend the departed to God, bring the joining of the betrothed to each other before God and welcome a child into the family of God concentrated in your words and gestures, your presence and person. This is even more likely in the sort of quasi-sacramental action which we are called upon to perform because in some way we are identified with, or even as, the Church – house-blessings, naming ceremonies, prayers – in that quaint liturgical expression – on 'various occasions', ranging from the death of a pet to the opening of a sports stadium. They are occasions which, rather than decreasing as the influence of the Church in the nation declines, seem to be increasing as our contemporary culture becomes more open to the spiritual realm and looks for people accomplished in its arts.

For many of us, this interface with the world in which we are seen as the public face of the Church forms the stuff of much everyday ministry. We find ourselves to be a person who can be trusted with intimate secrets in the street, painful memories on an occasional visit, deep-seated resentment of God outside the school gates, profound religious experiences as we sit opposite the stranger on a train journey. With very little warning windows are opened into people's otherwise quite closed lives, and the ministry of Christ in the Church is given a rare invitation to help and to heal.

Being a school governor, meeting other carers to discuss common problems, joining a local pressure group to campaign for a doctor's surgery in a forgotten part of town, place us in situations where we are expected to speak for the Church, declare its mind and bring its hope. This sort of interaction with the warp and weave of human society is the substance of most work-based ministries, whether in formally constituted chaplaincies, with their designated position in an institution, or the background ministries of self-supporting priests whose workplaces become their confessionals as colleagues discover that one of their number may just provide a new angle on an old problem.

Whether our theology has prepared us for it or not, it does not take long to dawn on us after our ordination that we are often seen as walking sacraments through whom the presence of Christ can be touched. Like the hem of his cloak we are evidence that he is passing by. Sometimes, as Jesus warned those who followed him, we evoke hugely antagonistic reactions well out of proportion with the failings of our own personalities or social skills. Often these simply have to be suffered. Occasionally they become opportunities for deeply creative ministry.

Our calling to build up the life of the Church is not an excuse to distance ourselves from the life of the world. In fact, it should propel us into the world so that we can model the priestly attention to the world which is the calling of all Christians as they serve the Christ who gave himself up for all. Neither can the concentrated form of the presbyter's priestly ministry be detached from the ministry of the priestly people through whom it is given. The priest's ministry is not to obliterate the presence of other Christians in any place but to make the Church obvious wherever it is. The priest is called to support and to nurture Christians wherever they may be found, helping them in whatever way is appropriate to actualize their priestly calling to be with and for others, living in the ways of God's kingdom and practising the presence of God in their places of work and leisure.

*Love for the Church as the mark of the priestly ministry of
the presbyter*

The calling to preside over the people of God, seeking to preserve, prosper and perfect their life in Christ, carries with it a
particular priestly attitude to the Church. Richard Baxter called
it 'a public spirit' and claimed that 'No [one] is fit to be a minister of Christ that is not of a public spirit as to the Church and
delighteth not in its beauty and longeth not for its felicity', and so
is ready to 'rejoice in its welfare and be willing to spend and
be spent for its sake'.[14] We see something very similar in John
Chrysostom who said that 'Priests must be sober and clear-
sighted and possess a thousand eyes in every direction, for they
live, not for themselves alone, but for a great multitude'.[15]
Ordained life is impossible without the deep love for the health
of the Church that Chrysostom, Baxter and many others spoke
of and lived by, despite the blows that the Church had dealt them
in different ways. This love for the Church lies at the heart of
many of the images that have been used to describe the ministry
of the priest over the ages.

There is an extraordinarily rich variety of images of priestly
ministry in the Church's tradition. Exploring them in the liturgies and writings of the centuries can feel like wandering through
a beautiful house or even searching the hidden depths of a pyra-
mid or some other archaeological site, where new treasures are
waiting to be discovered in each room. To help us find our way
we have chosen to use Gregory the Great's *On the Pastoral
Charge*. Other choices could have been made but maybe
Gregory's affection for the English makes him a good choice. He
was the sixth-century missionary pope who sent Augustine on
his mission to England after seeing faces of English slaves in
Rome and thinking that they looked like angels!

One of the images Gregory leads us to is of the priest as a
*mother*. He talks of the capacity of mothers to give birth and to
nurture life, even through its hard times, and encourages people
facing severe temptation to 'run to the pastor's heart, as to their
mother's bosom, and wash away, by the comfort of exhortation

and the tears of prayer' the troubles that overwhelm them. Motherhood is a rich image for ministry, with deep biblical roots. Paul's missionary ministry thrust him into experiences of birth and nurture. 'My little children,' he implored the Galatians, 'for whom I am again in the pain of childbirth until Christ is formed in you' (Galatians. 4:19); and he reminded the Thessalonians that 'We were gentle among you, like a nurse tenderly caring for her own children. So deeply do we care for you that we are determined to share with you not only the gospel of God but also our own selves, because you have become very dear to us' (1 Thessalonians 2:7–8). The yearning to see new life emerge, the dedication to see it grow healthily are hallmarks of motherhood. And mothers do not need to be to told that birthing and caring necessarily involve a sharing of 'one's own self'.

Alastair Redfern explores the stories of the two mothers who figure in the infancy narratives of Christ – Elizabeth and Mary.[16] Both were childless, though at different stages of their lives. The one was blamed for having no children and the other would be blamed for bearing a child. Both encounter the wildly creative activity of the Spirit that cannot be contained in the usual norms of life-making. Both only appear in a fleeting sort of way. Elizabeth fades from view when her new life appears. Alastair Redfern notes that not only is she 'self-effacing' but that she bears a self-effacing child who is content to decrease so that Christ can increase (John 3:30). Similarly, Mary is prepared to be a 'largely background figure' whose preoccupation is the development of her child. And like Elizabeth, the child she forms is as self-effacing as his mother, who points to his heavenly Father and gives himself to the world.

Of course, we must be very careful not to reduce womanhood to motherhood or to see motherhood entirely in terms of losing oneself in the other, just as we must be very cautious about images of priestly ministry that might appear to treat the priest as a cloth to be wrung out by others. Yet the energy of motherhood and the willingness of mothers to risk their lives in the giving of life are strong and powerful pictures of the calling of a priest. A woman about to give birth is driven by the instinct to ensure that everything needful is ready for the birth. And a woman who has children is constantly checking that everything now and at the next foreseeable stage is in place to ensure the health of her child. These are essential perspectives of the priest. We must be asking, 'What are the conditions for the health of the Church? What is needed for the birth and growth of people into Christlike life? How can it be provided? When do I need to move into the background so that the people of God can take their place in the foreground of the Church's ministry? When do I need to decrease, so that others can increase?'

Gregory balances the image of mother with that of *father*. As we would expect there are all sorts of gender assumptions in the way he compares the two, particularly when he says that priests should be like 'a mother by kindness and a father by discipline'.[17] Fathers, thankfully, give a lot of kindness and mothers certainly know how to wield discipline, and yet many of us have experienced mothers and fathers handling us in different, though complementary, sorts of ways.

My experience of my father was of someone who was thrilled by each new step I took. Whether it was learning to ride a bike, going into a pub for the first time or moving on from the safety of home to the new possibilities of university life, he was always anticipating the next stage, getting me ready for it and, although I did not realize it at the time, working hard to make sure that I was given the best chance possible to make it work. He seemed to like nothing more than to teach me how to do something and then to work alongside me as I clumsily tried to hammer in a nail or paint a wall. Sometimes there would be a slightly tense moment as I became as good at a particular task as he was, but without too much trouble he would soon hand over a project to me and allow me to get on with it, promising that he was there for me if I found myself in difficulty.

Interestingly, my father's experience of his father was the opposite. Rather than releasing him into adulthood, his own father tried to constrain him in childhood. The loss of his wife in childbirth, the poverty of the 1930s and the trauma of the war had left my grandfather protective and possessive, unable to learn 'How self-hood begins with a walking away. And love is proved in the letting go.'[18] There is little more depressing than seeing mature and gifted members of a church, some of them perhaps already trained for particular ministries, distrusted or disempowered by a priest who cannot take the risk of working with others in ministry. But there is something very invigorating in a church where gifts are being discovered, different ministries being discerned and where people are being trained and then released to fulfil their part in the priestly ministry of Christ's body. Where there are clergy confident enough to know that their priestly identity is fulfilled in the mentoring and mobilizing of others for ministry, the Church will grow into adulthood and come closer to its full stature in Christ. The 'walking-away' and the 'letting go' required of the priest is the sort of space-giving that a good father does for his child. It is a process of giving room for the other member of Christ's family to find the calling that God has given and then permission to exercise that God-given ministry. And, like Paul with Timothy, his son in ministry, we discover that there is still much for us to do as we continue to support those we have trained and released into Christ's work (Philippians 2:2). 'What are the conditions for the growth of the Church into maturity? How can Christians be stretched to serve God in the ministry to which God is calling them? What is needed in this place for the development of the Church into adulthood in Christ? How can the Church be raised and released to propogate its own life? How can I discern and shape and support the giftings of others?' These are critical questions for those called to preside over the priestly community.

Perhaps Gregory's favourite image is of the priest as a *physician*. The largest part of his *Pastoral Charge* consists of detailed advice on how to approach seventy-two different pastoral cases. Each case is paired with its opposite: the joyful and sad, the patient and impatient, the quarrelsome and peaceful and so on. Gregory is not trying to establish some sort of immutable case law – a set of pastoral precedents to which we can always turn in whatever situation. Quite the opposite in fact – his pastoral advice is finely honed to particular situations. He begins each section by repeating his overriding pastoral principle – 'different admonitions are to be addressed to . . .' and then he shows how different people, with different problems need to be approached in different ways. At the same time, though, he is conscious of the importance of maintaining Christian integrity and consistency so that the care given to one person will not only help that individual but will be good for the community as a whole: 'The speech therefore of teachers ought to be fashioned according to the condition of hearers, that it may both be suited to each for their own needs, and yet may never depart from the system of general edification.'[19]

With extraordinary insight Gregory skilfully diagnoses the way different dispositions can impede Christian growth and suggests treatment that goes to the heart of a problem, where necessary wielding the surgeon's knife with purposeful precision. He combines fine psychological judgements about healthy human living with deep spiritual instincts about how the ordinary qualities of a wholesome life find their origin and fulfilment in God. *Peace*, for example, that human virtue for which most of us strive, is merely 'a foot-print of peace eternal', and what, he asks, 'can be more mad than to love footprints left in the sand, but not to love Him by whom they are left'.[20]

Gregory is 'a lover of souls'. He knows that only God will fulfil the deepest longings of human hearts and that Christ's pattern of life is the definitive example of humanity fully alive, of life lived in welcoming openness to all that God intends for us. Committed to the 'cure of souls', Gregory attends to any signs of ill-health in people, any attitude or action that may restrict a person's growth into the life of Christ, and suggests forms of ministry suited to each situation. He knew that the health of the Church depends upon the health of its members. Paul's letters are a mirror image of Gregory's charge. He was passionate about the health of church communities and was able to analyse the communal dynamics of healthy churches with startling accuracy, while at the same time giving very particular advice about how the members of the community should handle their relationships with each other and their life in the world. Those who study the growth of the Church today tell us, as if we needed reminding, that healthy churches are growing churches.[21] It is not for nothing that the Church is called the body of Christ. Like human bodies, individual Christians and Christian communities have natural capacities to grow. 'What are the conditions for the health of the Church? What is impeding the growth of the Church? How can the diseases of the soul be cured? How can members of the Church be helped "to grow up in every way into him who is the head, from whom the whole body . . . promotes the body's growth in building itself up in love" (Ephesians 4:16)?'

The priest as a _navigator_ is another favourite image for Gregory. He describes the pastoral calling to be *with* people when they face 'a storm in the soul, in which the vessel of the heart is ever tossed by gusts of feeling, and driven without ceasing hither and thither, so that it is wrecked by transgressions in word and deed, as though by rocks that meet it'.[22] Much of his advice to pastors is about helping people to find their way through the difficult times of life, to steer their way through temptation and testing, to keep their sights set on the destination to which God is calling them. Again, Gregory has one eye on the person in particular need and the other on the well-being of the Church as a whole, but he knows that the ship as a whole cannot be steered unless all its parts are working well.

The navigator is a good image for the priest. It recognizes that Christian existence is never stationary. We are always moving in one direction. The only question is by which current we will allow ourselves to be propelled. It is an eschatological image that underlines that we are to be always on the move, looking ahead to the future that God has prepared for us and ready to set all the instruments by which we orientate ourselves, all the antennae we use to determine our direction, on the new way of living to which we are being called by Christ.

For Gregory navigators are similar to shepherds. They steer us through the vicissitudes of life, leading us into places of nourishment and then leading on to the next place in our journey with God. As we have seen, the shepherd is one of the foundational images of Christian ministry, inspired of course by the image of Jesus as the Good Shepherd. The relationship, however, between the ordained and Christ in the ministry of the Church has led some to explore a comparison between the priest and the sheep-dog. Sue Walrond-Skinner, for example, has some evocative things to say from her 'years of watching and working with border collies':

> The sheepdog possesses two all-consuming attractions: the sheep and her master. Her eye stays focused always on the sheep; her ear listens ceaselessly to the shepherd's call. Her attractions to both are profound . . . yet neither attraction can be worked out for her without the contrary pull of the other. She is held into a triangular relationship with the shepherd and sheep; her wild, compulsive instincts are only kept in check by her unswerving attention to her master.

> Sheepdogs lie about a lot. They are capable of putting every fibre of their being to work when required to do so, but they are instantly at ease, able to leave the sheep to get on with their lives, feeding, communicating, just 'being' together. The sheepdog does not interfere with or interrupt the life and work of the flock. The sheep are always the focus, the dog is merely an instrument which exists for their welfare and a tool that is usable by the shepherd in his own care of them.[23]

The dual focus on the people and on Christ is central to Gregory's pastoral method. The priest is to be 'next to each person in sympathy' and to 'soar above all in contemplation'. Identification and transformation, incarnation and redemption are the twin poles of our activity as we stand in solidarity with those entrusted to us and, listening to the voice of Christ, discern how they are to be led to where Christ wants them to be. And so we will be asking, 'What are the conditions for the movement of the Church in the right direction? How can Christians be helped to see their way forward in a culture increasingly alien to the central convictions of their faith? How can the Church learn to hear the echo of God's word leading it towards God's future, so that through the Church the world will be able to find its way to the new earth and the new heaven that God has prepared in Christ? And how can I be so with the people that they trust me to lead them?'

The final insight to draw on from Gregory pulls the others together. It is less of a pictorial image and more a descriptive noun. Gregory regularly refers to the priest as a *rector*, a Latin word that found its way intact into the English language. Derived from the verb *rego* (meaning, to keep straight or guide in the right direction), it literally meant a helmsman or a herdsman and was even used of an elephant driver! Gregory believed that the two basic roles of the priest were the 'office of pastoral teaching' and the 'sacred goverance' of the Church.[24] Clearly, then, *rector* carried strong associations for Gregory with governing the Church. Although we need to make sensible adjustments from the more paternalist culture of Gregory's day, the nuances of the word and the way Gregory actually describes the mindset of the *rector*, mean that even here he has much that is worth hearing.

Gregory is very clear about what needs to be avoided. Conscious that 'the business of governance destroyeth integrity of heart', he explains that priests must not be driven by any sort of 'ambition of pre-eminence', they should 'shun praise', and 'dread and avoid prosperity'.[25] Aware of the pressures to please others, he reminds us that our ministry is to lead the Church into a deeper love of Christ, not to covet the love that belongs only to him. Realistic about the narcissistic pitfalls of public ministry, he warns us against forms of self-love that lead people to honour themselves rather than God. Nevertheless, Gregory's equally clear belief in the need for good and firm leadership in the life of the Church seems to be the main motivation for writing his *Pastoral Charge*. He believes that the nurture, development, health and direction of Christian communities require the guiding and shaping ministry of the presbyter who presides over the people of God and leads them into more faithful service of Christ. *Orego*, the Greek equivalent of *rego*, means to reach out. That is the calling of the priest: to reach out for the vision of a holy people blessing the world with the news of God's reconciling love, to strive for this way of living to be seen and heard, touched and felt in the churches of our land, and to show that it can be seized only through the power of love. 'Do we know the power of love?' Chrysostom's question to Basil remains the true test of the priestly ministry of the presbyter.

# 3

# BEING FOR GOD

Could they have guessed, by Galilee,
the impact of Christ's word?
how lives would change, their world would be
transformed by what they heard?

Those simple, country, peasant folk
who heard their kinsman speak
of suffering for righteousness,
of blessing for the meek;

could they have guessed who this man was,
this man they'd known from youth?
a carpenter from Nazareth
the bearer of God's truth?

And dare we guess how Jesus' words
will challenge all we know,
how vast the vision, broad its scope,
how strong its undertow

that stirs the basis of our lives,
asks of us that we face
the challenge of beatitude,
to live our lives by grace?

O that the boundless love of God
Christ's burning, searing word,
would live in us, and then through us
transform our broken world.[1]

## Earthenware vessels

How on earth are we to fulfil this heavenly calling? How can we live with God and others so that others may live with and for others? How can we be not only *signs* of the priestliness of God's people but *effectual signs*, activators and animators of their calling to live holy lives of blessing? George Herbert, the seventeenth-century Anglican priest and poet, knew the problem.

> Lord, how can man preach thy eternal word?
>   He is a brittle crazy glass:
> Yet in thy temple thou dost him afford
>   This glorious and transcendent place,
>   To be a window, through thy grace.[2]

Sue, an ordinand whom we both knew, once went to a lecture given by Jürgen Moltmann, the influential German theologian. Inspired by Moltmann's theology, she attended a small book-signing event after the lecture. As Moltmann was signing her book, Sue mustered the courage to tell him how she was struggling to make the Christian faith relevant to the inner-city people among whom she was living and ministering. Moltmann was silent for some time. She thought he had not heard her or had chosen not to reply. Finally, he turned to her, looked at her with a piercing stare and said, 'You must divest yourself.' In this short moment and four words, Sue felt that she had been seen by the eyes of Christ and heard the gospel of the Lord.

Moltmann was calling for the radical repentance that lies at the centre of Christian faith. It is a turning from human pride. Karl Barth defined pride as the *original sin*, the root problem of humanity's relationship with God. Pride is the human principle that says 'we can go it alone'. We cannot be saved unless we turn from this confidence in our own capacities, until we empty ourselves of our own attempts to sort ourselves out and get ourselves right. 'For by grace you have been saved through faith, and this is not your own doing; it is the gift of God' (Ephesians 2:10). Abraham is the father of our salvation by grace through faith.

When all seemed hopeless, when the weakness of his own fleshly powers overwhelmed him, he heard God say, 'Abram, I will sort it'; and he believed the promise of God.

The dynamics of grace do not end with conversion. They begin with the call to follow Christ and they extend into every aspect of discipleship, including Christian ministry. We are saved by grace through faith and we minister by grace through faith. If the father of salvation by grace through faith is Abraham, the father of ministry by grace through faith is Moses. Moses was called to lead the people out of slavery to freedom in the promised land. God had seen the bondage of his people and had come to deliver them (Exodus 3:7–8). God had determined to bring his people to their rightful place in his purposes. God was going to set his people free to worship (Exodus 3:12; 4:23) and was calling Moses to play an instrumental part in these mighty works. Moses' response was archetypal, echoed throughout the generations of calls to ministry: 'Who am I that I should go?' (Exodus 3:11). God's reply to Moses is equally foundational and remains the word to all who have been called: 'I will be with you; and this shall be a sign for you that it is I who sent you: when you have brought the people out of Egypt, you shall worship God on this mountain' (Exodus 3:12). Moses' response is a statement of his own weakness. God's response is a promise of his presence – a presence that will be known to be true only in its believing, only in obeying the call, only in the doing of ministry. '*Only the believers obey*, and *only the obedient believe*', said Dietrich Bonhoeffer in his great work on discipleship.[3]

Moses' recognition of his own weakness is a *justifying* recognition. It justifies that God has made the right choice. It justifies that Moses is the right person for this work because it shows that Moses is in the right place to realize that the work will be completed not by his own abilities but by God's abiding presence and power. It is the place that leads to priestly praise and proclamation:

> For I will proclaim the name of the Lord;
> ascribe greatness to our God!

The Rock, his work is perfect
and all his ways are just.
A faithful God, without deceit,
just and upright is he. (Deuteronomy 32:3–4)

Moses' song exalts the Lord as the true God who is able to accomplish the unexpected. It is the same key in which Hannah, Mary and other biblical characters sang. 'There is no Holy One like the Lord, no one besides you,' sings Hannah, no one 'raises up the poor from the dust' and makes the 'barren bear seven children' (1 Samuel 2:2). Mary's soul too 'proclaims the greatness of the Lord' who has 'looked with favour on his lowly servant' (Luke 1:46–48). The Daily Office invites us to sing these familiar words of the *Magnificat* each evening as we gather the day before God in prayer. The day may have felt very unproductive. The powerful forces of the world may have seemed secure on their thrones and we, feeble against them. But the theological truth in the strange kenotic workings of God is that even on this day, when our ministry has seemed at its most barren, God has done great things for us and through us, simply because, with Mary, our faith has said 'Here am I, the servant of the Lord' (Luke 1:38).

Paul seems to have been suffering from some sort of 'physical infirmity' (Galatians 4.13) when he first brought the gospel to the Galatians. It may have been the 'thorn in the flesh' to which he referred when writing to the Corinthians. Certainly, the experience of weakness that appeared to debilitate his ministry led Paul to a deeper realization of the power of God.

Three times I appealed to the Lord about this, that it would leave me, but he said to me, 'My grace is sufficient for you, for my power is made perfect in weakness.' So, I will boast all the more gladly of my weaknesses, so that the power of Christ may dwell in me. Therefore, I am content with weaknesses . . . for whenever I am weak, then I am strong. (2 Corinthians 12:8–10)

Just as in the dynamics of salvation 'nothing in our hands we bring, simply to the cross we cling', so in the dynamics of ministry all we can do is to offer ourselves to God in our weakness, even offer our weakness itself to God, trusting that God's 'extraordinary power' (2 Corinthians 4:7) will be manifested through us. Yes, training for ministry is important, but the fundamental lesson to be learnt in any course of theological education is that 'our competence is from God, who has made us competent to be ministers of a new covenant' (2 Corinthians 4:5–6).

Aelred, the abbot of a large Cistercian monastery in Yorkshire during the twelfth century, had a profound sense of his own inadequacy for the responsibility that had been placed upon him. His *Pastoral Prayer* is a moving manifesto of ministerial weakness.

> O Good Shepherd Jesus
> good, gentle, tender Shepherd,
> behold as a shepherd, poor and pitiful,
> a shepherd of your sheep indeed,
> but weak and clumsy and of little use,
> cries out to you.
> To you, I say, Good Shepherd,
> this shepherd, who is not good, makes his prayer.
> He cries out to you,
> troubled upon his own account, and troubled for your
>     sheep.[4]

The prayer continues through several pages as Aelred wrestles with his calling.

> And you, sweet Lord,
> have set a person like this over your family,
> over the sheep of your pasture.
> Me, who take all too little trouble with myself,
> you bid to be concerned on their behalf;
> and me,
> who never pray enough about my own sins,

you would have pray for them.
I, who have taught myself so little too,
have also to teach them.
Wretch that I am.
What have I done?
What have I undertaken?
What was I thinking of?[5]

'The divine grace, which always heals what is infirm and supplies what is lacking, appoints [this person], beloved by God'; so says the archbishop in the Byzantine rite before he ordains a bishop, presbyter or deacon. This solemn statement, known fittingly as 'The Divine Grace', reminds all concerned that God is the one who is calling this person and that God will supply all that is needed. The people cry out, 'Lord, have mercy', and then the archbishop prays over the candidate calling for the 'great grace of the Spirit'. Following a similar pattern in the Anglican rite we sing:

Come, Holy Ghost, our souls inspire,
and lighten with celestial fire;
Thou the anointing Spirit art,
Who dost thou sevenfold gifts impart.

Prayer for the candidates' future ministry follows and leads into the ordination prayer during which the bishop prays:

Send down the Holy Spirit upon this your servant
for the office and work of a priest in your church.

Ministry by grace through faith provides the shape of the ordination liturgy. We are called to let it shape the ordained life. It is the pattern we see when Jesus fed the 5,000 in Luke 9. 'You give them something to eat', he tells the disciples. They are being called to a new event of ministry. 'We have no more than five loaves and two fish', they reply. They face and acknowledge their weakness, their inability to meet the people's needs by their own endeavours and powers. 'Make them sit down . . .', Jesus insists.

The call goes on, not despite but because of their acknowledgement of their own inadequacy. Their calling is simply to set the scene for Jesus to act, to prepare the way for the coming of the Lord. 'They did so.' Here is faith at work – the willingness to risk that God will act as we obey the call and do as Jesus tells us. 'And then taking the five loaves and two fish, he looked up to heaven and blessed and broke them and gave them to the disciples to set before the crowd.' The faith doing, the risk taking goes on as the disciples dare to believe that Christ is active in a situation and can transform it through the faithful ministry of his followers. 'And all ate and were filled.' Like Moses we discover the truth of the promise of God's presence and power as we do the work of ministry.

The Croatian theologian Miroslav Volf, talks about 'catholic personality, community and cultural identity' in his various writings on human reconciliation. We will make some explicit use of these ideas later. It is also possible to talk of *evangelical personality*. An evangelical personality is permeated with the grace of the gospel. It is a personality whose identity is based on and flows from the unimaginably abundant love of God, the ultimate affirmation of worth and value. This is the personality priests are called to model as they live with God and as they act for God by ministering to others in the love of God. It is a love dedicated to the formation of an *evangelical community* – a community of people open to the 'extraordinary power' (2 Corinthians 4:7) of God's love, a community willing to act in the power of God's love through their ministry to each other, and a community willing to make known God's great love for the world to all the peoples of the earth. It is a love that is seeking to create an *evangelical cultural identity*. Constrained by the love of Christ, evangelical personalities and evangelical communities are committed to the transformation of the culture of their localities and lands by ministering the love of God to the world. In the face of the enormity of the task, we do well to remember that God still sees the suffering of all that he has made, and yearns for the work of his hands to be set free from the tyrannies that hold humanity captive. And God still calls people to announce to Pharaoh that he has come to bring his people to 'a good and broad land, a land flowing with milk and honey' (Exodus 3:8), a land where the dynamics of grace have caused people to realize that only God is to be worshipped and that the idols of our self-sufficiency have bound us in slavery for too long.

As well as the experience of the 'power of love', John Chrysostom also looked for wisdom in the ways of God in those to be ordained. Wisdom is one of the marks of the evangelical personality of priests. We are to be skilled in speaking of and living by the hidden ways of God made known in Christ. We are to tell of the God who uses bread and wine, water and oil for eternal purposes. We are to preach of the God whose divinity is not denied but defined by the self-surrender to the conditions of humanity. We are to proclaim a God whose power is demonstrated in the helplessness of a crucifixion. We are to celebrate the God who chooses to create and who suffers the self-imposed limitations that come with freely sharing life with others. We are living proof that God has chosen 'what is weak in the world to shame the strong' (1 Corinthians 1:27).

Before we move on to other themes, there is one critical postscript to add. Although we are saved by grace through faith and not by our own goodness or strength, a change does occur in us as we are slowly, faltering step by faltering step, transformed into the likeness of Christ. The same applies in priestly ministry. Although it is always a ministry of faith in the grace of God, God is doing a work in and through us. We are in the worst position to judge the ways that the life and exercise of ministry is changing us into an authentic sign of the priestly people of Christ. But most of us will have known faithful 'stewards of God's mysteries' whose lives have been permeated with the light and beauty of God and can agree with the second verse of George Herbert's poem 'The Windows', the first verse of which began the chapter.

But when thou dost anneal in glass thy story,
   Making thy life to shine within
The holy Preacher's; then the light and glory
   More rev'rend grows, and more doth win:
   Which else shows wat'rish, bleak and thin.

*Beloved disciples*

> In those days Jesus came from Nazareth of Galilee and was baptised by John in the Jordan. And just as he was coming out of the water, he saw the heavens torn apart and the Spirit descending like a dove on him. And a voice came from heaven, 'You are my Son, the beloved; and with you I am well pleased'. And the Spirit immediately drove him out into the wilderness. (Mark 1:8–12)

We have talked quite a lot about being for others, about being, as Moberly put it 'an utterly loving pastor',[6] ready to give ourselves to our people and to our wider communities. In the background to all we have said is the model of Jesus, the Good Shepherd of Aelred's prayer, who laid down his life for his sheep and who calls us to follow in his way of lifelong loving of others. All this is true. Certainly Christian existence is a call to count others better than ourselves and to commit ourselves to their well-being. And most definitely Christian ministry is an all-embracing command to do as Jesus did, taking the towel and bearing the cross for the good of others. The Church is called to enter into 'the movement of Christ's self-offering', as the ARCIC statement put it, pouring itself out in obedience to God and to God's purposes for the world. If presbyters are to resonate with that which they signify and if they are to have any credibility as pastors who 'set the example of the Good Shepherd always before them as the pattern of their calling', they have to 'model their lives on the mystery of the Lord's cross'.[7] However, we can never enter into the movement of Christ's self-giving, unless we also enter into the movement of his self-receiving.

Mark's account of Jesus' baptism gives a profound insight into the self-receiving of Jesus. The heavens are torn open and the Spirit descends on Jesus and a voice addresses him as *the Beloved* in whom God is well-pleased. The heavens are indeed torn open and in the waters of the Jordan we see a freeze-frame of an eternal event. The Son eternally receives being from the Father in the action of the Holy Spirit. In an eternal moment without beginning or end the Source of all things speaks the Word by the breath of the Spirit; the Father begets the Son in the energy of the Spirit. And the Word speaks back in the breath of the same Spirit; the Son says 'Father' in the love of the Spirit. The eternal round of giving and receiving, the ultimate exchange of loving, is the way God is and it is manifested for us, incarnated in human conditions, as the heavens roll back and the Spirit rests on Jesus and the Father calls him the Beloved, in whom he is well-pleased.

This is the shape of Christian identity and Christian ministry. In Christ we too are called beloved. We too are given the Spirit. Christ's heirdom, Christ's anointing is shared with us. This is the baptismal gift to be received in Christian living and Christian ministering. These are the dynamics of salvation and ministry by grace through faith. Feminist critique of notions of self-giving that reduce some to expendable servants of others, exploited by those who have denied them their own autonomy and identity, are gospel-driven insights of great significance for those who minister in Christ's name. Jesus' ability to receive from God and from others ridicules our masochistic tendencies to give when our account has dried up and there is nothing left even to warm the house of our own lives, quite apart from lighting the darkness of others.

'Keep watch over yourselves', Paul told the Ephesian elders in Acts 20:28. Richard Baxter spent the first part of his *Reformed Pastor* urging clergy to keep watch over themselves, to attend to their own lives in Christ:

> See that the work of saving grace be thoroughly wrought in your own souls. Take heed to yourselves lest you be void of that saving grace of God which you offer to others and be strangers to the effectual working of that Gospel which you preach . . . Take heed to yourselves . . . lest you famish while you prepare their food.[8]

He urges them to be 'very careful that [their] graces be kept in life and action'.[9] In other words, we are not to rest content with our spiritual experiences of the past, even our call to ministry and the high moments or our ordained life; we are to seek to grow in faith and hope and love, deepening our roots into the Christ who has called us. The good advice to keep our spiritual lives in order, to keep exercising the spiritual disciplines which we commend to others, runs hand in hand with the need to attend to our mental and physical health, our emotional and social well-being. This is not the place to try to offer detailed guidance on how to do so. It is impossible to legislate in any meaningful way. Different personalities are nourished in different ways and what works for one age and stage in life may need to be adapted as life's journey moves on. But the strength that regular exercise, sensible patterns of sleep and good food give to our bodies is not be underestimated. The beauty of art, music, word and all the wonders of nature can feed our souls and inspire our imaginations in ways that cannot be foreseen. The joy of a network of relationships to sustain and stimulate us is a gift to be treasured and protected.

Simply wasting time is seldom really wasting time. For most of us it is just letting the rubber band unwind. Steven Croft recounts the story of the person who is frantically trying to cut down a tree but without much success. 'Why don't you stop and sharpen the saw', someone calls out. 'There's no time to sharpen the saw,' is the reply, 'I have to cut down this tree!'[10] Later, when warning of the dangers that come when we ignore the signals that tell us we are working far too hard and very inefficiently, Croft says:

> When we keep going through these early warnings we quickly find ourselves in the wastelands of stress: exhaustion, bad temper, depression, addictive and dependent cycles of behaviour, vulnerability to temptation, ill-health and damaged relationships.[11]

Sabbath is the biblical principle that lies behind this common sense. Sabbath builds rest and renewal into the rhythms of the created order. It is a radical theological conviction that 'There are some things that can be accomplished, even by God, only in a state of rest'.[12] In contemporary life when we can shop through the night, carry around almost all the facilities of an office in our bags or pockets, buy strawberries in the winter and hot cross buns at Christmas, the biblical patterns to the days, weeks and years can seem far away and really rather quaint. Yet if we do not break up our days they will break us up. If we do not allow ourselves to come up for air and breathe in the life of the Spirit, we will suffocate under the relentless pressures of the week. If we do not punctuate our time with changes of pace and focus, our well-meaning ministry will make as much sense as words outside a sentence.

Eugene Peterson describes how we often feel caught between the demands of attending to the needs of people and the call simply to attend to God, to grow in prayer and the word. There are often structural changes we can make that will help to free us for the fundamentals of the ordained life but the demands of people will never go away. By attending to people's need for ministry we are living the ordained life and fulfilling our calling. Even so, Peterson is right to remind us that our perennial temptation is to slip into the constant serving of others while ignoring the One who gives us the good things we are trying to share.

> Every profession has sins to which it is especially liable. I haven't looked closely into the sins that endanger physicians and lawyers, woodworkers and potters, but I have had my eye out for the snare of the fowler from which pastors need deliverance: it is the sin of reversing the rhythms. Instead of grace / work we make it work / grace . . . And that, of course, is why so few pastors keep a sabbath: we have reversed the rhythms. How can we quit work for a day when we have reversed the rhythms?[13]

Keeping sabbath means more than trying to protect one day as a day of rest. It means seeking sabbath space during the day, the year and the sequence of years. When John Wesley was asked how he could sustain the extraordinarily heavy preaching commitments across the country, he said, 'Don't forget, I spend a lot of time alone as I travel'. Augustine said, 'If I could not find my own self, how much less could I find you God'. Sabbath space allows us to find ourselves and, in finding ourselves, to love ourselves as God loves us.

After a long period of fairly relentless and demanding work I eventually took myself on retreat. As I gazed out onto the North Sea while staying in a Franciscan friary I was overwhelmed with the simple joy of 'brother wind' buffeting my body and 'sister water' filling the horizon with gallons of rolling beauty. It was good to be created, to be a creature with senses able to enjoy all that God has made. I had spent too long closed off from God's ministry of the earth to refresh my soul. I found myself again as a human being, a participator in God's marvellous creation.

Cuthbert's island of Coquet was just visible and I began to understand how God was able to use those wild northern missionaries to found communities, convert cultures and build churches. Like Jesus, he drove them into the wilderness by the Spirit and then, by the same Spirit, drove them out into the world. Sabbath space is not always comfortable. When the voices go quiet and the pace changes, we can very soon find ourselves wrestling with devils. These times of testing cannot be avoided. Abba Macarios, one of the founders of desert monasticism, saw them as opportunities to be clothed in the armour of the Spirit, so that, 'Having armed [ourselves] by all prayer and perseverence and supplication and fasting and by faith, [we] will be able to wage war against the principalities'.[14] At these times we find that the ministering angels are not far from us (Matthew 4:11) and that we are empowered by the Spirit for a new phase of ministry in the world.

Jesus was free enough to retreat into times of solitude with God but after his own desert experience he always did so as part of the new community of faith that formed around him. Jesus spent time with others, worked with others and received from others. He ministered with them, travelled the long road to Jerusalem with them and went to Gethsemane with them. They shared meals, prayed prayers, sang hymns, wept and rejoiced together. When they let him down in the last fatal week of his life, he forgave them and then, with all the possibilities of the new creation, he came back to them to reconstitute them as his fellow-workers. The interdependence between them and him was reinforced at his ascension. They were to be his witnesses, bearers of Christ's presence and he received their worship.

Jesus' capacity to be with others and to share ministry with others became embodied in the new Christian community baptized in the Spirit of fellowship: 'When you come together, each one has a hymn, a lesson, a revelation, a tongue, or an interpretation' (1 Corinthians 14:26). Christian ministries interpenetrate each other and the giftings of each believer imply and rely on the giftings of others.

In terms of its formal offices the Church soon discovered that it needs bishops and presbyters and deacons – and that each order needs the others. Ordination services are based on the assumption that we need the ministry of others before we exercise ministry and while we exercise it. Whether it is in the silence as the congregation prays for the anointing of the Spirit on a new bishop, or as presbyters join the bishop in the laying of hands on a new priest or as the bishop washes the feet of those about to be ordained deacon, the clarion call of the ordination service is 'receive from God the ministry of the Spirit through the ministry of Christ's people!'

The ordained life begins as it is meant to go on but it can become increasingly difficult to lay oneself open to the ministry of others, and especially from members of our own congregations. It can feel like an admission of failure for others to know, even see, us being ministered to in some way by others – the very people to whom we have been charged to serve. In fact, it is evidence of success. It is a sign of the sort of humility that comes with trust that ministry really is by grace and through faith. It is evidence that we are shaping the Church to be the Church, the priestly people of God. It is an example of the people of God fulfilling their promise to 'uphold and encourage us in our ministries'.

Receiving the ministry of others and working with the ministry of others, encouraging, enabling and equipping God's people to serve the Church and the world, are marks of the *catholic personality* of the priest. 'A catholic personality', says Miroslav

Volf, 'is a personality enriched by otherness, a personality which is what it is only because multiple others have been reflected in it in a particular way.'[15] Volf rightly sees this as the inheritance of all Christians as the Spirit breaks apart the walls that separate us from others but it has a special relevance to the life of the ordained. Multiple others are always reflected in the life and ministry of a priest. We are who we are because of a myriad of people who have cared for us and taught us. We are given the privilege to minister as priests because the Church has placed us in this relationship of responsibility for others. We are called to share life intensively with others, even to the point, Gregory tells us, of taking upon ourselves 'the infirmity of others', prepared to suffer with those who suffer and to rejoice with those who rejoice. Our ministry is to help form *catholic communities*. Catholic communities are environments of mutuality where people admit their need of each other and recognize the inter-penetration of their life and ministry. Catholic communities know that 'The eye cannot say to the hand, "I have no need of you"' (1 Corinthians 12:21). The 'other' for catholic communities extends beyond those among whom we worship to all of those who bear the name of Christ, allowing them space to be *other* and not the same, unique and not a clone. This is the catholic spirit that John Wesley learnt as he saw God working in different parts of the Church.

> It is true, that, for the thirty years past, I have gradually put on a more catholic spirit, finding more tenderness for those who differed from me, either in opinions or modes of worship.[16]

The Church is to anticipate and to activate the reconciliation of humanity that awaits us in the new heavens and new earth. Our mission is to be, as yeast in the dough, agents of catholicity in our localities and lands, to see them rise to the *catholic cultural identity* that only God's Spirit can properly form in human con-sciousness. It is a way of being human in which we affirm our common destiny in God's purposes and our particular character as diverse expressions of God's creativity. Cultural identity begins to be *catholic* when communities of human beings become secure enough of their membership of God's community of love to be able to view others with the love through which God sees them.

## Enjoying God

The Westminster Catechism's well-worn phrase that our chief end is to love God and enjoy God forever is as true today as the day it was written. The baptismal call to be with God is an invitation to joy. Christian life is the form of human living that seeks to live fully in and from the life of God. It is life lived *en joie* – lived in the joy in which God lives. We are placed *in* the divine joy. The joy of God is a priestly joy. It is the joy of the interpenetrating life of the joy-giver, the joy-bearer and the joy-sharer. It is the mutually indwelling life of the three persons of the Trinity, whose joy in living is the joy of living in and through each other. It is the life of joy that shouts the creation into being though an explosion of joyful sound, 'Let there be light.' It is the life of joy that chooses to form a people and to shape them in the ways of joyful living, and to inspire them to sing on behalf of all creation:

> O be joyful in the Lord, all the earth;
> serve the Lord with gladness
> and come before his presence with a song.
> > (Psalm 100, Jubilate)

It is a joy that comes to earth to redeem the earth as the angels sing:

> Glory to God in the highest heaven,
> and on earth peace among those whom he favours!
> > (Luke 2:14)

It is a joy that bursts from the grip of earth's death and causes people to sing, even today, the new song of the 'Day of Resurrection':

> Now let the heavens be joyful,
>   And earth her song begin,

The round world keep high triumph,
    And all that is therein;
Let all things seen and unseen
Their notes of gladness blend,
For Christ the Lord hath risen,
Our joy that hath no end.[17]

The presbyteral call to live our life with God in such a way that
we place ourselves *with* others and position ourselves *for* others,
so that they may more fully find their life in God, is a vocation for
joy. It is a life lived after the pattern of Christ. It is a life that lives
in the movements, the dynamics of God's life of joyful living. It is
a life that longs for others to have joy. It is a life based on God's
promise that 'everlasting joy shall be theirs' (Jeremiah 60:7),
even though now the suffering of this world has caused the 'joy
of their hearts to cease' (Lamentations 5:15).

Joy-giving is a costly thing. Priestly living is not easy living.
Wanting the best for people, wanting others to have the joy that
only God can give will require the best from us. Such a life is not
one of unbroken happiness. It exposes one to the suffering of
others and lament is as much its song as praise. And yet, even in
the lament, we remain, as Augustine reminds us, 'Easter people'
with 'Alleluia' imprinted on our hearts, even if it does not always
make its way to our lips. Christ *is* risen – and this makes a difference to all life. The Spirit is being poured out on all flesh and this
life-giving presence of God pours water even on the thirsty
ground of human life, as we await the renewal of all things in
Christ.

*Charismatic personality* is the inheritance of all Christians.
Through our baptism and by our faith we are bearers of the Holy
Spirit. We have been gifted by the Spirit of love with charisms of
grace. We are evidence of God's enjoyment of human life: God
enjoys us so much that he shares divine gifts with each one of us.
Charismatic personalities are attractive, drawing people towards
them, not because of the intrinsic merit of inherited psychology,
still less because of the social appeal of particular sorts of personality traits, but because they bear the imprint of God.

Charismatic personalities have allowed themselves to recognize the generosity of God and have opened themselves to the gifting of God. They may be loud, they may be quiet. They may be energized by company, or renewed in solitude. They may be skilful in any manner of things or reticent about their abilities. Whatever their natural assets, they will be people who have responded to the call to taste and see that the Lord is good (Psalm 34:8). Goodness is the magnetic force in human interaction. Goodness attracts. Goodness compels. Goodness has the power to change situations.

As we have seen, at the heart of the ordination service is the invocation of the Spirit of God upon those who offer themselves for the ministry of God's Spirit in the Church. Like many others, my ordination was preceded by a retreat. Almost as soon as it began, I became overwhelmed by the enormity of the events ahead – not just the ordination but the whole life of ministry. There were a series of addresses at various points in the day during the retreat. At each of them the retreat conductor encouraged us to wait, with expectation, for the gift of the Holy Spirit to be given to us at our ordinations. The confidence of his exhortation and the fragility of my feelings led me to talk to the conductor and to share my fears for the future. 'It's all right for you to say things like that', I remember myself saying, 'but I find that God usually misses me out when he's giving out the Spirit.' His reply was swift and sharp. 'How can you doubt the promise of God to give good gifts to his children: trust the Bible and if you cannot trust the Bible, trust the sacramental actions of the liturgy – the Church is asking, God is giving!'

And God gave. Ordination proved for me the faithfulness of God to give the Spirit to those who ask. It helped me to live in and to minister from the gifting of God. It gave me a desire to see others enter more fully into the baptismal inheritance of Christian life. It renewed my vision to help build *charismatic communities*.

Charismatic communities are collections of people who enjoy the enjoyment of God. They have dared to trust that God enjoys the praise of his people, that God has placed his joy in human beings and seeks to see that joy discovered and released in lives of mutual generosity. Such lives recognize that the gifts God gives are gifts to be shared. They are gifts given for the good of others. Charismatic communites are shaped by the ultimate charismatic community – the community of the divine generosity and communion. It is said that St Sergius, who founded the monastery outside Moscow where André Rublev painted his famous icon of the Holy Trinity, 'built the Church of the Holy Trinity as a mirror for his community, that through gazing at the Divine Unity, they may overcome the hateful divisions of the world'.[18]

Like the community of St Sergius, charismatic communities are committed to the creation of a *charismatic cultural identity*. Charismatic cultural identity enjoys the generosity of God. It looks at the creation and sees God's gift – a gift to be received with delight and to be cared for with love. It looks at another human being and sees a person loved into being by the kindness of God and designed for the giving and receiving of love. It looks at God and sees immensity and abundance and overflowing goodness and cries out:

> We praise you, O God,
> we acclaim you as the Lord:
> all creation worships you,
> the Father everlasting.
> To you all angels, all the powers of heaven,
> the cherubim and seraphim, sing in endless praise:
> Holy, holy, holy Lord, God of power and might,
> heaven and earth are full of your glory.
>                    (Te Deum Laudamus)

# PART 2

# THE SHAPE OF PRIESTLY LIFE

# 4

## BEING FOR WORSHIP

Ponder long the glorious mystery,
breathe, in awe, that God draws near;
hear again the angels' message,
see the Lamb of God appear.
God's own Word assumes our nature:
Son of God in swaddling bands;
Light of light, and God eternal
held in Mary's gentle hands.

Ponder long the glorious mystery
of the Lamb who once was slain,
now at God's right hand in glory:
he who in the grave had lain.
Once he bid the doubting Thomas,
'See my hands and touch my side.'
Now the angels gaze in wonder,
Jesus' wounds are glorified.

Ponder long the glorious mystery,
'This my body, this my blood.'
Bread and wine reveal God's presence,
love engulfs us like a flood.
Human longing meets God's yearning,
words fall silent, all is grace;
mystery with hope is brimming,
earth is held in heaven's embrace.[1]

## Called to worship

In the Byzantine rite of the fourth century, the archbishop prays that the person God has 'willed to undertake the rank of the presbyterate' will be filled with the Holy Spirit and so 'be worthy to stand blamelessly at your altar':

> to proclaim the gospel of your salvation,
> to exercise the sacred ministry of the word of your truth,
> to offer you gifts and spiritual sacrifices,
> and to renew your people by the baptism of regeneration.

Not everyone is comfortable with the idea of altars in church. Indeed, the word is studiously avoided in the Church of England's Book of Common Prayer. Be that as it may; the Byzantine prayer of ordination is talking about much more than ecclesiastical furniture when it speaks of 'standing blamelessly at God's altar'. It is referring to an encounter between God and human beings. Altar is liturgical shorthand for an environment of costly exchange, a meeting place with the holiness of God, a divine appointment before the one who demands my soul, my life, my all.[2] That is why the invitation to give one's life to Christ at an evangelistic event became known as the *altar call* in settings where a physical altar was nowhere to be seen. Presbyters stand on holy ground, ground sanctified by the promise of God's presence. Their ministry is to serve this promise. Doing so extends far wider than what is done in the church building or even among the community of the Church. It includes every opportunity for the opening of eyes and ears and hearts to the activity of God in the world. But it is concentrated in a liturgical ministry that 'proclaims the gospel of salvation' through a ministry of preaching and teaching, Eucharist and baptism. The Byzantine rite is clear that both word and sacrament are priestly activities. Using language drawn from the world of priestly worship, it says that presbyters are 'to exercise the sacred ministry' (*ierourgein*), and 'to offer gifts and spiritual sacrifices'. They are priestly because they are for God and with God and for and with others. They serve what the Orthodox theologian Alexander Schmemann, describes as the essential function of the liturgy, which is to bring the Church into being and 'to realise the Church by revealing her (to herself and the world) as the epiphany of the kingdom of God'.[3]

Worship is the priestly activity par excellence. To offer worship is the beginning of the sort of ecstatic life to which we are called. *Ecstatic* means to be taken out (*ek*) of a given place or position (*stasis*). When we worship we step out of the place of preoccupation with ourselves and into the place of praise of another. Of course, this sort of movement can happen towards a variety of objects. That is why worship is a serious and dangerous business. That is why the Old Testament is full of injunctions about false worship, worship that blindly leads us to love that which cannot love us. Hebrew faith was realistic about the powerfully seductive forces that seek to entice us to put our faith, hope and love into hopeless causes that bind us into loveless living where faith is reduced to fear. The Mosaic faith of God's people emerged from an encounter with the God who, refusing to be defined through the usual categories of human religion, demonstrated his presence in a fire that burned with compassion for a suffering people. 'I have come to set my people free ... free to worship' (Exodus 3:1–12). This is the covenantal *promise* to the people of God, the ordination *charge to* their ministers and the *warning* to all the Pharaohs of our world and the world beyond who keep God's people captive in slavery to systems and structures that deny their birthright and betray their destiny. The worship of this God is not another form of human dependency to be cast off as we find our own two feet in the world. It is not another opiate from which we need freeing. It is our dignity and our liberation.

The God who calls us to worship is free and fulfilled. God is complete and sufficient. God does not *need* our praise like some sort of supernatural power station, insatiably feeding on the energy of our worship to sustain its life. The God we worship is not the ultimately deficient personality whose every move from the first day of creation has been to extract the praise of others.

God's life is a life of praise and worship in which 'Lover, Beloved and Friend of Love' celebrate love in an eternal dance of joy. It is a love that beckons us, bids us welcome and bears all the cost of teaching us to dance with the same step:

> Love bade me welcome: yet my soul drew back,
>    Guilty of dust and sin.
> But quick-eyed Love, observing me grow slack
>    From my first entrance in,
> Drew nearer to me, sweetly questioning,
>    If I lacked anything.
>
> A guest, I answered, worthy to be here:
>    Love said, You shall be he.
> I the unkind, ungrateful? Ah my dear,
>    I cannot look on thee.
> Love took my hand, and smiling did reply,
>    Who made the eyes but I?
>
> Truth Lord, but I have marred them: let my shame
>    Go where it doth deserve.
> And know you not, says Love, who bore the blame?
>    My dear, then I will serve.
> You must sit down, says Love, and taste my meat:
>    So I did sit and eat.[4]

God's love is an expansive love, an eternal giving of love, a heaping of love upon love between Father, Son and Spirit, an 'overflowing, creative love, which freely perfects its own perfection and invites others to join this life through praise'.[5] The invitation to sit at the table of this life of love and to taste the intoxicating joy that comes only from sharing in the 'perfecting of perfection',[6] is a call to priestly existence, a call to live with, in and for God, the ultimate other, whose love for us is beyond our imagining.

This is the calling of God to humanity: to love and be loved by God, to honour God and find ourselves honoured by God, to render glory to God and discover our own glory as works of beauty fashioned by God's hand for the space at God's table. It is a radical, prophetic calling that challenges the idols of human achievement and autonomy. It sets before us an alternative vision of a life liberated from the circles of self-fulfilment that spiral inwards, imploding in self-destruction. It offers a way of living that spreads outwards, raising us to new heights of personal integrity and new breadths of social integration, as we are transformed by the transcending experiences of giving love to and receiving love from the source of all things. This is the calling that the Church has heard and is seeking to fulfil. This is the calling that presbyters are ordained to see realized in the life of the Church and proclaimed to the world.

Isaiah, son of Amoz, was probably a priest. While worshipping in the temple he was caught up into a vision of the Lord. Overwhelmed by the holiness of God he called out 'Woe is me! I am lost, for I am a man of unclean lips, and I live among a people of unclean lips' (Isaiah 6:5). One of the angelic host ministering to the Lord took a burning coal from the altar, touched Isaiah's mouth with the coal and then declared that his sin was 'blotted out'. Then Isaiah heard the voice of the Lord: 'Whom shall I send, and who will go for us?' 'Here I am, send me!' (6:8), Isaiah responded and then heard the Lord send him out to the people with God's word in his heart.

The *characteristics* of priestly life that we will be exploring in this second part of the book and the *fruit* of priestly life to which we shall be turning in Part 3, are all found in this short exchange between Isaiah and his God. While *worshipping*, Isaiah hears the *word* of the Lord and utters his *prayer* to the Lord. He is *reconciled* to God in a new way and, receiving the *holiness* God provides for him, *offers* his life to God and is *sent out* to bring the *blessing* of God to the world, even though it is a blessing that comes first through judgement. Those who have been called into the 'priesthood of the presbyterate' are to be worshipping people, shaped by God's 'word of truth' and sustained by lives of prayer. These characteristics of priestly life will lead to the fruit of holy lives that bring reconciliation and blessing to God's people, and proclaim the good news of salvation to the nations. Worship is therefore a concentrated experience of priestly existence in which its character is formed in us and its consequences initiated.

What is true for the priestly presbyter is true also for the priestly people. God's people are to be nurtured by the word and nourished by prayer. They are to be holy people, reconciled to each other and able to bless each other through their life together. And all this is for the world. The Church is to be formed by the word so that it can speak God's re-forming word to the world. The Church is to pray for the world, so that the world may find peace in the Prince of Peace. The Church is to be a holy people, at peace with itself, so that it can proclaim and demonstrate God's promise to bless the world by transforming it into a place fit for God to dwell, a world where 'a great multitude that no one could count, from every nation, from all tribes and peoples and languages' cry: "Salvation belongs to our God who is seated on the throne, and to the Lamb!"' (Revelation 7:10).

## Called to lead worship

There is always a propensity in the Church to disconnect the calling to lead worship from the ministry of the ordained. There is a good and healthy side to this. God has given musicians, for example, gifts of skill and sensitivity to steer worshippers through the outer courtyards of the temple into the holy of holies itself. Whether directors of music in cathedrals, leaders of charismatic worship bands or anything in between, the ministry of leading worship through music is critical for the health of the Church. And there are other forms of worship leading that are to be equally celebrated and used – from the leading of all-age worship by a well-prepared team to the wide-ranging liturgical ministry of readers and catechists.

The problem comes if the ordained begin to abdicate their charge 'to lead God's people in the offering of worship, offering with them a spiritual sacrifice of praise and thanksgiving'.[7] Like the bell in a north Wisconsin church with these words inscribed on it, we are to summon people to worship:

> To the bath and the table,
> To the prayers and the word,
> I call every seeking soul.[8]

We are also to preside over acts of worship. But the priestly call to tend carefully the worship of a congregation is more than this. It is a calling to oversee the culture and ethos of worship in the Christian communities we serve, to have our eyes set, with John Chrysostom, on 'one end: the glorification of God and the edification of the Church'.[9]

Whether presiding over the process of worship or actually leading people in worship, the calling of a worship leader is to be first a worshipper. Here again we are to set before us the pattern of Christ who is the *leitourgos*, the true leader of our worship (Hebrews 8:2), who proclaims God's name 'in the midst of the congregation' (Hebrews 2:12). 'We have confidence to enter the sanctuary by the blood of Jesus', the book of Hebrews goes on to tell us (Hebrews 10:19). The sacrificial death of Christ which has qualified us 'to stand in God's presence and serve him', was the expression of both Christ's priestly ministry *for us* and his priestly ministry *to God*. In the manner of all the great martyrs who have followed him, Jesus' death was an act of worship – a giving over of everything to God. It was the supreme shout of praise, the complete and efficacious gesture of prophetic defiance to all that would thwart God's purposes for good for his creation. Jesus in earthly life and death, in ascended glory and majesty, is our brother who worships God in spirit and in truth and who, as our priest, leads us to worship in his spirit and in his truth. Our calling is to be in Christ and to bring others to Christ, so that through *his* priestly ministry *our* praise will be perfected and *our* lives made holy offerings to God.

Liturgy has immense formative power. Aristotle recognized that we *are* what we repeatedly *do* and one of the ancient theological principles of the Church is *lex orandi, lex credendi*, we believe what we pray. This is why it is often hard leading worship out of our natural liturgical habitat. But the catholicity of our ordination means that we will often find ourselves taken beyond our liturgical comfort zones into styles of worship that are not of our first preference. Yet, even here, we may discover that some of our richest times of worship turn out to have been in the most unlikely of places. Congregations know a reluctant worship leader when they see one and we need to enter fully into the worship for their sake as well as for ours, not obscuring by our manner of celebration what we say with our lips. God has an amazing habit of sidestepping our expectations of what is 'best' for us and greeting us in the midst of our least-favoured form of worship.

Our priestly ministry involves a double calling to be worshippers ourselves and to lead others into worship so that we are all transformed. However there is more still: Robert Barron writes of the task not only of drawing others into worship but of making the liturgy dance, not for the sake of it – although liturgy should live – but so that we all share in the dance of God,

> The mystagogue is the one who has been entrusted with the sacred symbols and given the responsibility of making them speak. He is the artist whose task is to make a liturgy a great dance expressive of God's grace, a stunning saga at the heart of which is God's embrace of every aspect of our fallen humanity ... the mystagogical artist, in image, symbol and story, presents the truth that is God's love in Christ and draws the worshipping community to share in it.[10]

To do so leaders of worship have to be liturgists: liturgists in the deepest sense of people who offer *leitourgia*, who render service to God, by being *worshippers*, and liturgists in the more technical sense of people with some understanding of the dynamics of worship and some feel for the words of worship. This is especially important in our contemporary liturgical life when, throughout the churches, a vast range of liturgical resources is available. Gone are the days when all we had to do was to open the book at the right page and then work through it until the final page of the service.

We Anglicans, with our *Common Worship*, are not the only ones who have to acquire a deep sensitivity to the structure of worship and to the function of particular liturgical texts, so that we can make responsible choices among the many alternatives available to us. The new liturgical world calls us to attend to the dynamics of worship. It asks us to think carefully about the flow of worship. It invites us to ease ourselves into the skin of the liturgy, to see through its eyes, because it is only when we inhabit a liturgy that we can use it properly. It is certainly only then that we can attempt the sort of task the Second Vatican Council commended to the language and cultural groups of the Roman Catholic Church: to adapt, amend and add to what has been provided.

I once made the mistake of telling a German Lutheran theologian, who has a deep sensitivity to the function of liturgical texts in worship, that I thought the Gloria was a dispensable part of the liturgy. 'I completely disagree,' was his swift reply. 'When we have given glory to God, then we cannot give glory to the Führer.' The following Sunday I was attending the Church where the Gloria itself was not sung. But in its place was a series of worship songs that, in their own way, did the same thing – they gave glory to God and acknowledged 'the Most High, Jesus Christ, with the Holy Spirit, in the glory of God the Father'. Some good liturgical decisions had been made. Early in the service, in whatever way is appropriate to the congregation, we are to proclaim the divinity of God and so disown the idolatries of the age.

This appreciation of the liturgical dynamics of worship requires a deeper appreciation of the theological dynamics of worship – and theological in the fullest sense of the Trinitarian dynamics of God's life of worship. 'When we cry, "Abba! Father!" it is that very Spirit bearing witness with our spirit that we are children of God' (Romans 8:15–16). We are saved by grace through faith. We minister by grace through faith. We worship by grace through faith. The eternal spiral of love and joy, praise and wonder which constitutes the very being of God as Father, Son and Spirit honour each other, is extended through creation and redemption to embrace our praise. We are invited to step into the life of Christ, to hear the Father speak the Word of love and to join the Word's response in the song of praise. The invitation is delivered by the Spirit of God who 'comprehends what is truly God's' and bestows on us the spiritual capacities to share in the 'depths of God' (1 Corinthians 1:9–13). It is our baptismal gift, the right of our new birth in Christ simply awaiting our use, our enjoyment, our faith as we practise what Christ prayed: 'Father, I desire that those also, whom you have given me, may be where I am' (John 17:24).

Recognition that worship comes to us as a gift to be received and not a duty to be performed relieves us from the tyranny of excellence that can reduce us to despair. Most of us have high standards for worship. That is right and good. We should aim for the best for the Lord. But even when everything goes right something in our hearts tells us that we are still a long way off the sort of experience of worship for which we long. The dynamics of grace allow us to see things differently. They show us that our flawed and faltering worship is received by God with the same joy as a mother hears her child's words of love. God hears the sounds of our words of love in the same tone as Christ's eternal affection. God is able to see through their shortcomings to the salvation he has established for us in Christ, the perfect worshipper. By grace God counts our feeble praise as righteous, holy worship, because it is offered by those who simply cry out, 'Abba!', trusting that the Spirit of God's love will help us in our weakness (Romans 8:26).

Although the deepest dynamics of Christian liturgy are determined by the Trinitarian dynamics of God's life, they are also entwined in the dynamics of the worshipping community. In fact, these two realities – the life of God and the life of the community that seeks to worship God – are themselves closely related. The dynamic of God's love places God in constant interaction with the world brought into being by God's love. God chooses to be touched by the changing circumstances of the world. Hence, the permutations of a congregation's life matter to God. They influence the way God relates to the people, affect what God says to the people and shape God's expectation of the people in any given act of worship. So the situation of a worshipping community requires our attention and sensitivity. We are called to help *this* community in *this* place at *this* time to worship God. That means knowing about all sorts of general things like the age, culture and tradition of the worshippers. It also means tuning into more particular facets of a community's life, the dilemmas and difficulties, the pressures and pains, the concerns, issues, hopes, fears and joys of the people. Our worship can only be an authentic share in the worship of heaven when it respects and reflects the realities of our time and place. Contemporary liturgy allows us to use those patterns and words of worship that can lift a community beyond its immediate context to its wider context in the life of the whole Church and in the life of God. It also gives us great scope to enculturate the liturgy into the rhythms and rhymes of that community's daily living.

While on holiday once, I took my family along to the village church to join its morning service. It was a fine act of worship in many ways, a well-prepared parish communion ordered on good liturgical principles. The problem was that it just carried on regardless of an increasing level of commotion towards the back of the church. Soon after the service began an elderly parishioner began to look worse for wear. She started to keel over in the collect. By the epistle she was flat out on the pew. Although energetically fanned by a number of other parishioners, she was out for the count during the creed. It was by no means clear that she was still alive, which gave a whole new meaning to affirming one's belief in the resurrection of the dead. By the eucharistic prayer the paramedics had arrived and, thankfully, proved that she was still breathing. They carried her out to the ambulance just as I returned from communion. But it was not until the notices before the blessing that the goings on were even given a mention. I remember seeing a magnificent Celtic cross in the churchyard as we left for the beach. I could not help thinking that the powerful symbol of the eternal circle of God's love intersected by the emblem of a harsh event at a particular point in human history, had hardly been reflected in the liturgy we had just experienced.

The condition of the world is the wider context of the worship of a congregation. We always have the world with us when we worship. The life of the local community, the nation and the wider world affects the dynamics of an event of worship, as any who have missed the news the night before have often learnt to their cost. But attention to the life of the world is required by more than the common sense of knowing what is on the hearts and minds of our people. The priestly calling of the Church is to stand before God with and for the world, praying for its pain and speaking the praise that many cannot yet voice. In worship we are being trained to discern God's activity in our places of work, residence and rest, and then we are sent out to do the will of God in our time. Our worship has this priestly orientation because it is a participation in the worship of Christ who intercedes for the world to which he was sent and for which he died. The chapel of Tamil Theological Seminary in South India was built without walls. The seminary wanted its worship to be open and responsive to the world. Although the British climate does not allow such a clear architectural expression of the liturgical principle of openness to the world, part of the responsibility of those who preside over worship is to help the congregation's worship express the intensity of God's interaction with the world.

## Called to preside over the celebration of the Eucharist

Presiding at the Eucharist is the clearest expression of our place and purpose among the priestly people of God. The Eucharist is the great thanksgiving – *eucharistia* – of the great goodness of God. It is the promise of encounter with Christ. It is the place where the body of Christ – Jesus and his people – is manifested in its clearest form. As Christ's people gather for the sort of deep remembrance that absorbed the disciples on the way to Emmaus, they find Christ already with them, they listen to him unfold the scriptures to them, they join in his blessing of the Father, they see him in the breaking of the bread and then they go off to tell the world that he is risen. Here their fundamental identity as Christ's priestly people, offering the fruit of their lips in worship and the obedience of their lives in witness to the world, is renewed and reactualized. And among the people is one who presides: one who is called to guide the Church into a fuller realization of its calling by a truer enactment of its life in this great celebration of faith, hope and love. 'And to preside in the very deed that so expands the life of creatures', writes Robert Hovda in his classic book on presiding at the liturgy, 'is a function of unquestionable beauty and dignity.'[11]

Such a person, Hovda says, will be 'strong, loving and wise', with a depth of faith in Christ and 'a pastoral respect and reverence for people'.[12] Like a conductor of an orchestra the presider is able to hold the various parts of the liturgy together, enabling them to 'flow in and out of each other smoothly'.[13] Like an actor, the presider is 'a body person, at home in the flesh, moving gracefully and expressively, gesturing spontaneously, communicating by the rhythm of the whole person, knowing how to dress up and wear clothing'.[14] Like an athlete in a team-sport, the presider 'facilitates, discretely yields the focus to the one who is operating at a particular moment, guides, prompts when necessary, leads the congregation in attending to the action'. Good presiders 'feel the freedom' of their role. They know their way around the liturgy. They feel the pulse of the people. They listen for the breath of God. They can move with the dynamics of worship, giving space for spontaneity, room for silence and are trusted by their people to lead them towards moments of encounter with the Christ, the head of the body.

The first stage of the Eucharist involves the gathering of the people of God for worship. They have gathered before but they are gathering afresh. This is a new event in the life of the Church. This moment in the history of the Church has not happened before. This is a reconstitution of the Church in the presence of God. The task of the liturgy and the ministry of the presider is to form this people once again into a worshipping community – a body able and willing to work together. We know from the earliest Eucharists at Corinth that it has always been possible for people to *come* together without *being* together. Paul told the Corinthians in no uncertain way that whatever they were doing with bread and wine, it was not the Lord's Supper. The celebration of the grace of the Lord Jesus Christ and the love of God requires the *fellowship of the Holy Spirit*. As we said in Chapter 2, the Spirit is the true administrator of the Church who takes a collection of individual people and separate groups of people and forms us into one body of mutually related ministries. The presider's ministry is to assist the Spirit of fellowship, a ministry that may, as we shall see in Chapter 8, involve facilitating reconciliation.

The relationship between the presider and the people is established in the Greeting. *Dominus vobiscum* are the Latin words from which 'The Lord be with you' is derived. They can also be translated 'The Lord is with you'. Right from the outset we affirm that this is the people of the Lord, Christ's treasure 'bought through the shedding of his blood on the cross'.[15] They are here because Christ has promised to meet them again and to shape them more fully for his purposes as his priestly people. 'And also with you,' is the reply. We too are members of this priestly community. Appointed by the priestly community to preside over its life in Christ, we are here to preside at this eucharistic celebration of the Church's identity and ministry. It is not so much a case of leading the service as *leading in service*, assisting the community to maximize its encounter with Christ. We are here to steer this unique event in the life of the Church in which this worshipping community is being drawn deeper into the Trinitarian dynamics of God's life of giving and receiving. Throughout the liturgy the unbounded self-giving of God to us allures us into the giving of ourselves to God. God's word and our response, gift and welcome, grace and faith are interwoven in an intricate design in almost every part of the Eucharist. The presider is there to oversee the liturgy, to oversee it, literally to *see over* and through it, to the interface between the dynamics of God and the dynamics of the congregation so that, at this time and at this place, Christ's people can engage fully with the reality and activity of God. 'All remember Christ's death, all give thanks to God, and repent and offer themselves an oblation to Christ, all take him for their Lord and Saviour, and spiritually feed upon him,' said Thomas Cranmer, and rightly. The presider's calling is to turn these liturgical principles into liturgical practice.

When the people have gathered as a worshipping community, they are ready to engage with God's word. We can only be the people of God when we allow ourselves to be formed and re-formed by God's word. 'There is only one means and one very cure has been given us after any trouble, and that is the teaching of the Word. This is the best instrument and best climate.' These words of John Chrysostom were certainly true for the disciples on the Emmaus road. The community that had grown up around Jesus had fallen apart. It could only be put back together by the teaching of scripture unlocked by God's word of grace that tells us the Messiah suffered for our sake. In the Liturgy of the Word, the presider stands in direct continuity with Timothy who was advised to 'give attention to the public reading of scripture, to exhorting, to teaching' (1 Timothy 4:13).

Fulfilling this calling does not mean that we do all the preaching, and certainly not all the reading. Presiding over the Liturgy of the Word in the Eucharist is the expression of our general responsibility to ensure that the diet of the people and the climate of their lives, as Chrysostom would have it, are firmly based on scripture. As we attend to God's word, read, sung and proclaimed in the Eucharist by the various ministries of the Church, we show that we stand as much under the word as any other member of the Church, and we model the receptivity to God's word that is vital for the development of the congregation's life in Christ. When we do read or preach as presiders, we put into practice our calling to 'fashion your own life and that of your household according to the way of Christ, that you may be a pattern and example to Christ's people',[16] and by searching the scriptures with our congregations we lead them deeper into Christ's life.

As we participate in Christ's life we not only join Jesus praising the Father, we also hear the Father speaking the word. In Christ we hear God's word, 'You are my beloved' and, in Christ, we become bearers of the word, 'Go on your way. See I am sending you out . . . Whenever you enter a town and its people welcome you, say to them, "The kingdom of God has come near you"' (Luke 10:11). We hear the word and bear the word because, like Mary, overshadowed by the activity of the Holy Spirit, God has promised to form the life of Christ within us and longs for us to respond, 'Here am I the servant of the Lord; let it be to me according to your word' (Luke 1:38).

The ancient Georgian ordination rite prayed that presbyters would 'fulfil apostolic service by true teaching', so that they would be able 'to present to you your Church'.[17] That is what we are called to do when we preside over the Liturgy of the Word at the celebration of the Eucharist and in the whole of the life of the congregation. God has chosen to create a holy people through whom the ministry of Christ can operate. We are to work to see that the Church hears the word of God and responds to the word of God.

The intercessions offer an immediate chance to respond to the word, but the sacramental action and then the Dismissal provide a fuller opportunity for the sacrificial response of lives given over to the service of God for which the word calls. The main actions of the Liturgy of the Sacrament are concentrated in the presider but they assume a dialogical relationship between priest and people and the interplay of a range of other ministries. The bread and wine that the presider *takes* are brought, in some churches at least, by the people. The thanks that the presider voices are as much the praise of the people as the intercessions are the prayer of the people. The bread that the presider breaks is seen by the people and, of course, the gifts of God are given to the people of God.

These simple actions of Christ with bread and wine, repeated by the Church at the Eucharist, are ritual summaries of Christ's action with his people. We have been taken, chosen by Christ for his purposes, called to be his people. Christ gives *thanks* over us, rejoices in us and in so doing blesses us, sanctifies us. 'I thank you, Father, because you have hidden these things from the wise and intelligent and have revealed them to infants' (Luke 10:21). As Jesus praises God for us we are declared righteous, set apart as holy people, consecrated as servants of God. And then Christ *breaks* us – not in the sense of breaking us apart but in the sense of redistributing us, preparing us to be shared with the world. This is Christ's purpose for us, to *give* us to the world as a priestly people living for the praise of God and working for the salvation of the world.

The Eucharist is an intensive moment of Christ's extensive

action among us. Christ has committed himself to a long historical process to perfect a priestly people but in the Eucharist a veil
is lifted off the future and we are permitted to taste 'the powers
of the age to come' (Hebrews 6:5).

> Ponder long the glorious mystery,
> 'This my body, this my blood.'
> Bread and wine reveal God's presence,
> Love engulfs us like a flood.
> Human longing meets God's yearning,
> Words fall silent, all is grace,
> Mystery with hope is brimming,
> Earth is held in heaven's embrace.

As we proclaim the Lord's death until he comes, we offer our
sacrifice of praise and we call upon the Spirit to act through
bread and wine. By gesture and voice, words and song, the
presider's ministry is to build a framework upon which the
people of God can place their great proclamation of priestly
praise and prayer. *Anamnesis*, the grateful remembrance of all
that God has done throughout time and space, *epiclesis*, the
invocation of the Spirit to act at this point of time and space are
the corporate actions of the Church, orchestrated by the
presider. As a sign of the priestly identity of the whole Church
the presider not only co-ordinates the voices of this celebration
but also connects them with the eucharistic worship of the
Church at all times and in all places.

In the eucharistic prayer we practise priestly praise and in the
holy communion we practise priestly living. Martin Luther was
insistent that we have communion with Christ and all his people.

> Then do not doubt that you have what the sacrament signifies,
> that is, be certain that Christ and all his saints are coming to
> you with all their virtues, sufferings, and mercies, to live, work,
> suffer and die with you, and that they desire to be wholly
> yours, having all things in common with you.[18]

Life lived with and for others is the reality and the opportunity of the Lord's Supper. Christ comes to us as the priest who gave his life as a ransom for many and who ever lives to intercede for the world. The one with whom we have communion brings us into communion with God, with God's Church and with God's world. The breadth of our common life with Christ is extraordinary. It reaches beyond those we can see and hear around us, through to the whole Church, living and departed, and then further still to all with whom Christ stands in solidarity as their true priest who has offered for them the sacrifice for sin and continues to bear their burdens. The implications of this communion are equally staggering. How can we be out of sorts with our neighbour who drinks from the same cup of salvation? How can we not share the eucharistic bread with those who are in communion with Christ? How can we not tell the world that Christ has given his life so that we can share his life and sit at his table? How can we rest when vast swathes of the human population die of hunger and thirst while we eat the bread of tomorrow and taste the new wine of the kingdom? Can we not hear the tears of Christ as Lazarus – the poor man at the gate and the friend of Christ – dies? Perhaps the hardest challenge for the presider is to keep people's hearts open to the challenge of Christ's invitation to share his life *and his work*.

The Dismissal is the final stage of the eucharistic celebration and the next stage in living the eucharistic life. Traditionally deacons, as signs of the serving ministry of the Church, send the people out 'to love and serve the Lord'. Before doing so it is usual for the presider to pronounce God's blessing on those who, having heard God's word, offered God praise and received God's Son, will now obey the word through a faithful ministry to God's world in the name and power of Christ. That is the fruit of our priestly ministry: the formation of a missionary people.

# 5

## BEING FOR THE WORD

Through the seasons of our wonder,
through our searching of God's ways,
prospects far beyond our dreaming
open to attentive gaze.
Each new haven on our journey,
each new path with God begun,
turns our steps to love so glorious,
love that moves the stars, the sun.

Vast the splendour of creation,
deep the mysteries of grace,
full the scope of Christ's redemption,
fine their edges that we trace.
Jesus, light and truth incarnate,
Word made flesh, our great high priest,
once with friends, and now for ever
host at heaven's earthly feast.

Glimpsing pure and dappled beauty,
holiness made manifest,
unexpected hints and guesses
of God's life in Christ expressed,
listening for God, we follow,
drawn by love's insistent voice,
known beyond our comprehension,
welcomed home, our hearts rejoice.

In the seasons of our wonder,
in our probing of God's ways,
words eclipsed and thoughts confounded
point us to profounder praise.
Earth reverberates with glory:
foretaste of God's kingdom come,
beauty that astounds and charms us,
Love, compelling, bids us come.[1]

## Formed by the Word

As Christians we are *for* Jesus Christ, the Word of God to whom
God's word in scripture points. Being for the Word means living
with holy wonder in a world in which the Word of God took
human flesh, a world in which the Word speaks, whispers,
shouts and serenades today. But we cannot be for the Word
unless we are also people committed to being for the word of
God in scripture. Therefore, our own immersion in scripture is
essential for any ministry among the people of God, people who
are themselves called to be people of the word. Given that the
word of God is living and active, sharper than any two-edged
sword that pierces to the very core of our being (Hebrews
4:12–13) this is a life-changing business. We lay ourselves open
to God whenever we turn to the word.

We tend to think of Joshua as a military leader, but he is intro-
duced as a young man who spent long hours in the tent of meeting, staying even when Moses left (Exodus 33:11), and he is
described by God as a man in whom the Spirit dwelt (Numbers
27:18). God's first word to Joshua, when he took over responsibility for leading the people into the promised land after Moses'
death, was not the detailed military strategy for which he might
have hoped, but the charge to meditate day and night on the law,
and to be careful to act in accordance with it. In Joshua's life,
word and work belonged together, as all ministers in secular
employment know.

Sometimes we talk of being *immersed* in the word of God.
Another image is Aidan Kavanagh's description of being

*marinated* in the word so that we cannot help but spread the fragrance of Christ wherever we go (2 Corinthians 2:14–16). Then, when we fulfil our charge to proclaim the word of God, to call hearers to repentance, to teach and encourage by word and example, there will be an integrity between our words and our life. George Herbert, in his poem 'The Windows', to which we referred in Chapter 3, catches this beautifully:

> Lord, how can man preach thy eternal word?
>   He is a brittle crazy glass:
> Yet in thy temple thou dost him afford
>   This glorious and transcendent place,
>   To be a window, through thy grace.
>
> But when thou dost anneal in glass thy story,
>   Making thy life to shine within
> The holy Preacher's; then the light and glory
>   More rev'rend grows, and more doth win:
>   Which else shows wat'rish, bleak, and thin.
>
> Doctrine and life, colours and light, in one
>   When they combine and mingle, bring
> A strong regard and awe, but speech alone
>   Doth vanish like a flaring thing,
> And in the ear, not conscience ring.

Being for the word, being marinated in the word, God's story annealed in us with the colours burned in as they are annealed into glass: that is our vocation. Therefore we promise to be 'diligent in prayer, in reading holy scripture, and in all studies that will deepen our faith and fit us to bear witness to the truth of the gospel against error'.[2] The Mozarabic ordination liturgy prays for presbyters to carry out their reading in their work and improve their work by reading. In the twelfth century, William of St Thierry beautifully explained how our quest for theological understanding only begins to bear genuine fruit when it is motivated by our love of God and of God's ways:

When the object of thought is God and the things which relate to God and the will reaches the stage at which it becomes love, the Holy Spirit, the Spirit of life, at once infuses himself by way of love and gives life to everything, lending his assistance in prayer, in meditation or in study to human weakness. Immediately ... the understanding of the one thinking becomes the understanding of the one loving.[3]

Truth and love, doctrine and life, an embodied form of wisdom, is the goal for which the biblical writers strove and the great theological figures of the Church have searched. Doctrine without life can be legalistic, while life without doctrine can be diffuse. In the ordination service the bishop tells the congregation that priests are called to be 'formed by the word'. Our vocation is to combine a passion for God's living word with a joy in living in God's world. Committed to live lives of wonder, searching and probing God's ways, we will be windows through which God's light and glory can shine.

Moses is described in Psalm 103:7 as being a person to whom God revealed not only his acts, which anyone who looked could see, but God's ways – the meaning of God's acts – which are so much harder to comprehend. Not being content with simply observing what is happening but being willing to explore below the surface through study, reflection and prayer, in effect living with attentive wonder, is integral to the priestly ministry. While without wonder we are prone to jaded stagnation, wonder keeps us constantly open to being delighted and drawn on by God, living with our senses attuned to the life-giving word of God. Then we can help to fill and fire people's imaginations with wonder, creating an enthusiasm for living in a world in which the word of God sets life alight and joins us to the story that reaches from ancient times until now.

We are ever moving onwards, as the Rule of Benedict describes so ecstatically in the Prologue, 'as we progress in this way of life and in faith, we shall run on the path of God's commandments, our hearts overflowing with the inexpressible delight of love'.[4] Running has an urgency about it and, although it can be an urgency born of fear, in this context it is clearly the urgency of exuberance. It is the same delight that lies behind the passionate love of God's law that exults, 'I find my delight in your commandments because I love them' (Psalm 119:47). This word is living and active, so that we too will discover with Barbara Brown Taylor, an Episcopal priest in the United States that:

> For all the human handiwork it displays, the Bible remains a peculiarly holy book. I cannot think of any other text that has such authority over me, interpreting me faster than I can interpret it. It speaks to me not with the stuffy voice of some mummified sage but with the fresh, lively tones of someone who knows what happened to me an hour ago. Familiar passages accumulate meaning as I return to them again and again. They seem to grow during my absences from them; I am always finding something new in them I never found before, something designed to meet me where I am at this particular moment in time.[5]

Delighting in the love of God's word, we can be vulnerable enough not to seek to master the word but to be mastered by it, to engage with it and so be transformed. God never speaks for the sake of it. Instead God's word accomplishes God's purposes (Isaiah 55:10–11), and never merely marks time. Maria Boulding, a nun and hermit from Stanbrook Abbey, describes how even though the word does not always clarify situations or inform us about matters in quite the way we might hope, it is nonetheless performative and creative: changing and converting and renewing us, since it is the presence and self-communication of God.[6] God calls us to live with and be transformed by the creative and mysterious word of God ourselves, and as we do so to invite others into that living engagement with the performative word. When so many in our world and our churches are looking for false certainties, it can be threatening to be confronted with the word that is creative and renewing, not merely comfortable. The Holy Spirit has always been disruptive, sending the prophetic word to disturb our complacency and engaging us, too, in the priestly ministry of bringing comfort through necessary disturbance. If we are to be for the word, we have an immense pastoral task given to us as we help people keep track of what God is doing among them.

Being for the word involves knowing the word: studying the written word, meditating on it, allowing it to change us. We have never read any particular scripture too many times; we can never skip the word of God on the basis that we have heard it before. Instead, it is as we give ourselves to the priestly task of listening to God and listening to the parish, or other location in which we serve, that we will begin to hear the unexpected word that is life-giving for our people today. The psalmist says, 'Today when you hear his voice, harden not your hearts as your forebears did in the wilderness' (Psalm 95:7–8). Today, wherever we are, whatever the season, we are face to face with the word of God in all its explosive power and we are told to be attentive: sit up and take notice! Then we will begin to see the fulfilment of the charge we are given when we are ordained, to pray that 'our hearts may be daily enlarged and our understanding of the scriptures enlightened',[7] so that our lives and the lives of those we serve will be shaped by God's word. Growth in holiness and in the knowledge and love of God ask of us that we are ever open to the exhilarating yet sometimes demanding process of the Holy Spirit in enlarging our hearts. That comes about, in part, as our understanding of the scriptures is enlightened. Our people need us to be open to enlargement and enlightenment of both heart and mind through our exposure to God's word, and at the welcome of the newly ordained the people charge the new priest to 'Let the word of Christ dwell in you richly'.

In the fourteenth century John Myrc wrote a series of versified 'Instructions' for the clergy of his time. He exhorted them to study scripture, to know what God wanted them to preach and teach, and to learn how God wanted them to be.

If you are not a learned cleric,
you must study this written work;
for here you can find and read

that which it is incumbent upon you to know;
how you will preach to your parish,
and what it is necessary that you teach them,
and of what character you must be
if you wish God to be near you.[8]

Unlike so many medieval clergy whose opportunities were very limited, we are familiar with the Bible. Committed as we are to a daily rhythm of reading and meditating on the word of God, we will find that the same reading, the same psalm, brings different life as we encounter it in different circumstances. A story from the Gospels will meet us in a different way when we hear it in its seasonal context from the way it will speak in the midst of a daily lectionary trek through a Gospel. The account of the transfiguration of Jesus is read on the Feast of Transfiguration, which is also Hiroshima Day with all the ambivalence that evokes, on the last Sunday before Lent where it comes as the culmination of the revelation of Jesus Christ that we have been following since Epiphany, and in the midst of ordinary time in the daily lectionary. We encounter the transfiguration differently each time; the same sermon cannot be preached on each occasion and we have never exhausted the perspectives that shed light on it. We will hear God's word through the same lectionary readings very differently in a church where hope is rampant from one where tragedy has struck in one of its many guises.

Our task is 'to enlarge our understanding of the scriptures and thus to fashion our own and our people's lives on the word of God', as an earlier Anglican liturgy put it.[9] Our forebears knew this well: Joseph Hall, the seventeenth-century divine, saw his vocation as teaching people the skills for divine meditation that could enable them to practise true piety. His writings on the art of divine meditation amplify how meditation – pondering God's ways revealed through scripture and life – is 'the very end God hath given our souls for'. Often our problem is that we live as though God has given us 101 tasks to do that can be allowed to squeeze out this 'very end'. When this happens – as it will – Hall stands as a wise reminder that meditation is a wellspring of ministry that cannot be neglected. Some of his contemporary seventeenth-century Anglicans, knowing the very close link between preaching and the preacher's own personal meditation on the word, spoke of preaching as 'meditation shared with an auditory'.[10] If this is taken to heart, then sermon preparation can be recast from a rush to get words on paper into meditative reading and reflection on the word. As meditation helps us to bear the fruit of centredness or collectedness, so we in our ministry bear the life-giving word to others.

All this sounds ideal, if not idealistic! For most clergy, particularly those whose ministry takes them into the secular workplace, the time to meditate on the word of God is probably at a premium. The Daily Office provides for daily exposure to the word of God, but how to build this necessary meditation into our lives is one of the constant challenges of our vocation. We may need to learn that failure (in this or in anything else) is not terminal with God. Nevertheless, if a pattern of sustained engagement with God's word, through prayerful, systematic, rhythmic and deep exposure to scripture, is not in place then it will be difficult for us to become people in whom 'the word of Christ dwells richly' (Colossians 3:15). Patterns of prayer and Bible reading that satisfied us in the past will need to be reconsidered as we grow into the ministry to which God has called us, since what was sufficient once may not be adequate now (1 Corinthians 3:1–2). Without a routine grounding in God's word we will falter or dehydrate, and our ministry will accordingly cause others to fall or their thirst to go unquenched.

The Anglican Ordinal (1550/1662) has some salutary words from the bishop addressed to those to be ordained,

> Seeing that ye cannot, by any other means, compass the doing of so weighty a work, pertaining to the salvation of man, but with doctrine and exhortation taken out of holy Scripture, and with a life agreeable to the same, ye perceive how studious ye ought to be in reading and learning the holy Scriptures, and in framing the manners, both of yourselves, and of them that specially pertain unto you, according to the rule of the same Scriptures.

The Reformation emphasis on doctrine and exhortation taken out of holy scripture is familiar to us, as is its emphasis on godly living shaped by the scriptures. But that challenging word 'learning' sits there as a demanding reminder of the vision Cranmer had for the reformed Church in England. He wanted people to *learn holy scripture*. While this includes committing it to memory, it seems to be broader than that, hinting at learning as committing it to life so that we are led forth ('educated'), in scripture. Few ordination courses today require the learning of scriptures. Instead, we too often are content to stop short on the one hand at hasty exegesis which informs our study but misses the wisdom that shapes our lives, or on the other hand, at devotional reading of a short passage of scripture followed by some Bible reading notes. We need the best of both worlds, with both informed study and devotional engagement, since our preparation to preach in the life-shaping manner that Cranmer envisaged requires that we learn God's word in a way that transforms us.

## Messengers of the word

Exposure to God's word is essential to our preparation to proclaim the word. So, too, is exposure to words. Reading for pleasure, listening to the spoken word, watching plays and films are all ways of developing our resources for proclaiming the word. Language should be beautiful if we speak of a beautiful God, but to speak in this way we need to hear and read in this way. Our diet of terse e-mail communication may be convenient, and the specialist language of technical manuals or business documents may be necessary but, lest either diminish our ability to think and speak with grace and imagination, we need to ensure a balanced diet that keeps words alive and lively. Time to read a well-written novel or poetry, and to savour the words and images that in turn nurture our own imagination and vocabulary, is time well spent.

Our vocation as described in the Ordinal includes being messengers, watchmen or sentinels, and stewards of the Lord. This is a prophetic as well as pastoral vocation. Prophetic ministry is an extension of the ministry of caring, and it is a calling that requires us to be open to hear and to interpret the sometimes challenging and provocative word of God. At times we are called to speak words of comfort, to serve people gently, to offer comfort and consolation. At other times we are asked to proclaim God's challenge and disruption to the status quo. Both are at the bidding of the Holy Spirit who can be disruptive, driving rather than leading us into what seems like a wilderness (Mark 1:12; Luke 4:1), as well as being the giver of peace and calm. In the imagery of the Celts, the Holy Spirit at times appears more as a wild goose than a dove, coming on us as a rush of violent wind and tongues of fire rather than as gentle breath (Acts 2:2–3; John 20:22). This disturbing power of God, not our own stirring of people's emotions, brings life and transformation. Caring for people means that we too have to be exposed to this unsettling and at times unruly word of God, living faithfully and helping others to live faithfully in the place of unsettlement.

Mary Grey's evocative phrase, 'kneading hope'[11] articulates the prophetic and pastoral tasks that we are given. As any bread maker knows, kneading is a hands on, time-consuming and physically demanding task which repeats the same movements time and again with the same lump of dough. Yet without that kneading there is no bread; without the kneading of hope there is no life. Kneading is not always comfortable. The pastoral aspect of priestly ministry, the diaconal vocation that we never outgrow, kneads hope through compassionate service and care; the priestly vocation kneads hope as we lead our people on paths that they have not yet seen for themselves, or need encouragement to tread.

What our world needs, what our people need, is to be taught to dance and sing their lives to the music of the word of God. But in many churches today any spark of life is being quenched by concerns about small congregations, repair bills and the other hard practical issues of church life where the geographic distribution of churches no longer reflects the realities of life. It is not surprising that faithful people find their vision faltering as survival seems barely assured. In these situations, kneading hope is a demanding responsibility. We share the prophets' call to keep

alive the ministry of imagination, to keep on dreaming alternative possibilities to the apparently inevitable. As those charged
with the cure of souls, we need to be exposed to the word of God
ourselves in order to keep our own hope and imagination alive.
God's word will relentlessly push our own boundaries back with
the expansive love of God, while at the same time securing our
centre in God. Dreaming dreams with God for our churches can
be hard when they are locked into despair or unyielding routine,
and we are faced with the challenge to trust that the Holy Spirit,
the wild goose and the gentle dove, can breathe new life. It is at
times like these that we are called back to the word.

The early ordination liturgies emphasized the call of the presbyter to preach and to teach, a calling that is as true today as it
ever was. Michael Ramsey worked on the principle that in
preaching we should be simple rather than erudite since our aim
is to be understood, not to blind our people with theological
science. There is no short cut to the task of kneading hope
through preaching the word of God week in, week out, among
the people we are called to serve. Weekly kneading of hope opens
a different perspective on preaching to the preaching that is
called for at a one-off event, be it celebration or funeral. There
we are asked to preach the word knowing that the sermon, along
with the rest of the liturgy, must do its task of bringing word and
world into dialogue for this one occasion. On the other hand,
preaching regularly to a congregation each week allows us to
adopt a longer perspective. While each sermon should be complete in itself, it is only part of the ongoing formation of the congregation and all the work does not have to be done in one week.
The lectionary keeps us moving through the story of God's ways
with the world, particularly the story of Jesus, and thus spares us
the impossible and dangerous task of trying to make each week's
part of the story into the denouement. The lectionary, or other
systematic reading of scripture, allows for life to be ordinary,
and reminds us that the chance to relish the ordinary is a gift.

Daily prayer and reflection on the scripture read systematically will immerse us in the story of God and integrate us in God's
word. This lies at the heart of what has become known as –

somewhat formidably – the 'Daily Office'. The Daily Office is simply a way of structuring prayer, praise and scripture reading in a common framework which people can follow together, whether or not they are physically in the same place. For Anglicans the Daily Office has always had a strong emphasis on sustained engagement with scripture both through hearing scripture read and using scripture in prayer. *Common Worship: Daily Prayer* both continues this respect for the place of scripture in prayer and allows for a variety of ways of distributing the reading of scripture through the day. It builds upon Thomas Cranmer's conviction, which he inherited from Benedictine patterns of prayer, that formation in God's word lies at the heart of Christian living.

Regular, daily engagement with scripture as we begin or end the day, or sometime during the day's demands, teaches us to listen to scripture in the light of the ordinary events of the day. In the morning we listen for help to see the day ahead with the eyes of faith, and then we join with Zechariah as (in the words of the Benedictus) we commit ourselves to 'go before the Lord to prepare his way'. In the evening, we listen for help to see how God has been at work in the joys and frustrations of the day, and we join with Mary as (in the words of the Magnificat) we rejoice that God has 'cast down the mighty from their thrones and lifted up the lowly'. At the close of the day, we listen for help to see that God has been with us even in the unexpected places of the day, and we join Simeon as (in the words of the Nunc dimittis) we affirm that 'our own eyes have seen the salvation which God has prepared in the sight of every people'.

## Listening to the word and to the world

Hope has to have a voice and has to be heard. If we are to help to keep hope and imagination alive for ourselves and in others, Walter Brueggemann suggests that the sermon must be a modelling of a conversation in which all partners speak. He warns that if the human voice, the voice of our listeners, has been silenced by alienation or suppressed rage, then the voice of God alone will not evoke praise or permit transformation.[12] We should remember that we can only preach the word of God as such a conversation if our own voice, too, has not been reduced to silence. If we have silenced it, it will speak anyway, in potentially destructive ways. Thus we are brought back to our own being for God, being for the word, being for prayer. Without becoming self-centred, we need to remember that the health of our ministry depends upon our own relationship with God and God's word: if we keep that healthy and lively, all else can follow.

The task we are given of fashioning our lives and the lives of our people on the word of God involves us in learning to know and to articulate the voice of our hearers so that they can hear themselves in the conversation. This means listening to the world our congregation lives in, knowing that world through living close to the ground our people tread on in the parish, the hospital, the prison, the school, or wherever else we are set. For those clergy who have been deployed to a different area this world may be unfamiliar, even strange, while for others, particularly for those called to Ordained Local Ministry, it may be very familiar. The challenges are different. In an unfamiliar world the problem can be the difficulty of entering into the different context fully, while for those ordained to serve in their home context the problem can be learning to see it with the eyes and heart of a priest in addition to the eyes and heart of a local resident. Our vocation is to oversight, to 'seeing over' a situation so that we discern what is really going on, what God is doing.

Whatever the situation, our example is the Word made flesh who dwelt among us. As we get to know our hearers' world and what makes them tick, then we can help them to hear God and to hear their own voice in the conversation that the sermon begins. Our responsibility as preachers includes both knowing the world around us into which we preach, and exploring the word so tenaciously that we draw from it the words that will be life-giving to those entrusted to our care. Our preaching will be most effective when it flows from a relationship of love and trust with those who hear us, as Gregory, from whom we heard in Chapter 2, reminds us, 'the seed of the word springeth easily when the kindness of the preacher watereth it in the breast of the hearer'.[13]

While God speaks through scripture and in our prayer, we will also find ourselves hearing God in sometimes unexpected ways. As part of our ongoing preparation for preaching as well as our sheer enjoyment of God's creative gifts, there should be space in our lives for the arts, sports events, hobbies, laughter, current events and whatever else both re-creates us and keeps us rooted in the world in which we live. We should listen to and enjoy our world at large and our local patch which includes our particular people, with all their gifts and idiosyncracies. Each congregation is unique and there is no substitute for visiting people in their homes if we are to know and care for them, as George Herbert describes the 'parson in circuit' in his rather quaint, but knowing, language:

> The country parson upon the afternoons in the weekdays takes occasion sometimes to visit in person now one quarter of his parish, now another. For there he shall find his flock most naturally as they are, wallowing in the midst of their affairs, whereas on Sundays it is easy for them to compose themselves to order, which they put on as their holy-day clothes and come to church in frame, but commonly the next day put off both.[14]

'Wallowing in the midst of their affairs' may mean being, as one local ministry ordinand describes himself, chaplain to the local pub. It may mean serving tea in a hospital or following in the footsteps of many clergy who have taken part in the local pantomime. For many it involves daily work in a factory or research institute and being known and available as an ordained person to colleagues who would never set foot in a church. Whether it is sheer enjoyment or grinding hard work, we are perpetual students when it comes to learning to listen to God through and with the people and the situations in which we live.

As we go through life learning to listen, we have to learn, too, to reflect on the word theologically, however it comes to us. Grappling theologically with the word and world in which we live is essential if we are to speak the word of God in the face of triumph or tragedy: someone has to preach the sermon at the funeral of a murdered child, at a celebrity wedding, on the Sunday

after a momentous village event or the destruction of the World
Trade Center. The liturgical tradition is immensely helpful here
in containing the grief or the joy and holding our lives within
God's larger story. The word of God spoken at a funeral in
Christmas week cannot avoid the clash of the mourners' grief
and the world's joyful anticipation, but the message of the angels
has never been spoken to people who live in unconflicted peace.
Mothering Sunday falls in Lent each year, Holy Innocents comes
straight after Christmas, and on rare occasions the Annunciation
falls on Good Friday – a theme explored in 1608 by John Donne
in his poem 'Upon the Annunciation and the Passion Falling
Upon One Day':

> Tamely, frail body, abstain today; today
> My soul eats twice, Christ hither and away.
>          . . . this doubtful day
> Of feast or fast, Christ came, and went away; . . .
> She sees at once the virgin mother stay
> Reclused at home, public at Golgotha.
> Sad and rejoiced she's seen at once, and seen
> At almost fifty, and at scarce fifteen,
> At once a son is promised her, and gone,
> Gabriel gives Christ to her, he her to John.[15]

Paradox has never been a problem to God, and wise theological
thought will help us to trace God's ways in the midst of it. Most
of the time the preparation for the extraordinary lies in faithful
and attentive listening and reflection on the ordinary, week in,
week out.

The poet and priest, R. S. Thomas captures this essential blend
of listening to God and to the people in his perceptive but ultimately tragic poem, 'The Minister'. This poem, which repays
reading in full,[16] tells of the enthusiastic young minister called to
serve in a Welsh chapel where the moor and the wind shaped the
people's hearing of the word:

> There were people here before these,
> Measuring truth according to the moor's
> Pitiless commentary and the wind's veto.

Elias Morgan, BA, the young man called to this bleak place, came with pale cheeks and bowed shoulders from years of study, and a deep inner zeal to thaw the darkness around these people. He had all the training to hear the word of God, but unlike Herbert he had no training in listening to the people and the place. Too late he says of himself:

> . . . indeed, my knowledge
> Would have been complete, had it included
> The bare moor, where nature brooded
> Over her old, inscrutable secret.
> But I didn't even know the names
> Of the birds and the flowers by which one gets
> A little closer to nature's heart.

In the end, Morgan is defeated by his deafness to the people and their land:

> Need we go on? In spite of all
> His courage Morgan could not avert
> His failure, for he chose to fight
> With that which yields to nothing human.
> He never listened to the hills'
> Music calling to the hushed
> Music within; but let his mind
> Fester with brooding on the sly
> Infirmities of the hill people.

## Preaching the word

Listening is part of the story. We also need to find appropriate ways to proclaim and preach the word of God, recognizing that preaching can take different forms in different churches and contexts. On the one hand, John Donne could write, with his tongue in his cheek, that he had come to the conclusion that Puritans preached long sermons because they imagine 'it is their duty to preach on till their auditors [hearers] wake'.[17] On the other, keeping people's attention was apparently not a problem for a

Mr Rogers, who lived around the same time at Dedham. He was in the habit of 'taking hold with both hands of the supporters of the canopy over the pulpit, and roaring hideously to represent the torments of the damned. [It] had an awakening force attending it'.[18]

Kneading hope through preaching need not be so dramatic. George Herbert knew this: when, faced with 'thick and heavy' people, he preached from scriptural texts that he described as 'moving and ravishing' because he wanted his people to be transported and enchanted, nor merely entertained or informed,[19] and Izaac Walton described Herbert's preaching as essentially 'plain and practical'.[20] According to Izaac Walton, John Donne also allured and entranced people with the gospel as he drew large crowds to hear his sermons at St Paul's in the early seventeenth century. His sermons have been described as avoiding polemical points of doctrine in order to concentrate on the essentials of the Christian faith.[21] Richard Baxter's advice was that 'all our teaching must be as plain and evident as we can make it . . . He that would be understood must speak to the capacity of his hearers and make it his business to make himself understood.'[22] However, this was no excuse for not stretching the people, 'See that you preach . . . some higher points, that stall their understandings and feed them not with all milk, but sometimes with stronger meat.'[23] We can learn from these earlier preachers that there are many ways to fulfil the charge given at ordination to 'unfold the word', preaching both in season and out of season. 'Unfolding' asks of us a greater creativity and sensitivity than simply presenting our hearers with a set-piece sermon that they can take or leave, and we can only preach the word out of season – when people may resist what they hear – if we have taken care to build a relationship as we unfold the word in season.

Unlike Herbert and Donne who appear to have chosen their own text, as do some preachers today, the choice of text is not always up to us. Many denominations share a lectionary which holds us to the whole of scripture and does not give us the option of picking and choosing as though the Bible were an anthology, or a collection of verses to be underlined and taken out of context. Whether or not our congregation follows a lectionary, priestly ministry makes us responsible to the word of God and for the word of God. The Church does not have the luxury of avoiding the hard edges of the biblical tradition, or the hard situations in life to which the word of God speaks. Lancelot Andrewes said in an Ash Wednesday sermon in 1619, 'our charge is to preach to men *non quae audire, sed volunt audisse* "not what for the present they would hear, but what in another day they would wish they had heard".' Twenty-five years earlier, in Lent 1594, he had described priests as 'the Lord's remembrancers', bringing the people to God in prayer, both private and public, and God before them in preaching. In the same vein, John Donne wrote in his poem, 'To Mr Tilman After He Had Taken Orders', about the task of those who bear the word of God:

> Mary's prerogative was to bear Christ, so
> 'tis preachers' to convey him, for they do
> as angels out of clouds, from pulpits speak;
> if then th'astronomers, whereas they spy
> a new found star, their optics magnify,
> how brave are those, who with their engine, can
> bring man to heaven, and heaven again to man?

For Donne the preaching task is to convey Christ, to bring heaven and earth to each other. How, then, do we preach the word once it has taken root in us? There is no one way: John Donne preferred to take a text of no more than two or three verses and dissect it, bringing other scriptures to bear on it, reflecting on it rather than giving an exposition. In contrast, Herbert, who considered Donne's approach to be 'crumbling the text' and treating it as a dictionary, took longer portions of scripture and aimed for sermons (of no longer than an hour!) that were presented with attention to the congregation's various needs, illustrated by stories and sayings which would be easy to remember, and applied to their situation.[24] In the nineteenth century the Anglican priest Frederick Robertson drew large congregations to his church in Brighton where he always began from the biblical text, rather than using scripture to illustrate or support a line of thought from an external source. This is the authentically Anglican way of preaching, shaped by the word read systematically. Although the preacher may refer to current issues and events, they are rarely the inspiration for the sermon. Instead, faithful reflection on the word provides the context in which these issues can be pondered theologically and held in the light of the whole word of God.

Ellen Davis has said of Robertson's preaching that the single most important factor in its powerful effect was his broad and profound knowledge of the Bible, which enabled him to find the truth in any one passage and present it simply, because he looked at it from a perspective informed by the whole of scripture. Robertson taught the truth suggestively, not dogmatically, so that it could be discerned by one's spirit rather than merely evaluated intellectually as propositions to be taken or left without touching the hearer's life.[25] This points us to another facet of kneading hope, since the word discerned by the spirit can be internalized by the hearers until it becomes life-giving and transformative. There is certainly a place for the intellectual presentation of the gospel, but week by week our preaching should also tend and feed Christ's people. How we do this is influenced in part by our knowledge of our hearers.

When we tell the story of God and the world we invite people into this story, not just to observe it but to participate in it within the framing story of creation and redemption. Too often we ignore the Old Testament in our preaching, and it is disturbing to discover how many Christians at the heart of their church's life know the Old Testament only as a series of unconnected stories about a few famous people, rather than as the record of God's dealings with a people, as the coherent story of God's ways with a wayward world. How can we, as people who proclaim the word of God, reduce God's word to snippets? The story of David and Goliath is a gloriously dramatic story for children, but if it remains for adults nothing more than a dramatic but isolated event we are selling people short and the story ceases to be formational, only episodic. When the word is confined to accounts of isolated events that show the central character as so faithful and holy that we wonder if they are like us, it is no wonder that we despair at being able to hear our story in the greater story. Told that way, there seems to be no room in God's word for our mundane and undramatic everyday life. One of my abiding memories is reading the books of Ruth and Susanna to a group of women on a retreat. They had never heard the books read in their entirety and many did not even know the stories, but that evening they were as attentive as a group of children listening to a story and they quickly made connections with their own lives. In our proclamation of the word of God in the Old Testament it is our privilege to invite people into the story of oppression and injustice, of struggle with and resistance to the hard call of God, of deliverance and of responsibilities. To that much fuller story, people can bring their own experiences, hopes and fears, thus meeting the God who redeems and transforms, knowing that God can work with their struggle, resistance and fear too. Therein lies hope.

The question for each one of us, as we fulfil our charge to preach the gospel of Christ, is how best to enable people to hear the word of God so that it can be unleashed in them to do its transformative work. For those who preach in the context of liturgy, the liturgy itself helps people to absorb a scriptural vocabulary, for good liturgy is simply scripture turned into prayer.

In addition to awareness of its liturgical context, preaching should always recognize that people come with their own stories, joys and sorrows, so that the preacher's task is, in part, to enable them to make the links between the gospel and daily life. At its best, Anglican preaching aims for conversion of life, for daily conversion to a more godly way of living, and therefore preaching has to help people enter into the scriptural world so that they can hear its call to conversion of life. Thus Thomas Cranmer, in the first homily that was distributed for use in the new, reformed English Church, wrote,

And in reading God's word, he most profiteth not always that is most ready in turning of the book, or in saying of it without the book; but he that is most tuned into it, that is most inspired with the Holy Ghost, most in his heart and life altered and changed into that thing which he readeth; he that is daily less and less proud, less wrathful, less covetous, and less desirous of worldly and vain pleasure; he that daily (forsaking his old vicious life) increaseth in virtue more and more.

We can open up the scriptural world, we can hold out the hope born of a godly imagination and passion for the kingdom of God, we can give people the opportunity to be faithful, we can invite them to share in God's life, and we can empower people. However, we cannot do their work for them or take away their responsibility to act for themselves on what they hear. Our privilege is to keep the word alive in people's hearts and minds, to give them the vocabulary of faith, to teach and encourage by word and example. The calling on us to serve the people with joy, to build them up in the faith and do all in our power to bring them to loving obedience to Christ, does not allow us to keep them as spiritual infants who are dependent on us, or to shackle them to an inauthentic response. In this our own response to the word, our own example, will speak as loudly as our words. Our life during the rest of the week may be just as much a sermon as the brief time we spend in the pulpit on a Sunday.

For ourselves, our vocation is to become people of the word, people who know our baptismal calling, who live with our imaginations fired and filled by the lively and performative word of God in a world which tries so relentlessly to reduce everything to security and certainty. In the face of our culture's fixation on its own means of control, our vocation is both prophetic and pastoral: we proclaim and are ourselves open to the powerful and transformative word of God. We are asked to nurture ourselves in God's word, so that we and others know the truth that earth, indeed, reverberates with glory, the foretaste of God's coming kingdom. Astounded and charmed by God's beauty, we are invited, compelled, by love to 'come, buy and eat! Come, buy wine and milk without money and without price' at the table of God's word (Isaiah 55:1).

# 6

## Being for Prayer

Holy Spirit, come among us,
come in gentleness and love;
once you came empowering Jesus
God descending as a dove.
Once you came on the disciples –
rushing wind and tongues of flame,
come, descend, O Holy Spirit,
come in Jesus' holy name.

Holy Spirit, praying for us,
keep us in God's perfect will;
come, anoint us for God's service,
come, our open hearts to fill.
As the wind sweeps o'er the water –
unseen power that leaves its trace,
come, disturb our lives and make them
true reflections of God's grace.

Holy Spirit, guide and guardian,
teaching us the ways of God,
fire and cloud to lead us onward
as we tread where Christ has trod.
Should you drive us to the desert,
should you send us to the poor,
it is Jesus we are following,
Holy Spirit, come once more.

Holy Spirit, come, renew us,
breathe on us breath from above;
Advocate with us for ever,
draw us with eternal love.
Fill our hearts and burn within us,
redirect our wandering gaze
'til our eyes are fixed on Jesus
and our lives proclaim God's praise.[1]

## People of prayer

Whatever else people want of us as priests, they want us to pray
for them. Equally, being a person of prayer is a priority that most
clergy set for themselves, part of what they see as their vocation.
We need look no further for an example of a leader who prayed
for his people than Paul, who could say to the Philippians, 'I
thank my God every time I remember you, constantly praying
with joy in every one of my prayers for all of you ...'
(Philippians 1:3–4). And yet this is an area where, almost without exception, the ordained admit to feeling they fail to meet
their own expectations or hopes, quite apart from the expectations of those they minister among.[2] Too often we end up feeling
not only failures, but guilty about our inability to pray as, in our
better moments, we wish to do. It is so easy to be afraid that if
our congregations knew the paucity of our prayer life then they
would lose all the trust and respect they might have in us.

However disciplined our prayer life, whatever our devotional
feelings or lack of them, we cannot pray on our own, in our own
strength. Hence the wisdom behind the response we make at
ordination when asked if we will be diligent in prayer, 'by the
help of God, I will'. Paul reminds us that 'The Spirit helps us in
our weakness; for we do not know how to pray as we ought, but
that very Spirit intercedes with sighs too deep for words. And
God, who searches the heart, knows what is the mind of the Spirit,
because the Spirit intercedes for the saints according to the will of
God' (Romans 8:26–27). It is only because of the empowering of
the Holy Spirit coming among us, praying for and in us, drawing

us with eternal love, that we are enabled to fulfil our charge to be diligent in prayer, to intercede for our people, to lead them in prayer and worship, and to teach and encourage them by word and example. At ordinations we pray for the Holy Spirit to come with abundant grace, and it is in prayer that we daily live into that grace, enabling us to live the life we pray. Only then can we, and our people, have the spiritual strength to meet the demands placed upon us as well as the vitality and openness to receive the unexpected delights that flow from the generosity of God.

Many clergy recognize the feeling that we have to apologize for spending time in prayer when we could be 'doing' something more productive. When this temptation strikes us, as it will, we can look to our forebears in the faith to help us keep our balance in life. Theophan the Recluse knew that,

> Prayer is the test of everything; prayer is also the source of everything; prayer is the driving force of everything; prayer is also the director of everything. If prayer is right, everything is right. For prayer will not allow anything to go wrong.[3]

James Montgomery's hymn reminds us that,

> Prayer is the soul's sincere desire / uttered or unexpressed;
> The motion of a hidden fire / that trembles in the breast.
>
> Prayer is the simplest form of speech / that infant lips can try;
> Prayer the sublimest strains that reach / the majesty on high.
>
> Prayer is the Christian's vital breath / the Christian's native air,
> His watchword at the gates of death / he enters heaven with
>     prayer.

Montgomery suggests that prayer is our natural environment, not something we do under duress at certain times. Indeed, if prayer is our vital breath, we can say that if we do not pray we will die. How different all this is from prayer as a task. Fire trembling, fire hidden in the breast, fire waiting to fan into flame:

these are vivid images worth pondering in relation to our prayer as priests, particularly in the light of what John Wesley said of his preaching, 'I set myself on fire and people come and watch me burn.'

George Herbert's poem, 'Prayer (1)', is a rich mine of treasures on prayer as he piles image upon expansive image, each of them begging for joyful reflection.

> Prayer the Church's banquet, Angels' age,
>     God's breath in man returning to his birth,
>     The soul in paraphrase, heart in pilgrimage,
> The Christian plummet sounding heav'n and earth;
> Engine against th'Almighty, sinners' tower,
>     Reversed thunder, Christ-side-piercing spear,
>     The six-days world-transposing in an hour,
> A kind of tune, which all things hear and fear;
>
> Softness, and peace, and joy, and love, and bliss,
>     Exalted Manna, gladness of the best,
>     Heaven in ordinary, man well dressed,
> The milky way, the bird of Paradise,
>     Church-bells beyond the stars heard, the soul's blood,
>     The land of spices; something understood.

This glorious and powerful vocation is ours as gift, ours as right. How much we miss if we reduce our understanding of prayer to intercession. We share in the prayer of Christ who did, indeed, pray for his disciples and those who would believe through them (John 17); and praying for others is a very loving thing to do for them. However, the Church, in its wisdom, keeps a much wider and richer understanding of prayer before us. In the Anglican liturgy, in addition to the commitment to be diligent in prayer, there are also the more specific charges to lead people in prayer and worship, to intercede for them, and to bless them in the name of the Lord. These are wonderful responsibilities and privileges, expressions of our love for the people we are called to serve. But undergirding all this is our commitment to be diligent in prayer.

The root of the Latin word we translate as 'diligence' carries the meaning of choice, love and delight. We have lost that original sense of lightness and freedom, seeing diligence too often as something plodding and austere. We forget that it is our 'duty and our joy at all times and in all places' to offer thanks and praise to God.

Prayer, then, is the intimacy of our life in God. Prayer is being 'lost in wonder, love and praise', and it is also the short glance in God's direction; it is the gasp of wonder and thanks for a beautiful sunset, and it is the ache or the exaltation as we listen to the evening news. It is the cry of help when there is no time to articulate anything more and it is the silence of being with God in ecstasy or distress. Nothing in life is too mean or too majestic to be swept up in prayer. Prayer, like breathing, is not spasmodic or subject to our moods and fancies. Rather, prayer, like breathing, provides the underlying rhythm that is essential for life. Rowan Williams writes of the 'there-ness' for Christians of prayer, just as the sea is there at Margate,

> If you have the charge of priesthood laid upon you, then the Sunday liturgy, the Daily Office and private prayer are simply there, and there is no way around them, even if you should want one. They are part of the bargain, and they grow on us as we increasingly sense in them something of the sovereignty of God. In this way they become both a commitment and a joy, even if there are times when we would rather be doing something else. The 'there-ness' is not a matter of law or rules, but a part of the essence of being Christian.[4]

When the bishop lays hands on us, much as we might wish it, we do not suddenly become paragons of prayer. There are no extra hours in the day that we can fill with prayer, and the distractions in prayer do not flee from us. Instead, we are called to be priests and people of prayer as we are, called to offer all of life in prayer – life in its seediness and shame as well as its wonder and delight. Hannah, when challenged by Eli about her apparently unseemly behaviour as she prayed in the shrine at Shiloh, told him bluntly,

'I have been speaking to God from the depth of my grief and resentment' (1 Samuel 1:16, Jerusalem Bible). Would that we were honest enough to do the same, rather than wait until we feel 'holy'. We need to remember that God meets us where we are, not where we think we should be or where we are pretending to be. God takes us as we are and works in and with us to make us people of prayer.

As the boundaries of our prayer life are expanded we will discover new horizons, and as God's light penetrates we will find our lives being transformed. To grow in prayer is to grow in relationship with God. Kenneth Leech writes,

> There is no need to rush around feverishly looking for a prayer life: we need to slow down and look deeply within. What is the point of complaining that God is absent if it is we who are absent from God, and from ourselves, by our lack of awareness . . . At heart, prayer is a process of self-giving and of being set free from isolation. To pray is to enter into a relationship with God and to be transformed by him.[5]

Because being a priest is a vocation not merely an occupation, our prayer is not merely a functional means to secure the resources we need to do the work. It is life-changing. We should not pray if we are not willing to be transformed: it is simply too risky and we will exhaust ourselves in kicking against God. Even if we can only see it with hindsight, transformation does happen when we pray faithfully. The daily rhythm of prayer creates growth that is imperceptible to the self but evident to others. Our people will know whether or not we are people of prayer. We will not have to tell them.

We are called to live gratefully and inquisitively in God's world, never too jaded to see the glory of God in the dust of the streets, never too sated to awake each day in heaven. And we are to so love the beauty of enjoying it that we cannot restrain ourselves from drawing others into that joy. The baptismal liturgy of the Episcopal Church of the USA includes the prayer that the newly baptized may have 'a discerning and inquiring mind'. Our vital breath, prayer, involves living with this discerning and inquiring attitude. Michel Quoist, the French priest whose book *Prayers of Life* revolutionized prayer for many, wrote, 'If only we knew how to listen to God, if only we knew how to look at life around us, our whole lives would become prayer. For it unfolds under God's eyes and no part of it must be lived without being freely offered to him . . . for everyday life is the raw material of prayer.'[6]

If everyday life is the raw material for prayer then we should make sure we appropriate it, blending it with our own particular discipline of prayer. The people we meet, the newspapers and news programmes we hear are readily available raw materials for prayer if we but think to pray with them, pausing long enough to enter into the situations we encounter through them and asking ourselves what those caught up in them might want to pray. As with so much else, attentiveness is the key – attentiveness to our world and to ourselves. John Wesley's life of prayer was grounded in a scheme of self-examination in which he asked himself questions at the end of the day: 'Have I been simple in everything I said or did? Have I prayed every hour for humility, faith, hope, love and the particular virtue of the day? Have I prayed for the particular duty of the day? Have I used a Collect at 9, 12, 3 and before and after eating? And have I duly meditated?'[7]

In 1931 R. Somerset Ward, a priest and spiritual director, wrote of the danger of getting our perspective wrong:

> It is in this tide of (divine) love that I see both the origin and cause of prayer. It is because we are caught up by that divine love that we pray, and it is in the measure in which we surrender to that love that we pray well . . . It is obvious at once that we shall pray best when we are most closely identified with the great tide of the divine love. It is a common reason for failure in prayer that we are more aware of the subject of our prayer than of its object; we are apt to think more of what we shall pray for than of how we shall pray.[8]

He wrote of prayer 'glorify[ing] daily life with the glow of heaven',[9] a wonderful concept of heaven glowing in our daily lives. Our priestly ministry calls us to live on that boundary between earth and heaven, to be at home in both worlds which overlap in anticipation rather than exist separately, to be able to speak of each in the other. If preaching is about speaking of the ways of God to earth, prayer is about speaking of the ways of earth to God.

We are called to be people of prayer, people for whom prayer is not just something we do, but the environment in which we live, because we live in God. The rhythm of prayer is like the rhythm of the ocean, the ebb and flow of the tides, the waves that break on the shore moving shingle and sand around, the constant sound of water, the occasional rollers, the occasional ripples on the surface of an otherwise calm sea. Like a seabird on the ocean, we may bob up and down on the ocean of prayer being moved along by it, like a fish we may live and breathe in it moving around in the depths and shallows, or like a dolphin or seal we may move more powerfully in it, occasionally breaking the surface in playful fun. Prayer is all these things and more.

St Seraphim's words, 'Be at peace, then thousands around you will find salvation,'[10] are words to take to heart, to incubate in our hearts until they are brought to birth and grow in us. We are not called to frenetic activity, born either of rootless itchiness to be indispensable to God and our people or of fear of failure. We are to be people who are centred in God, at peace, able to live peacefully with the sometimes disturbing but always life-giving presence of God amid the turmoil of our world. Michael Ramsey has words of wisdom on this in a letter written in 1961,

We already belong to the heavenly country. We are on its frontier whenever we lift up our souls to God in prayer, whenever we feed upon our Lord in Holy Communion, whenever we reflect his love in our actions. It is as those who belong already to the heavenly country that we are alert to our present duties, sensitive to the world's troubles yet serene in the way we meet them.[11]

Two Anglicans, separated by 300 years, remind us of our

priestly vocation to pray. First John Donne in a sermon on 'Prayer and the Divine Mercy', then Michael Ramsey in a letter, speak of our being for prayer:

> [Prayer] may be mental, for we may think prayers. It may be vocal, for we may speak prayers. It may be actual, for we may do prayers . . . So then to do the office of your vocation sincerely is to pray.[12]

> While the life of the church expands with new and tremendous demands upon the energies of the clergy and laity, how will the spiritual strength come? It can only come from the deepening of the life with God. If we give our minds solely to thinking about the multiple problems which press upon us we can exhaust our spirits in the process. We are stronger to face the problems with freshness of heart if our souls are knowing the joy and serenity of a deeper communion with God. That is why the prayer of a priest is so supremely important, as the source of his ability to train the people in the way of prayer.[13]

## Persevering in prayer

Two poet-priests, George Herbert and R. S. Thomas, write in their different ways from a position of faith that is nevertheless realistic about the pressures to doubt and despair. Despite his occasional struggles, Herbert's poetry radiates his prayerful approach to life based on his confidence in God's willingness to hear us, as we see in the first verse of 'Prayer (2)',

> Of what an easy quick access,
> My blessed Lord, art thou! How suddenly
> May our requests thine ear invade!
> To show that state dislikes not easiness,
> If I but lift mine eyes, my suit is made:
> Thou canst no more not hear than thou canst die.

This assurance that even the glance towards God is seen is the encouragement we need to go on praying through the winter seasons of life. This may, at times, demand of us persistence in the face of seeming silence, as R. S. Thomas captures in 'The Belfry',

> I have seen it standing up grey,
> Gaunt, as though no sunlight
> Could ever thaw out the music
> Of its great bell; terrible
> In its own way, for religion
> Is like that. There are times
> When a black frost is upon
> One's whole being, and the heart
> In its bone belfry hangs and is dumb.
>
> But who is to know? Always,
> Even in winter in the cold
> Of a stone church, on his knees
> Someone is praying, whose prayers fall
> Steadily through the hard spell
> Of weather that is between God
> And himself. Perhaps they are warm rain
> That brings the sun and afterwards flowers
> On the raw graves and throbbing of bells.

We are called as priests to watch.[14] Watchmen were the people who watched through the darkness of the night so that others could sleep in peace, looking and listening for danger and then for the stirrings of the dawn. They could not be distracted from their task. For hour after monotonous hour they had to focus on the darkness with the intention of discerning signs of movement, and then discerning what that movement meant. Priests are called to watch on behalf of their people, watching with them through the darkness of their night, noticing the signs of life that they might miss and interpreting their meaning. This can only be done through prayer, through conversation with God, through knowing the darkness for ourselves so that we are not intimidated by it. But watchmen also watched the daytime skyline for signs of life that were not part of the normal routine, the unexpected and unusual activities that needed to be reported. As those charged with oversight, we too are to watch the busy skyline where God has placed us, knowing the routine and therefore recognizing the unusual which may be a sign of God's new life stirring among us. We are to have one eye on the horizon of what God is doing, one eye on the everydayness of life. We need to develop, through prayer, a new way of seeing-over on behalf of those for whom we are called to serve and care.

The liturgical tradition of prayer can be very helpful because it involves a rhythm of prayer that sweeps us up, along with all the rest of creation. The eucharistic liturgy reminds us that even when we pray on our own we are joining with the angels and archangels and with all the company of heaven, and yet even in our most vulnerable moments we are safe with this jubilant crowd around us. Psalm 84 paints the wonderful picture of the swallow finding a place to lay her young at God's altars. It is easy to forget that this is no quiet altar in a village church but an altar of sacrifice in the midst of the noise of the temple crowd, the stench of blood, the smell of fear as the animals are brought to be slaughtered. Here, the fledgling sparrow is safe. Here, as we stand before God, whether it is in the midst of noise and jubilation, silence and reflection, we and our people are safe as we bring ourselves and them to God in prayer. Sometimes all we can do is name them before God and leave them, as it were, in the nest by God's altar.

The commitment to pray in church, or in our own prayer place, is a helpful reminder that at its heart prayer is simply being with God. Theophan the Recluse wrote in a letter, 'the principal thing is to stand with the mind in the heart before God, and to strive towards him with longing'.[15] When we are full of joy, prayer may come easily in terms of words and actions. When we are broken-hearted, tired or confused it may be that all we can do is present ourselves, physically, in our prayer place without articulating words. In those moments, our presence, our showing up, is our prayer. We may find ourselves on our own, kneeling in turbulent silence, or with others who say the Daily Office around us and for us.

As the words of the Daily Office wash over us on those occasions when we cannot articulate our own prayer, we are nonetheless caught up in the prayer of the Church through the ages. Our own feelings should never be the barometer of prayer. At times the words may seem very foreign to our experience: the liturgy gives us words of rejoicing and our heart is breaking, or we may find ourselves wailing with the author of Lamentations when we are bursting with joy. This is the prayer of the Church, and for someone, somewhere – perhaps someone who has asked us to pray for them – these words express all they would say if they could. So when we are thrilled by good news and yet find ourselves complaining with the psalmist that God seems far from us and our enemies surround us, we are praying for the elderly widow in a high-rise block who is afraid of the drug pushers outside her door, or the person who feels abandoned by God as they watch a loved one dying in hospital. And when we are inarticulate in our grief, the psalmist can loan us words that countless people over the years have similarly borrowed and made their own, reminding us in the process that our current feelings are not the last word on the matter.

Facing this reality of the emotional cost to us of ministry in the midst of devastation, we are confronted with our own need for restoration – for our own time with God when the needs of others are not the subject of our prayer. It is easy, when we are in a situation where others are looking to us for help and comfort, to overlook our own needs but we have to be attentive to our own aching and emptiness if we are to have the ongoing resources for ministry. We can burn out. Small wonder that Jesus, surrounded as he was by crowds with seemingly endless needs, and a group of disciples who were, at times, remarkably capable of enervating rather than energizing him, sometimes took off into a lonely place to pray, having risen early or spent all night there.[16] Jewish people prayed in the morning, at noon, and at night[17] and we tend to forget that this disciplined structure was in place throughout Jesus' ministry, and the life of the early

Church. For ourselves, we need to know and turn to our underlying structures of prayer that sustain us through the times when
life and prayer demand our perseverance.

## The disciplines of prayer

The foundations of prayer that we have laid down over the years
before ordination remain the foundations of our prayer life after
ordination, the patterns of prayer that are most helpful for us
will not change instantly – although for all Christians there
should be growth and development in the way we pray. A spiritual director is an invaluable ally in nudging, cajoling, guiding
and directing us into new paths with God. There is a large element of discipline in prayer: we have vowed to pray. When all
else fails and we are not feeling profoundly moved to pray, then
the discipline of saying our prayers needs to kick in. Canon C26
of the Church of England reminds us of this: 'Every bishop, priest
or deacon is under obligation, not being let by sickness or some
other urgent cause, to say daily the Morning and Evening Prayer
either privately or openly.' In addition, the Canon states that
ministers are to be diligent in daily prayer and intercession.
Demanding as it may sound, this Canon is pointing us back to
the truth that James Montgomery and George Herbert understood so well, that prayer is fundamental to our being and that
without it we will shrivel up like an unwatered plant. We neglect
prayer at our peril, because in it is the life and nourishment that
we need and our people need us to have. There is no way round
the fact that if we want a life of prayer then the only way to
achieve it is by praying. That is true for us as priests, it is also true
for our people, and part of being for prayer involves shaping
communities of praying people.

When we pray together, the liturgy can catch us by surprise.
After a night of severe storms that brought down trees and
caused structural damage, in the half-light of a late October
morning the early congregation at Salisbury Cathedral said
Psalm 144. We found ourselves saying with the psalmist of old,
'we are but a puff of wind'. And if we are a mere puff of wind,

then who is this God whose voice shakes the cedars of Lebanon (Psalm 29) and whose thunder is heard over the whirlwind (an amazing concept from Psalm 77)? The morning after the night before, this was riveting imagery, glorious and vivid.

But so often we deprive the liturgy of its power to engage us. In the lands where Christianity took root, evening – the time of the setting of the sun and the lighting of the lamps – fell at much the same time each day. It was not time for bed but for a change in focus, a drawing in from the outside world of the day to the domestic world of the evening. Today we can dispense with darkness instantly and permanently at the flick of a switch. Evening Prayer invites us to let go of our control of things, to light the lamps, to change our pace, not to eliminate the darkness but to live with it comfortably as a part of our lives. Compline, the night office, is gentler still. There are no long psalms or readings as the office is the prelude to sleep, capable of being committed to memory and prayed in the dark if necessary. In monastic communities it is followed by the silence that will be broken next morning with the words 'O Lord, open our lips, and our mouth shall proclaim your praise' as the daily cycle of prayer and work begins again.

In contrast to the marking of the hours in the Anglican form of the Daily Offices, Celtic prayer takes as its anchor points the tasks of the day. Alexander Carmichael spent years walking the Scottish Highlands in the nineteenth century recording the centuries of prayers that were being forced out of existence by the English following the enclosures. Thanks to him we have a vast repertoire of Celtic prayers. Celtic prayer is very Trinitarian, adopting a repetitive rhythm of praying three times using similar words, often addressed to Father, Son and Spirit. Thus,

Come I this day to the Father,
Come I this day to the Son,
Come I this day to the Holy Spirit powerful;
Come I this day with God,
Come I this day with Christ,
Come I with the Spirit of kindly balm.[18]

Parents have discovered that this repetitive way of praying is enjoyed by children, while chaplains report that it is helpful to psychiatric patients who find security in it. The repetition can draw us into a rhythm of prayer as we do repetitive actions. Prayers for washing, dressing, cleaning our teeth, getting into the car, turning on the computer, stacking the hymnbooks, sorting the post, folding the newsletters and all the other daily tasks of life may replace the prayers for lighting the fire, milking the cow or following the plough, but the underlying principle is the same – that all the tasks of life are avenues for prayer.

Despite their geographical separation, the Orthodox and Celtic traditions have some common roots and both recognize the value of rhythm. For all of us the rhythm of walking can be a catalyst for prayer, as the Orthodox tradition of the Jesus Prayer ('Lord Jesus Christ, Son of God, have mercy on me a sinner') shows so well. This ancient prayer became more widely known in the nineteenth century when a monk walked thousands of miles across Russia learning to pray constantly. The words are often combined with breathing in (e.g. on the first six words) and breathing out (e.g. on the last six), so that our breathing becomes part of our praying. There is no substitute for walking round the area in which we minister, praying for people in their homes or places of work as we pass them, noticing detailed things that are so easily missed in the car but are important hints on how to pray for people.

When I lived in the US I found myself yearning for the British landscape. On one occasion I was talking about this with a friend from the mid-west and commented that when I flew over that landscape it seemed a totally placeless environment to me. He told me that he knew every tiny undulation along long stretches of road that to me would seem monotonously flat, that within the sameness there was infinite variety, that the flatness opened 180 degree vistas of sky that spoke to him of the expansiveness of God's world. He loved its flatness with the same passion that I loved southern England's rounded hills, and we both knew our localities in immense loving detail. Do we know our localities in prayer and love them and their people with such passion? Flying over the mid-west is not the same as living there and letting its sense of place engulf us. Flying over places in prayer is no substitute for incarnational living and praying.

As we ramble around God's world, we need to keep our senses attuned to the world in all its glory so that we cannot help but pray in joy. This way of prayer does not require beautiful surroundings. Watching ants with a transfixed toddler on a broken concrete step in a run-down steel town, being attentive to unexpected architectural details in a street of shabby inner-city buildings, seeing a weed in bloom on a derelict site, have all been for me hints that I am in the presence of the God who has not abandoned any part of creation. No matter where we are, the ground is holy. We cultivate awareness of living on holy ground through the everydayness of life, not through withdrawing from life. Bonaventure said that if we do not see God's power, wisdom and goodness in the splendour of created things then we are blind.[19] Later, John Calvin wrote that the most perfect way of seeing God is to contemplate God's works in which God is near and familiar to us.[20] A long line of poet-priests have written lovingly and perceptively of the world in which they lived.

One person who let creation turn him to prayer and praise was Thomas Traherne, the seventeenth-century Rector of Credenhill, near Hereford, whose hitherto unknown works were discovered in the twentieth century. In his *Centuries of Meditation* he writes,

> Your enjoyment of the world is never right till you so esteem it that everything in it is more your treasure than a king's exchequer full of gold and silver. And that exchequer yours also in its place and service. Can you take too much joy in your Father's works? He is Himself in everything. Some things are little on the outside, and rough and common. But I remember the time when the dust of the streets were as precious as gold to my infant eyes, and now they are more precious to the eye of reason . . . Your enjoyment of the world is never right, till every morning you awake in Heaven: see yourself in your Father's palace; and look upon the skies and the earth and the

air, as celestial joys: having such a reverend esteem of all, as if
you were among the angels. The bride of a monarch, in her
husband's chamber, hath no such causes of delight as you . . .
Yet, further, you never enjoy the world aright, till you so love
the beauty of enjoying it, that you are covetous and earnest to
persuade others to enjoy it . . . [21]

Gerard Manley Hopkins is another lover of God's creation. His
diaries reveal the attention to detail that yield the ecstatic rejoicing in God's creation evident in poems like 'The Kingfisher', and
here in 'God's Grandeur',

> The world is charged with the grandeur of God.
> It will flame out, like shining from shook foil;
> It gathers to a greatness, like the ooze of oil
> Crushed . . .

Hopkins' journal tells us what was in his mind when he wrote
'God's Grandeur'. 'All things therefore are charged with love, are
charged with God, and if we know how to touch them give off
sparks and take fire, yield drops and flow, ring and tell of him.'[22]
We are back to the idea of the fire, the flame: the trembling of
prayer, the grandeur of God that burns us. It is not a new idea,
Abba Joseph, one of the Desert Fathers, was asked by a disciple
about prayer:

> Abba Lot went to Abba Joseph and said to him, 'Abba, as far
> as I can, I say my little office, I fast a little, I pray and meditate,
> I live in peace and as far as I can, I purify my thoughts. What
> else can I do?' Then the old man stood up and stretched his
> hands toward heaven. His fingers became like ten lamps of fire
> and he said to him, 'If you will, you can become all flame.'[23]

To be at peace, like St Seraphim, means to be living in holy space,
living with the awareness of God's love and presence surround-
ing and holding us. This may be mediated by a particular physical place but it is not restricted to that. Moses found himself

unwittingly walking on holy ground in the midst of the familiar desert landscape, his place of work that was unremitting in its austerity, while Jacob woke from sleeping with his head on a stone to say, 'God was in this place and I, I did not know it' (Genesis 28:16). It is helpful to have a particular place for prayer, even if it is not our only place for prayer. But for some of us, at least some of the time, this is not always possible. It is worth remembering that the call to Moses was to turn aside in the midst of his daily work and find that ground to be holy, it did not depend on him praying in an already sacred place. Jesus' teaching to his disciples to go to their room and shut the door to pray has to be understood in terms of first-century domestic architecture where there were no private rooms in poor people's homes. We may not be driven to put a towel over our heads as Susanna Wesley apparently did when wanting her numerous children to allow her some privacy for prayer, and we will not always be in surroundings that encourage us to pray, but if all the world is God's world, then all the world is a place in which to pray. The pattern of our prayer may look different in different circumstances – celebrating the Daily Office in church is not an option for the commuter, although there may be a church near to work, or for the mother of young children. However, walking the dog or jogging may provide an opportunity to settle into a rhythm for prayer that bears some resemblance to the way of the nineteenth-century Russian pilgrim as he walked thousands of miles. Here again, a spiritual director can be helpful in creating a personal rhythm of prayer.

Most of our people need to be helped to pray in their own circumstances, to turn aside like Moses to see what is going on, to recognize that God is in this place. Sometimes this may involve us seeing God's glory that is ever present but perhaps not yet perceived by others, and helping them to see it too. It means recognizing the glow of heaven amid the grime of earth, becoming more and more familiar with holy space, with God's presence even in seemingly forbidding places.

*Prayer for others*

Priestly ministry immerses us in the everyday life of many people and that becomes the raw material for our prayer. The danger is that in becoming so immersed we are consumed. Writing to the Diocese of Canterbury on the theme of the call of the bishop to be intercessor for the people, Michael Ramsey said,

> We need as a church to be deeply involved with the world around us, with a keen sensitivity to the conditions of our time. Yes: but we also need to be far more ready to go apart with God, waiting upon him in quietness, and learning what is meant by the words of an ancient Christian writer: 'as the soul is to the body, so are Christians in the world'.[24]

On another occasion, Ramsey wrote, 'No work of the Christians as the soul of the world is more important than their work of prayer, bearing the world's needs upon the heart in God's presence.'[25] Sometimes all we can do is to appear before God with our people on our hearts. At other times, this priestly ministry of bearing others before God can be helped by talking *with* God about people who are on our hearts, rather than by talking *to* God. When we talk with God about people we may find ourselves simply thinking about them in God's presence, even dreaming dreams with God for them as we begin to see things in the light of God's redemptive love. Our own perspectives are transformed as, in God's presence, we put ourselves in their shoes, wonder what they may be feeling, what they might want of us, whether they are next door or across an ocean. We may, particularly as ministers, find ourselves in dialogue with God about what is going on behind the scenes of the presenting prayer request. If we embark on intercession as dialogue, God could ask us to be the answer to our own prayers and we could end up being changed by our prayers. The answer to our prayer for others may be that our compassion is enlarged, that God carves out in us the place which others need if they are to find a home, a safe place where they can experience God's love in their particular situation.

This may mean that we become more involved or, equally, that we do nothing except let God create in us a place of prayer that gives the other person strength because they know that someone is holding them in God's presence. John Wesley's 1733 Collection of Prayers for every day of the week includes this prayer for Monday morning, 'Grant that I may assist all my brethren with my prayers, where I cannot reach them with my actual service.'

At times our prayers may include 'actual service', often of a very practical kind. George Herbert, who was in the habit of walking to Salisbury Cathedral for prayers and then staying on with friends to make music, arrived one day in a dishevelled condition after helping a man who had fallen off his horse. Given his normally immaculate turn out, his friends were shocked at his seeming lack of concern at his appearance and one criticized him for getting himself involved in 'so dirty employment'. According to Izaac Walton, Herbert's biographer, he dismissed it, saying,

> For if I be bound to pray for all that be in distress, I am sure that I am bound, so far as it is in my power, to practice what I pray for. And though I do not wish for the occasion every day, yet let me tell you that I would not willingly pass one day of my life without comforting a sad soul or showing mercy; and I praise God for this occasion; and now let's tune our instruments.[26]

At other times, we are called to pray for people as we minister to them. How we pray then will reflect the environment of prayer in which we live as well as our pastoral sensitivity. While working in a hospital, I was called to a teenager who held her stillborn child of twenty-three weeks in her arms. During our conversation, I asked her daughter's name then gave thanks for the short life she did know in the womb and the joy she brought her mother, to which the tears of bereavement bore painful witness, before commending her to God. For the teenager, this short unscripted prayer became a healing encounter with God.

Meanwhile, on another ward, the familiar words of the Book of Common Prayer were the lifeline to God for an elderly and confused person yearning for something familiar and secure to keep hold of in a world that had seemingly careered out of control.

If we are genuinely to pray for others, we have to find ways to be sustained ourselves. We will face situations that are so draining, so sad, so significant, that we cannot shut them out of our lives when we go home. In these situations we have to pray not only for other people affected, but also for ourselves because we are being changed by the encounter and need to work with God on what is going on. This may not always involve prayer as we think of it most readily. Instead, after a hard day of emotional strain, repetitive manual work – stitching a patchwork quilt, hammering nails, polishing a car, weeding the garden, pacing up and down with the lawn-mower – can become part of our prayer as we let the thousands of tiny stitches, each blow of the hammer, each uprooted weed, become prayers for the people who have come home with us in our memory. Years later that quilt, that piece of furniture, that flowerbed, can be a reminder of events that have gone but of stories, names and faces that remain as we find ourselves praying again for people who had slipped out of our conscious memory.

The psalms can be our lifeline too. Not only the psalms as written in the Bible, but the psalmody as a genre that transfers across the centuries and cultures. The psalmists tell us, loudly and clearly, that nothing, nothing is beyond saying in God's presence, nothing is beyond celebration or lament if God is in the conversation. We can let our defences down before God, because God always has the last word and we know that God will not allow our sometimes confused ranting – essential as it is at the time – or our deepest lament to be definitive for ever. The psalmists keep God in the dialogue, and their tenacity can be a challenge when we face situations where everything in us wants to break off the conversation with God. Psalm writing can be a healing way to deal with our troubled experiences because of the genre's capacity to keep God and human experience in dialogue. 'Psalm 42 for Deborah'[27] was written after the tragic death of a young woman. She had responded well to treatment for a life-threaten-ing illness but then tripped and sustained brain injury. I sat with her and her family as she gasped for the water she could not have by mouth, trying to force our hands to her lips, seeming to know who we were but unable to communicate anything except her desperation for water. Never before has the longing of Psalm 42 been so devastatingly brought alive. One way to process her dying agony and to nurture in me the spiritual resources to help the family was to stay with that imagery and the psalm's structure,

As a deer longs for flowing streams,
so she longed for water, O God.
When will her thirst be quenched?
when will she find relief?
Our tears have been our food, day and night,
since her life collapsed around her.

These things we remember
as we pour out our souls:
how she walked with anticipation out of the hospital
five days ago:
her family celebrating her remission.
Why is she here, O hidden God?
why are we around her bed, disquieted in our depths?
Hope in God, for we shall again praise you,
our help and our God.

Our souls are cast down within us;
therefore we remember you
from the Medical Ward and from Intensive Care.
Deep calls to deep
in the thunder of your waterfalls;
all your waves and your billows have gone over us.

By day the Lord commands his steadfast love,
and in the night – as we sit and hold her hand – his song is
    with us,
a prayer to the God of our life.

We say to God, our rock,
'why have you forgotten her?
why must she lie here, brain-injured
because of a simple fall?'
As with a deadly wound in his body
her father's guilt taunts him
and he says to himself, continually,
'why was I not there to save her?'

Why are you downcast, O my soul?
why are you disquieted within me?
Hope in God, for I shall again praise him,
my help and my God.

Writing this psalm was cathartic. It was also hard because, having decided in this instance to follow the biblical train of thought
closely, I had to find a way to follow the psalmist from lament
to praise when everything in me cried out to lament, lament,
lament, and to abandon the transitions to hope.[28] The gift we
have to offer as priests is that of theological perspective, of theological prayer. As people of prayer who carry our people on our
hearts before God, we can bring the hard-won certainty that we
can 'hope in God, for I shall again praise him', a certainty we
may only come to on our knees. Again, R. S. Thomas puts this
experience into poetry, in 'In Church',

Often I try
To analyse the quality
Of its silences. Is this where God hides
From my searching? . . .
. . . There is no other sound
In the darkness but the sound of a man
Breathing, testing his faith
On emptiness, nailing his questions
One by one to an untenanted cross.

The vocation of a priest is to pray, to ever redirect our wandering gaze in the direction of the one who himself prayed, so that we and our people may receive mercy and find grace to help in time of need.

# PART 3

# THE FRUIT OF PRIESTLY LIFE

# 7

## BEING FOR HOLINESS

Lift up your hearts! The Lord is here!
Sing, church of God, sing out for joy,
lead all creation's song of praise,
your richest harmonies employ.
Called to a life of holiness,
to bear the beauty of your Lord,
display to all God's glorious love,
our God forevermore adored.

Come, holy God, refine your church
hallow to us our poverty,
we would be rich in holiness,
servants of him who sets us free.
Our listlessness transform with power,
our meagre love with love divine,
come Holy Spirit, breath of God
as wind disturb, as fire refine.

Still, gracious God, you give to us
for holy people, holy things,
the timeless sacrament of love,
foretaste of joy your coming brings.
As earth joins in the praise of heaven
so heaven's joy arcs back again,
across the ages rings the cry,
'Our Saviour comes, Christ comes to reign!'[1]

*Introduction*

In Part 1 we saw how presbyters are called by Christ to be signs and animators of the true identity, life and ministry of the Church. They are to indicate the character of the Church by their example and they are to activate the life and ministry of congregations by presiding over the community and leading it deeper into God in worship and deeper into the world in mission. The Church is called to be a royal priesthood offering its praise to God and giving itself to God for God's work in the world. It is a calling to live with God and for God, and to live with others for others. Among the priestly people of God presbyters are appointed to hold this fundamental calling of the Church before the people of God and to nurture this calling by shaping and forming Christian communities to be the holy people of God. This is the root of the priestly calling of the presbyter.

We explored the shape of priestly ministry in Part 2. We saw how presbyters are called to structure their lives around the worship of God, engagement with God's word and dependence upon God in prayer. By embodying lives of worship and prayer that are receptive to God's word, presbyters model the basic pattern of Christian living and sustain their ministries of leading God's people in worship, opening God's word to them and deepening their lives of prayer so that the people of God may be a worshipping people, attentive to God in prayer and faithfully communicating God's word in the world.

Now in Part 3 we turn to some of the fruit that is formed in us as we live these sorts of lives. Out of the many expressions of Christian living that could have been considered, we have chosen to focus on some fundamental features of priestly identity: holiness, reconciliation, blessing and mission. In Jesus' high priestly prayer he prayed for his followers to be 'sanctified in the truth', made one with each other and placed into the oneness of Christ and his Father, *so that* 'the world may believe' (John 17:20–21). Jesus lived a holy life, a life turned towards God and others, a life that sought to honour the glory of God and to see God's glory manifested in those he met and to whom he ministered. This ministry of establishing human beings in their true light as people created to express the glory and beauty of God in human form, involved restoring the broken relationships caused through complex patterns of sin and suffering. The result of the reconciliation that followed was not only the re-creation of individual life in dignity and hope but the appointment of new ministry in which the restored person became a source of blessing to others sent out into the world to live in and speak of the kingdom of God.

Zacchaeus is a good example. His life was a tragic story of betrayal and hurt in which he had become increasingly closed off from others and reduced to a pale reflection of all that he had been created to be. Caught up in the economic ramifications of political oppression, he had allowed greed and deceit to weave their web around him and trap him into a life divorced from God and neighbour. The encounter with Jesus changed everything. Salvation came to his house. A person of theft, driven by the desire to acquire, becomes a person of blessing, overwhelmed by the generosity of Jesus and ready to give. The deeper identity of Zacchaeus was revealed. Once beguiled into becoming a servant of the Roman empire, he was now shown to be truly a 'child of Abraham' (Luke 19:9).

This is what Christ does. He turns us into holy people who can bring blessing to the world because we have been reconciled to God and to others. This is our calling as human beings. It is the full stature of humanity. Hence, the ministry Christ exercises in the Church is the ministry to which he is calling the Church to exercise in his name in the world. Christ is forming his people into a holy people who, having being reconciled with God, are committed to a ministry of reconciliation for the blessing of the world. This is the full stature of the Church. The ministry of the ordained is to signify and animate this calling of the Church. We are to make visible this calling, not so that other members of Christ's body need not do the same but precisely in order that they may do the same. Thus the Church prays for those being ordained priest to be renewed in holiness and given wisdom and discipline to work faithfully with those committed to their charge.[2] We are called into 'the pain of childbirth until Christ is formed in [the Church]' (Galatians 4:19). This is the full stature of the ordained ministry.

## Called to be holy

'Train yourself in godliness' (1 Timothy 4:6). This exhortation to Timothy in the New Testament Church has been repeated to those called into ordained ministry in the Church through the centuries. From the ancient Armenian liturgy with its expectation that the ordained will exhibit a 'correct life and spotless conduct' to the nineteenth-century Baptist leader Charles Spurgeon's insistence to his students that 'We must seek the highest degree of godliness, *because our work imperatively requires it*',[3] holiness has been seen as *the* requirement of the ordained. True to this strong tradition, it is likely that one of the earliest western ordination rites prayed for the presbyter to be transformed in love, rather than, as in later forms, to be able (in the somewhat awkward expression) to 'transform the body and blood' of Christ.[4]

Richard Baxter defined holiness as 'a devotedness to God and a living to Him'.[5] The fact that the Hebrew origins of the idea of holiness lie in the people of Israel's call to be 'set apart for God', remind us that holiness is not in the first place about moral character. Essentially it is about being set in a relationship of commitment and fidelity to God. Primarily, therefore, holiness is a gift. We are called into relationship with God, set within a covenant of God's faithfulness that provides an environment in which we live and move and have our being. Because the environment is the space that God opens to us in this world to live in his love and blessing, it is a place of change in which we are summoned to the sort of faithfulness to God and to others that God shows to us. '*Be holy, as God is holy*' is the consistent call of the scriptures to the people of God. It is a vision of renewed humanity that continually recurs in the spiritual tradition of the Church. William of St Thierry is one of many who confidently asserts that 'to this end alone were we created and do we live, to be like God; for we were created in his image'.[6] This is not a dutiful repetition of scriptural ideas, it is the expression of realities which William had seen and had come to expect. Like many other spiritual writings, his 'Golden Epistle' develops a systematic description of how Christians may reach unity with God through a life of love for God. For William this is not an empty pipe-dream. It is a statement of what we are to expect as faithful followers of Christ.

Christ is the fulfilment of the challenge of the covenant to holiness. In his life and ministry he devoted himself to God. In his suffering and death he went to the cross in obedience to God, voluntarily assuming the role of God's servant who suffers for others and of God's priest who offers the perfect sacrifice for sin in the form of his own willingness to do the will of God. In Christ's risen and ascended life he stands before God as the representative figure of humanity, a pure picture of what we are meant to be as human beings and he continues his life of joyfully serving the purposes of God.

We are baptized into this holy life. As we receive God's gift to us of Christ's life we are counted worthy 'to stand in God's presence and serve him'.[7] Through our ongoing relationship with Christ, the holy status which is applied to us by baptism and faith becomes the state which is actually formed in us by the Spirit's work in us, transforming us into the image of Christ 'from one degree of glory to another' (2 Corinthians 3:18). It is a continual process requiring what William Law, the eighteenth-century Anglican who had a significant influence on John Wesley, called 'the perpetual inspiration of the Spirit'. This, of course, is true for all Christians. It is the heart of the gospel; but the ordained have a particular opportunity and responsibility to enable people to see this dynamic of Christian life at work. 'If you are to walk in all holiness and purity, as becometh ministers of the gospel, you must be daily baptized into the Spirit of God',[8] Charles Spurgeon made clear to his students.

'Dr Moule helped me, as he helped so many others, to see embodied in a life the holiness and love which are the essentials of the Christian Faith in action.'[9] These words were written about Handley Moule, the influential evangelical leader at the turn of the last century who inspired generations of ordinands and clergy as college principal and then as Bishop of Durham. Towards the end of the last century, despite the dramatic changes in society in the intervening years, including the place of the Church in it, the deep appeal of a holy person was again evident in the genuine sense of sadness and respect following the death of Cardinal Basil Hume. 'He was goodness personified, a true holy man with extraordinary humility and an unswerving dedication. He did much to inspire people of all faiths and none', said the Prime Minister, Tony Blair, capturing the mood of many.

There is an immense ecclesiological and missionary significance in our calling to be holy. Most of our churches have high expectations of our efficiency and competence. They expect us to be able to do certain things and to be busy doing them. There is no shortage of opportunity and encouragement to put our lives into the highest gear and fill every waking hour – and many others when we should be asleep – with good and honourable ministry. There are times when this may be necessary for a limited period but it is very easy for us to be hoodwinked by the activism of our culture into thinking that this is what the Church really needs from us. In fact, it does not take much for members of a congregation to spot when the high-octane fuel on which we try to run is fast burning out. Our activity may remain but if our spirituality begins to run dry then it is the very people we are desperately seeking to serve whom we are most letting down. 'We wanted a person of energy and vitality to do things. God showed us we needed someone of holiness to show us how to be,' wrote an ordinand when reflecting on a recent appointment in her parish.

People are Christians because they have glimpsed a life of beauty and integrity, authenticity and goodness, in the extraordinarily attractive and compelling figure of Jesus Christ. They have signed up to life in the Church because they want to follow Christ and, in following him, become like him. Amid all that can divert the people of God from their primary calling to walk with Christ along the way of Christ, the priest is to stand at the crossroads and say, 'This is the way Christ has called us to walk, let us go there together.'

The missionary significance of the call to holiness for priest and people is also critical. Gandhi once said, 'If you do not see God in the other person, there's no point looking any further.' People look at the ordained and read the Church. If they do not sense something of the holiness of God in us, they may not look any further. 'The world is better able to read the nature of religion in a man's life than in the Bible,'[10] noted Richard Baxter. Despite the apparent marginalization of the Church in contemporary society, there is little that the media find so thrilling as the moral failing of a cleric. Indeed, outrage at hypocrisy in religious leaders has a long and honourable history, stretching back to the indignation of the prophets at the false leaders of Israel. Dante's hell is full of clerical characters from popes downwards who have failed their people by preaching one thing and acting quite differently. The tragedy when priests do not live up to their calling 'to be what they proclaim' (as the Anglican Ordinal in New Zealand puts it), is not only the damage done to the individuals immediately affected by whatever has gone wrong. The ramifications go wider and deeper, reinforcing a loss of confidence in the Church.

On the other hand, when people brush against the holy they are never quite the same afterwards. Perhaps it is only in a fleeting encounter, but they have met someone who stands for another world, a different set of values that are strangely compelling. They have sensed another way of ordering life and, for a moment, everything seemed to make sense, to fit into place. In this person something of the divine could be sensed, and it felt good to be in touch with such deep reserves of affirmation and love.

In our day when there are few fixed points for people to make their ethical choices, the significance of Christian communities that seek to embody the ways of God is of critical missionary importance. The prophetic call for 'another Benedict' at the end of Alasdair McIntyre's seminal analysis of the moral confusion of our age is one of the many examples, Christian and otherwise, of the need for faithful people who are committed to the creation of ways of living built upon deeply rooted principles of goodness and compassion.[11] Where conversions are happening in our

culture today they seem to involve encounter with, and acceptance by, some form of Christian community, whether a large,
vibrant congregation or a small, caring group of believers in the
neighbourhood or at work, or some other expression of authentic communal life.

## The characteristics of holiness

There is a tangibility about holiness that is steeped in the incarnation. It is our vocation to be increasingly conformed to – and
an image of – Christ who is the Good Shepherd, and to live pure
and holy lives amid all the demands of daily living. At ordinations since the seventeenth century, Anglicans have sung to the
Holy Spirit, 'Anoint and cheer our soilèd face with the abundance of thy grace'. The amazing truth is that, when we live for
Christ, God's grace makes holiness visible in even the soiled and
the cheerless. One of the emphases of the Reformation, particularly stressed by Luther, was that holiness is lived out in ordinary
life, doing ordinary things. In the nineteenth century, John Henry
Newman, who did not agree with Luther about everything, liked
to say in a similar fashion that perfection is not doing extraordinary things, but doing ordinary things well. Making holiness
visible in the ordinary things of life, embracing and integrating
all of life within our vocation, is a priestly ministry.

In a sermon on 'Holy ground', Rowan Williams points us to a
view of holiness that is not static but ecstatic, not dependent
upon perfection but upon faithfulness:

A human being is holy, not because he or she triumphs by
willpower over chaos and guilt and leads a flawless life, but
because that life shows the victory of God's faithfulness *in the
midst* of disorder and imperfection. The church is holy – and
this congregation here present is holy – not because it is a
gathering of the good and the well-behaved, but because it
speaks of the triumph of grace in the coming together of
strangers and sinners who, miraculously, trust one another
enough to join in common repentance and common praise – to

express a deep and elusive unity in Jesus Christ, who is our righteousness and our sanctification. Humanly speaking, holiness is always like this: God's endurance in the middle of our refusal of him, his capacity to meet every refusal with the gift of himself.[12]

So, one vital characteristic of holiness is that it is manifest in the mess of life as well as its glorious moments. One way of exploring what being holy means in practice is to use the framework of the evangelical virtues of poverty, chastity and obedience. Far from being the preserve of monastics, the virtues are essential to us as people who bear the priestly calling to be holy so that we can enable others to be holy. 'We must begin by purifying ourselves before we purify others; we must be instructed to be able to instruct others; we must become light to illuminate others; we must draw close to God to bring God close to others; we must be sanctified to sanctify and lead by the hand and counsel prudently,' said Gregory of Nazianzus in his fourth-century catechism.[13] It is our being, as well as our doing, that is at the heart of our priestly identity and character.

Poverty is usually construed in terms of deficiency or shortage but it actually has far more to do with simplicity and adequacy. That immediately puts a positive construction on it, freeing us to live gratefully and graciously. Unlike poverty that is enforced rather than chosen and is not a virtue, poverty that is freely embraced enables us to live with openness to God and to others. Knowing our poverty and being open to God are two sides of the same coin as we come face to face with the truth of ourselves, with our limitations and strengths, our inability to be omnicompetent and our riches in Christ. Acceptance of our limitations is integral to holiness. Quoting Johannes Metz's book, *Poverty of Spirit*, in which he suggests that we have only two choices in life – to accept our innate poverty or to be a slave to anxiety – Macrina Wiederkehr observes,

Anxiety robs me of my peace. It comes from forgetting that I am not in control. The moments when I have been most deeply in touch with God are those moments when I have been able to embrace my utter poverty. When I accept my poverty, my total dependence on God, I become vulnerable and God can more easily reach me because I'm not busy resisting being reached. When I am not resisting my poverty, I can more easily experience God in other people also, for I am more willing to allow them to minister to me. I am able to sit at their feet. Until we learn to sit at one another's feet, we will starve at our lavish banquet tables.[14]

People who know their poverty are not afraid to offer hospitality to others, sharing not only possessions but themselves: wounds, warts and all. Henri Nouwen describes hospitality as the ability to pay attention to the guest[15] and it comes from being at peace with ourselves. Hospitality finds a welcome for everyone at their own level. Some people need space to sit on the fringes. One measure of the holiness of our churches is the number of those people whom society and culture consider inferior, even embarrassing, who feel comfortable being around the Church because they know that they too have a home here. On this measure, some of the greatest health and holiness is to be found in the poorest and smallest inner-city churches.

If we are to welcome people, paradoxically we also need to have limits. From monasteries we can learn about the essential protection of boundaries that enable generous hospitality. The section on hospitality in the Rule of the Society of St John the Evangelist states,

> If we let our life as a brotherhood be overwhelmed by the claims of guests we could endanger the resources by which we can serve them. We can be confident of the rightness of boundaries which contain and foster our own life together. Every house shall have a private area to which guests are not normally invited and there shall be interludes during the year when guests are not normally received.[16]

This should be equally true of clergy family life which needs boundaries. Without boundaries there is chaos and invasion of privacy; with boundaries there is a safe place in which we can nurture our personal and family life, and grow in holiness. Even Jesus, with his boundless embrace of others, set limits on his availability at particular times by taking himself off simply to be alone with God.

Creativity is an aspect of holiness that is celebrated rather than stifled by poverty because we share in God's life-giving creativity. Christian ministry offers endless opportunities to be creative ourselves and to draw out creativity in others who thought their poverty was final. Somewhat reluctantly, I once visited a hospital patient about whom everybody complained because of her temper. Soon, I was teaching her to knit during my visits. Her excitement and enjoyment were matched by the gradual emergence of trust that freed her to tell stories of her life, thus defusing deep pain and resilience to God by cautiously giving them voice; so much so that the nurses commented that she had become more peaceful in herself. Years later, I remember that knitting as a testimony to God's creation of new life and hope in the most poverty-stricken place.

Although poverty is not about deficiency, it does confront us with areas of our life where we feel lack. For those who cannot have children, this aspect of poverty may be raw at times of baptisms – just as for some single, divorced or widowed priests weddings may be difficult, and all of us can find that funerals occasionally trip us up in our own grieving. However, since poverty also keeps us open to God, we may find that, in the mystery of God's economy, our perceived lack becomes a strange and holy gift to us and to others. Mercifully, with God, holiness is often carved out in the raw situations of life when our poverty is most evident. Holiness does not consist in denying or repressing our deep-seated desires or griefs but in ensuring that they are tended, and in living creatively with our poverty. Much of the most powerful and life-giving ministry has been born of poverty, many of the holiest saints have been most profoundly aware of their poverty and thus of their need of God's grace. That is the miracle of redemption.

Our vocation is, at times, incredibly demanding. Often holiness may simply mean doing the best we can as each situation arises, with no clear indication of what is right and no time to stand back and consider the situation, just a commitment to be faithful in the situation in which we find ourselves. Caring for ourselves means that we need to watch for signs of burn out when exhaustion and emptiness overwhelm, when we are giving more than we have the resources to sustain, or are ignoring our needs for nourishment and rest, for laughter and stimulus. At the heart of all of these is a denial of the very humanity in which holiness is manifest. We may make excuses – the parish or prison or hospital makes so many demands on us, we have no one to turn to ourselves, our people need us. All may be true but they should be wake-up calls to take a long, hard look at how we sustain ourselves in ministry. Left uncontrolled, they will destroy us or feed a messiah-complex; tended, they can become gateways to holiness. Godly poverty is not starvation, but openness to God, and the harder our situation, the more we need nurture.

When starvation does threaten, there are prayer resources in poetry that often parallel the psalms. Some of these poems from the Christian tradition take us to rock-bottom places where holiness is being forged in desperate circumstances. Gerard Manley Hopkins' sonnets of desolation are powerful windows on distress that was in large part brought about by the demands of his ministry in bleak surroundings. In 'No Worst' he agonizes:

> No worst, there is none. Pitched past pitch of grief,
> More pangs will, schooled at forepangs, wilder wring.
> Comforter, where, where is your comforting?
> Mary, mother of us, where is your relief?
>     . . . Here! creep,
> Wretch, under a comfort serves in a whirlwind: all
> Life death does end and each day dies with sleep.

George Herbert's 'Grief' articulates the absence of the comfort that he normally finds in poetry, and only in the last word reminds us that this is a prayer as well as a lament:

O who will give me tears? Come all ye springs,
Dwell in my head and eyes: come clouds, and rain:
My grief hath need of all the wat'ry things,
That nature hath produced . . .
Verses, ye are too fine a thing, too wise
For my rough sorrows: cease, be dumb and mute,
Give up your feet and running to mine eyes,
And keep your measures for some lover's lute,
Whose grief allows him music and a rhyme:
For mine excludes both measure, tune and time.
　　　　Alas, my God!

R. S. Thomas, in 'Waiting for It', is, as ever, to be found clinging tenaciously in prayer in the midst of doubts:

. . . Now
in the small hours
of belief the one eloquence

to master is that
of the bowed head, the bent
knee, waiting, as at the end

of a hard winter
for one flower to open
on the mind's tree of thorns.

Where is the holiness in this? It lies, in part, in the fact that these poems are prayer to a God whose apparent absence is not definitive, prayer by people who know their poverty and are committed by their ordination to remember that 'You cannot bear the weight of this calling in your own strength, but only by the grace and power of God. Pray that your heart may be daily enlarged and your understanding of the scriptures englightened. Therefore pray earnestly for the gift of the Holy Spirit.'[17] If we are 'fully determined, by the grace of God, to devote ourselves wholly to God's service, so that as [we] daily follow the rule and the teaching of our Lord and grow in his likeness, [then] God may sanctify the lives of all with whom [we] have to do'.[18] For this to happen we have to know and accept our poverty and model to others that acceptance of poverty is an ingredient of, not a barrier to, holiness.

The second evangelical virtue, chastity, is about living holy and faithful lives so that others may similarly live. It is about becoming a whole and holy person at peace with ourselves and trustworthy for God and others. Chastity frees us in our relationships with one another, since we do not use or abuse another person for our own benefit, or sacrifice others (too often our families) for any cause. The commitment to chastity enables us to sustain mature and holy relationships that respect the other person and maintain appropriate boundaries. Chastity is often confused with celibacy and while it is true that there is a sexual element to chastity as it relates to the priestly vocation (since chastity holds us to marriage vows of lifelong commitment, or to a vow of celibacy should that have been taken), chastity is much broader than that. It is quite possible to be chaste in relation to these vows and unchaste in other relationships as we manipulate and take advantage of people in non-sexual ways to meet our needs for power, prestige, security or emotional satisfaction. In fact, it is also possible to be sexually chaste in marriage but to be unfaithful in all sorts of other ways. Respect for the marriage bed should be the sacred symbol of respect for the person with whom one shares the bed – a lifelong sign of commitment to live for the well-being of another. Indeed, sexual chastity in marriage goes further than sexual fidelity. It expresses deep psychological and spiritual attitudes that are driven not by the desire for personal gratification but by the celebration of the strangely individuated oneness with another that marriage is designed to bring. And in the way of the gospel, union with another is a profoundly integrating experience for oneself.

How do we live chaste and holy lives? We are called to be lovers of souls, people who live and love with enthusiasm. Chastity is about being 'of virtuous conversation and good repute', capable of maintaining intimacy yet not controlling the other. Neither chastity nor celibacy negate loving: Donald Goergen quotes an unnamed Roman Catholic priest as saying, 'I am convinced that we have got to have personal, loving relationships. If someone is afraid of loving they cannot be a celibate. Celibacy only makes sense if a person knows how to love. No one can love in general if they do not love in particular.'[19] Holiness involves maintaining healthy relationships with family and friends that meet our needs for intimacy. This prevents us from looking to meet our needs in inappropriate places. We are responsible for maintaining boundaries in our ministry, and it is axiomatic that the people to whom we offer pastoral care in the course of our ministry are not people to whom we also look for intimacy or care: we must not muddy the waters for those who look to us as priests.

Our vocation involves much caring for others and it cannot be all one-way traffic. There is a paradox that while we are often the first to allow other people to be weak and let their defences down, we are often the last to allow ourselves to do the same. Chastity means that we are chaste with ourselves, not demanding more of ourselves than we can give. If we do nothing but care for others our ministry will, eventually, cease to be life-giving. Instead we will either burn out or we will care for others in order to meet our need to be needed, thus manipulating others for our own ends. Giving and receiving of love is at the heart of the Trinity, and we are called to share in this dance of love not to go it alone. For those who are married, our spouse and immediate family are primary sources of love and care, while single people may need to be more intentional about identifying sources of care and cultivating an openness to receive it if our ministry is not to be diminished. Holiness does not require loneliness, which is a very different experience from solitude.

In our priestly pursuit of holiness there are always decisions to be made between our own desires and the needs of those we are called to serve. Do we pursue what fulfils us or what best helps others? Our answer will affect everything from major vocational decisions to daily routine questions of visiting. It is in these nitty-gritty decisions of life that holiness is forged in us. Certainly, to grow in holiness we need to own and be able to

speak appropriately of our desires and passions, to search out
their meanings, to pray their yearnings, to live or deny them
chastely and with fire, to make wise and godly decisions. God
often works with not against our passions, so we are well-
advised to know them and to be able to answer the question,
'What do I desire?' or (as Jesus often asked) 'What do you want
me to do for you?' However, our desires and passions are not
only focused on ourselves: Jesus was clearly a passionate person
– passionate for God, for his friends, for the world – and we cannot fulfil our vocation to be holy unless we are people of similar
passion. Our vocation is one of service and following Christ who
laid down his life for his people, and chastity calls us to fidelity in
and to that vocation. We do not have a job that we can change
when it suits us, but a vocation to live. At times this may curb our
freedom of choice since the needs of others are a major concern
in our ministry.

The World Council of Churches' report on *Baptism, Eucharist
and Ministry* reminds us that our lives are signs to the body of
Christ,

> The Church needs persons who are publicly and continually
> responsible for pointing to its fundamental dependence on
> Jesus Christ, and thereby provide, within a multiplicity of its
> gifts, a focus of its unity . . . [The] presence [of ordained
> ministers] reminds the community of the divine initiative and
> of the dependence of the Church on Jesus Christ.[20]

If we are people committed to holiness of life, every retreat that
we make should be a reawakening and redirecting of our desire
for God and for our God-given desires. Chastity is the essential
safeguard for our desires and also the catalyst for faithful action
in response to the needs of others. Our vocation is about passion
for God, or, as Archbishop Oscar Romero put it, ambition to
greatness for God,

> I believe that the saints were the most ambitious persons. And
> this is my ambition for all of you and for myself: that we may
> be great, ambitiously great, because we are images of God and
> we cannot be content with mediocre greatness.[21]

Obedience, the third evangelical virtue, is also about fidelity, about ongoing formation, about openness to staying in the place of transformation because we are committed to the holy God who has called us by name. Obedience is responsive. Pope John XXIII's spiritual director told him he should always obey with simplicity and good nature, and leave everything else to the Lord. The Rule of Benedict begins with the word 'listen' and obedience begins with listening to God: listening in the sense not only of hearing but of acting in accordance with what we hear. That is where fidelity comes in because very often God's timescale is not ours and we discover the obedience that endures for the long haul, perhaps not seeing the end of our labours. As Eugene Peterson says,

> Apocalypse ushers us into the long and the large. We acquire, with St John and his congregations, fidelity to place and people, the faithful endurance that is respectful of the complexities of living a moral, spiritual and liturgical life before the mysteries of God in the mess of history . . . Impatience, the refusal to endure, is to pastoral character what strip mining is to the land – a greedy rape of what can be gotten at the least cost and then abandonment in search of another place to loot. Something like fidelity comes out of apocalyptic: fidelity to God, to be sure, but also to people, to parish, to place.[22]

Obedience means that when we stumble or make mistakes, we pick ourselves up, dust ourselves down and keep going, preferably learning from the experience for future reference. That is in part what the prayer in the Ordinal, that we grow stronger and more mature in our ministry, is about. To help us in this maturing we need role models. At the same time, we are role models for others and it can be a salutary challenge to ask ourselves, What do I model? Can I honestly ask others, as Paul did, to imitate me? (Philippians 3:17). Are we holiness walking? Do people see in us a determination to devote to God our best powers of mind and spirit, a deceptively simple phrase from the ASB Ordinal with its implicit challenge that we may offer our not-so-best powers? For many people, known and unknown to us, look to us – as astonishing as it sounds to say it – as the human face of God, the presence of God in their worlds. They will be deeply disappointed unless they can find in and through us the one 'who is close to the Father's heart, who has made him known' (John 1:18).

Obedience can be expressed through a Rule of Life, so long as we remember that a Rule is something we do 'as a rule' and is not an unbreachable set of regulations that carry harsh penalties for transgression. A Rule of Life can be a helpful framework for growth in holiness as well as a container for our scatteredness. Benedict's Rule provided for a basic balanced rhythm in life, guiding monastics towards holiness while also respecting their humanity (expressed in simple things like the timing of the night office to ensure adequate sleep and the opportunity to meet bodily needs). We all have a rhythm of life in some form or other, perhaps by default, and we do well to examine what it is and how it guides us to holiness. A Rule can help us to maintain balance in life and centre ourselves in whatever keeps us open and attentive to God. Obedience should mean that we are drawn rather than driven in our ministry, that we know God's ways with us in the past and can respond to the nudge of God in the present. Obedience, as expressed in a Rule of Life, recognizes that we are the temple of the living God (2 Corinthians 6:16) and embraces questions of what we do with our bodies – exercise, rest, diet; with our minds – what we read, our engagement with culture; what we do with our spirits – our prayer life, spiritual reading, joy and experience of beauty. We may find that we have to let some things go in order to give space for others just as gardeners have to thin out some plants in order to create space for others to thrive.

Holiness flourishes in ordered and uncluttered lives, we do not have to fill every waking moment with activity. St Seraphim's words, already quoted in Chapter 6, speak of poverty of spirit that is life-giving and holy: 'Be at peace, then thousands around you will find salvation.' We cannot be at peace and in a permanent rush. Diaries are essential to the maintenance of balance, safeguarding times of being off-duty and relaxing, times for prayer and for family. If time management is not our forte, there is plenty of help in books and seminars, and our spiritual directors should be checking in with us on this.

Holiness is always life-giving, not life-denying and we have to be at once firm and gentle with ourselves, finding and holding ourselves to a path in life that nurtures holiness. Pope John Paul II wrote to seminarians and priests, 'We must not forget that the candidate . . . is a necessary and irreplaceable agent in . . . formation. All formation, priestly formation included, is ultimately a self-formation.'[23] Henri Nouwen amplifies this, saying that we have to be able to articulate the movements of our inner life, to name our varied experiences and no longer be victims of ourselves. Only then can we offer ourselves as a source of clarification to others.[24] This requires the self-awareness that John Donne described nearly four centuries ago,

> . . . the copy, the pattern, the precedent which we are to propose to ourselves is the observation of God's former ways and proceedings upon us; because God has already gone this way, this way I will await his going still . . . Something then I must propose to myself to be the rule and the reason of my present and future actions . . . I can propose nothing more available than the contemplation of the history of God's former proceedings with me . . . Because this was God's way before I will look for God in this way still.[25]

How can we grow in holiness in this way? Henri Nouwen advises that one way is to keep a journal,

> Writing can be a true spiritual discipline. It helps us to concentrate; to get in touch with the deeper stirrings of our hearts; to clarify our minds; to process confusing emotions; to reflect on our experiences; to give artistic expression to what we are living; and to store significant events in our memories . . . We have to believe that our stories deserve to be told. We may discover that the better we tell our stories, the better we will want to live them.[26]

Have we ever considered our living as worthy of artistic expression, as significant enough to be recalled, as formative of our holiness? Like Traherne and Hopkins, whose writings are only extraordinary because they are so gloriously and attentively ordinary, we too can harvest and store formative times from daily life.

One way to increase our attentiveness can be the traditional practice of a review of the day when we recall events that were in danger of flying past unnoticed at the time – the conversation, the memories provoked by a letter, the sparkle in someone's eye, the unexpected beauty of a vista from the top of the bus, the moment that disturbed, the occasion for sin. It is a way of gathering up the crumbs so that 'nothing may be lost' (John 6:12): something done by people who know their poverty. There are many ways to do this. Bishop Thomas Ken's hymn, 'Glory to thee, my God, this night', originally his personal prayer at the end of the day, can be used as a framework for a review of the day. Another approach is the Ignatian examen, or the use of Compline's quiet space for evening reflection. It may also be helpful occasionally to set aside time for a review of the year, or – if we have never done it – a review of our life.

As children we were formed by stories told to us. As adults we are formed by God's stories, and – if we will but release them – our ongoing stories told day by day will form us as people who expect to find the Holy Spirit at work, whose fears are undermined by stories of God's power and whose hopes are stoked with stories of God's faithfulness. Priests are called, with all God's people, to tell the story of God's love,[27] to be storytellers but also those who enable others to become God's storytellers. Our pastoral ministry involves us in listening to many stories while our prophetic ministry involves us in facilitating the telling of stories to people who desperately need to hear the good news of hope and transformation.

> As a community of believers . . . we need both doctrine and storytelling . . . To be the church, to care for the church and to see its future (and even its diversity) among us – in short, to

sustain a vital tradition of spiritual formation – we need both the intellectual rigour of doctrinal theology and the rigorous immediacy of powerful stories . . .

We live the life of faith in and through the stories that testify that God is real, that growth is possible, that hope has meaning, that none of our suffering and none of our failures will ever finally destroy us, that nothing can separate us from the love of God. Christian community is a reservoir of such stories, a reservoir dug millennia ago by the storytellers of scripture but one to which every little congregation keeps adding, week by week, when we listen to each other's stories alert to recognising the sly, improbable interference of the Holy Spirit, the unscrupulous wit of a God determined to deconstruct our terror that life is indeed cold, nasty, brutish and short.[28]

Stories of God's actions free us to live with hope, to be holy people who model hope in a world where it is in scant supply. Hope derives from the fact that the Holy Spirit is active in the world, creating holiness everywhere, drawing us into the dance of God's life and love. Called to holiness, we live that holiness with humility, close to the humus, the earthiness of everyday life, so that others become holy.

## The cost of holiness

Holiness is not come by easily but requires sacrifice. Richard Baxter wrote in the seventeenth century to his fellow ministers about the demand that holiness makes upon them,

Self-denial is of absolute necessity in every Christian, but of double necessity in a minister, as he hath a double sanctification or dedication to God; without self-denial he cannot do God an hour's faithful service. Hard studies, much knowledge and excellent preaching are but more glorious and hypocritical sinning, if the end be not right.[29]

You can no more be saved without ministerial diligence and

fidelity than they or you can be saved without Christian diligence and fidelity. If you care not for others at least care for
yourselves . . . the day is near when unfaithful ministers will
wish they had rather been colliers or tinkers, or sweepers of
channels, than pastors of Christ's flock![30]

If we are to be holy, we must deal with our sin. Christ's priestly
action in not only sharing our life and identifying with sin, but
also in giving himself for us, is the only way in which sin can be
dealt with. We are sanctified through the offering of the body of
Jesus, once for all (Hebrews 10:10), and to that truth we must
keep returning. Again Baxter has wise advice, we do not only
keep sin out but we fill our lives with acts and attitudes that will
nourish goodness and holiness in our service of our people. He
knows, perhaps from experience, that if we do not do this not
only we but others will suffer as we fail to offer them the spiritual food that they have a right to expect:

> O brethren, watch, therefore over your own hearts! Keep out
> sinful passions and worldly inclinations: keep up the life of
> faith and love; be much at home: and be much with God. If it
> be not your daily, serious business to study your own hearts
> and subdue corruptions and live as upon God – if you make it
> not your very work which you constantly attend, all will go
> amiss, and you will starve your auditors . . . above all be much
> in secret prayer and meditation. There you must fetch the
> heavenly fire that must kindle your sacrifices. Remember that
> you cannot decline and neglect your duty to your own hurt
> alone; many will be losers by it as well as you. For your people's
> sake, therefore, look to your hearts . . . If [they] be then cold,
> how [are they] likely to warm the heart of [your] hearers?[31]

Baxter's words about the heavenly fire are similar to those of
Charles Wesley who prayed in words that capture the sacrificial
imperative of holiness and the balance of the Holy Spirit's work
and our own work in our growth in holiness:

> O thou, who camest from above
> the pure celestial fire to impart,

kindle a flame of sacred love
on the mean altar of my heart.

There let it for thy glory burn
with inextinguishable blaze,
and trembling to its source return
with humble prayer and fervent praise.

Jesus, confirm my heart's desire
to work, and speak and think for thee;
still let me guard the holy fire
and still stir up thy gift in me.

Ready for all thy perfect will
my acts of faith and love repeat,
till death thine endless mercies seal
and make the sacrifice complete.

We see in George Herbert's poem, 'Aaron', which alludes to the old covenant priestly ministry of Aaron, the same understanding of the need for and cost of priestly holiness, coupled with an awareness of his own sin and the foundation of his holiness in the sacrifice of Christ. Herbert's church at Bemerton, on the edge of Salisbury, surprises many visitors because it is so small. We tend to think that a poet and priest of the stature of Herbert should have had a large, even magnificent, church since it was the church building that inspired so much of his poetry. Instead, he served in a very small, simple church among a small congregation. It was in these simple surroundings that holiness was forged in him as a priest, and it was for this small congregation that he prayed for the holiness of life that would enable him to say, as in the last line of 'Aaron', 'Come people; Aaron's dressed.'

Holiness on the head,
Light and perfection on the breast,
Harmonious bells below, raising the dead
To lead them until life and rest.
Thus are true Aarons dressed.

Profaneness in my head,
Defects and darkness in my breast;
A noise of passions ringing me for dead
Unto a place where is no rest.
Poor priest thus am I dressed.

Only another head
I have, another heart and breast,
Another music, making live not dead,
Without whom I could have no rest:
In him I am well dressed.

Christ only is my head,
My alone only heart and breast,
My only music, striking me ev'n dead;
That to the old man I may rest,
And be in him new dressed.

So holy in my head,
Perfect and light in my dear breast,
My doctrine tuned by Christ (who is not dead,
But lives in me while I do rest),
Come people; Aaron's dressed.

Here, Herbert is pointing us to the vocation of the priest to *be* holy, not just to speak of holiness. Priesthood demands everything of us; our vocation is to be what we proclaim, to make present the love of Christ and to lead and inspire the people of God to live the holy obedience of Christ, that we may see in Moberly's words, 'the reproduction in her of the Spirit of Him who sacrificially offered himself. It is Christ himself who is being formed in her.'[32]

How do we live into these truths about holiness? The Jewish way of blessing things was through receiving from God and offering to God in thanksgiving. We do this in the traditional Jewish form of blessing if we use the prayers at the preparation of the table:

Blessed are you, Lord God of all creation:
through your goodness we have this bread to set before you,
which earth has given and human hands have made.
It will become for us the bread of life.

Indeed, the whole eucharistic prayer that follows is a giving thanks to and receiving from God. And, of course, the moment of communion itself is an intensive opportunity to receive from God the gift of Christ's holiness and to offer ourselves to God in gratitude. 'We present ourselves to this table', said John Knox's 'Forme of Prayers', 'to declare and witness before the world, that by him alone we have liberty, and life: that by him alone thou dost acknowledge us thy children and heirs; that by him alone we are possessed in our spiritual kingdom, to eat and drink at his table.'[33]

There is a cost to holiness, it is a cost we are called to pay daily as we follow Christ. But there is also a delight in holiness which, for those called to priestly ministry, includes the delight of seeing Christ formed in others. Richard Baxter, again, said it well:

The ultimate end of our pastoral oversight is that which is the ultimate end of our whole lives; even the pleasing and glorifying of God, and the glorification of his Church . . . and the nearer ends of our office are the sanctification and holy obedience of the people of our charge, their unity, order, beauty, strength, preservation and increase, and the right worshipping of God, especially in the solemn assemblies . . .

The world is better able to read the nature of religion in a man's life than in the Bible . . . it is therefore a necessary part of our work to labour more in polishing and perfecting the saints that they may be strong in the Lord and fitted for their Master's use.[34]

Polishing and perfecting the saints, ourselves included, is a life-long vocation to holiness.

# Being for Reconciliation

Once we had dreams, dreams of a new beginning
When we had fought the war to end all war,
A world of peace, where people live in freedom,
A world where justice reigns for evermore.
And yet, and yet, each year as we remember
We know too well how subtly dreams can fade.

In this our world where peace is often fragile,
Where war and hatred grip, where children die,
Too easily our hearts are dulled to suffering,
Our ears are deafened to the hopeless cry;
We fail to grasp the call to be peace-makers,
We act in fear and let the vision fade.

Still we need dreams, O God, make us your dreamers,
Inflame our passion for a world made whole,
A world where love extends to all a welcome,
Where justice, like a powerful stream, will roll.
Come, Prince of Peace, our fading hope rekindle,
'Your kingdom come' we pray, let peace be made.[1]

Sitting silently on a kerb outside the ambulance bay of a hospital
at two o'clock on a sultry July morning, next to an angry,
numbed young woman and wondering how on earth you came
to be there, is one consequence of the call to be people of reconciliation. The gangs of an American city were having a turf war,
and for a few nights the pager held by the on-call chaplain at the

hospital was a persistent, shrill reminder that we are called to be in the midst of the pain and the suffering that attends alienation. That night a young teenage boy had been shot. An hour earlier his family and friends had gathered in the family room where anger had bounced off the walls. Now that I had taken them to see his body laid out in a small room nearby, they were wandering around the entrance to the hospital trying to absorb the fact of his death. Tomorrow night it would be the same story, just a different cast.

A church office and another young woman weeping into her life the truth of her husband's infidelity; a funeral, and two sides of the family maintaining the silent clamour of antagonism that has been perfected to an art form over the years; a young person struggling with feared family reactions should he come out as a gay person; two sisters in a convent who cannot stand each other yet are both vowed to this life; a community fearful and angry at the prospect of a sex offender being released from prison in its midst; a prison, and a mother unable to forgive herself for murdering her child. These are the raw materials of being for reconciliation: enormous and difficult situations that may demand more than we feel we have to give.

Being for reconciliation confronts us with sin. There is no way round it. Sin, in all its messy and merciless manifestations, does not allow us to brush off its consequences or to be romantic about human nature. Historically, one of the main roles of the priest has been to encourage people to be reconciled to God and to others. Now that society is less interested in sin, often preferring to read in the tabloids about its sensational consequences, this aspect of the priestly ministry has tended to be sidelined. Reconciliation is only needed where there is alienation. As Christians, we worship the God who took the initiative and faced human alienation head on. Therefore, we should not be surprised to be thrust into its path today, and the question is not when, but how, do we face it? Being for reconciliation forces us to face our own sin and our own limitations. Probably as never before, we will be aware of our own wounds and weaknesses, our own vulnerable places and our consequent anger and defensiveness. We have this treasure, this proclamation of Jesus Christ through whom we are reconciled to God, in clay jars that bear the chips and stains of daily life; we do not have it in cut-glass crystal vases for display purposes only.

## God's reconciliation

Reconciliation is God's act, at God's initiative.[2] We do not reconcile ourselves to God, we are called to 'be reconciled to God' (2 Corinthians 5:20), to be the recipients of God's act of reconciliation. Miroslav Volf, writing on reconciliation and drawing on his experiences in his native country, the former Yugoslavia, in the 1990s says, 'When God set out to embrace the enemy, the result is the cross'.[3] In Christ God has taken the initiative and has removed any barriers from God's side to a relationship of reconciled friends. The ministry of reconciliation to which we are called is the proclamation of that open door and the invitation to walk through it. Each Christmas when we sing Charles Wesley's carol, we act as heralds of the good news of reconciliation.

> Hark! The herald angels sing,
> 'Glory to the newborn king,
> Peace on earth and mercy mild
> God and sinners reconciled!'

God has stopped at nothing to reconcile us, 'Beyond offering forgiveness, Christ's passion aims at restoring such communion – even with the enemies who persistently refuse to be reconciled.'[4] This is more than mere pardon, because reconciliation restores the communion that was broken by the sin. Pardon says, in effect, 'you will not be punished for your sins' whereas forgiveness and reconciliation say the much more demanding words with which we are sent out after every Eucharist, 'Go in peace to love and serve the Lord.' Reconciliation opens up the whole world of living in peace with God, with others and with ourselves and it involves change on both sides of the divide, the forgiven and the forgiver.[5]

Our ministry of reconciliation flows from the fact that God has not written the world off simply because something has gone wrong. From the Desert Fathers comes the story of a soldier who asked Abba Mius whether God accepted repentance. The Abba asked, 'Tell me, my dear, if your cloak is torn, do you throw it away?' He replied, 'No, I mend it and use it again.' Abba Mius then said to him, 'If you are so careful about your cloak, will not God be equally careful about his creatures?'[6] We are called to share in God's carefulness. Nathan Mitchell is quoted as describing reconciliation as 'a public announcement of the central paradox of the Christian faith: the fact that the words "God", "love" and "sinner" must be put together in the same sentence.'[7]

## Reconciliation in God's Church

Reconciliation is a joyful and gracious gift of God. When we undertake our charge to baptize and to preside at the celebration of the Eucharist we are acting as ministers of reconciliation. Baptism is the foundational sacrament of reconciliation, since in baptism we are washed by the Holy Spirit and made clean, clothed with Christ, called by God to live into our baptism and the promised fullness of life. But baptism does not only affect the individual; every time someone is baptized the Church is changed, fundamentally. In baptism the Lord adds to our number those whom he is calling and we welcome the baptized into the fellowship of faith, knowing that we are children of the same heavenly Father. The Church as the baptismal community is the context of reconciliation. As the first fruit of reconciliation of all humanity and all creation it is the effectual sign of the reconciliation of the world.

If baptism is the foundational sacrament of reconciliation, Eucharist is its ongoing sacrament and it is full of rich symbols of our reconciliation in Christ. The early liturgies recorded in the *Didache* made this very clear: 'as this broken bread was scattered over the mountains, and when brought together became one, so let your Church be brought together from the ends of the earth into your kingdom'. In the eucharistic prayer nearly 2,000 years later we pray 'as we eat and drink . . . unite us in the body of your Son.' Lest we forget the implications of this prayer, in Salisbury Cathedral the order of service for Holy Eucharist prints Augustine's powerful reminder that the Eucharist is more than words and actions, it is transformative:

> Receive, therefore, and eat the Body of Christ,
> you who are already made members of Christ within the
>     body of Christ.
> Take and drink the Blood of Christ.
> Lest you should fall apart,
> drink that which binds you together.
> Lest you should seem cheap to yourselves, drink that which
>     bought you.
> As this, when you eat and drink it, is changed into you,
> so you are changed into the Body of Christ by an obedient
>     and holy life.
> You are receiving that which (unless you receive unworthily)
>     you have begun to be.
> Make sure, therefore, that you do not eat and drink
>     judgement to yourselves. . .
> He who receives the mystery of unity and does not preserve
>     the bond of peace
> receives the mystery not for, but against, himself.

The whole eucharistic liturgy points us to reconciliation. We gather as one from many places; we confess our failure to love God and to love our neighbour, that we have lived unreconciled lives; together we hear God's word to us; we proclaim our common faith; we express our reconciliation as we share the peace and are reminded that, 'we are the body of Christ, in the one Spirit we were all baptised into one body' and are called to 'pursue all that makes for peace and builds up our common life'. In the Book of Common Prayer the same idea is expressed in the bidding, 'Ye that do truly and earnestly repent you of your sins and are in love and charity with your neighbours, and intend to lead a new life . . .' Together we make our offerings for those in need; we pray together '*Our* Father'; we share a common meal as

our Lord commanded; and, as we saw earlier, we go in peace. 'By
breaking the bread we share not only in the body of the crucified
and resurrected Lord, but also in the multi-membered body of the
Church. The Eucharist tells us that each member is not external
to the other members.'[8] To be a people of reconciliation is to be
a baptized, eucharistic people.

Despite the fact that we are united with Christ in baptism and
sustained in Christ by living the eucharistic life, at times we live
as though we were not united to Christ and in Christ to one
another. We are exhorted to 'seek peace and pursue it' (1 Peter
3:11), a charge that is not limited to the ordained. However, our
responsibility for the people entrusted to us means that we
should be proactive in maintaining and restoring the peace of
God, and, to that end, the Bishop asks those to be ordained
priest, 'will you, knowing yourselves to be reconciled to God in
Christ, strive to be an instrument of God's peace in the church
and in the world?'[9] We are to seek for God's children in the
wilderness of this world's temptations and to guide them
through its confusions – as the Church of England's liturgy puts
it – bringing people home, walking alongside them until they are
reconciled to God and restored to the company and unity of the
faithful. We see the ideal outworking of this in the writings of
George Herbert,

> . . . in his visiting the sick or otherwise afflicted, [the parson]
> followeth the Church's counsel, namely, in persuading them to
> particular confession, labouring to make them understand the
> great good use of this ancient and pious ordinance and how
> necessary it is in some cases; he also urgeth them to do some
> pious and charitable works, as a necessary evidence and fruit
> of their faith at that time especially; the participation of the
> holy Sacrament, how comfortable and sovereign a medicine it
> is to all sin-sick souls.[10]

As those entrusted with Christ's people, we have to keep a broad
perspective on reconciliation, aware of its often complex communal dimension. However, while keeping the community in mind,

we cannot downplay the personal aspect of sin and the need for repentance and reconciliation. For most people confession in personal prayer, along with the opportunity to confess their sins in the context of public worship in which they hear the words of absolution, is adequate. Others find it helpful to make a regular confession in the presence of a priest. There are some people, however, who need to seek counsel if forgiveness and reconciliation are to be received. This may apply in the case of very serious sin or after a long period away from the Church, or it may apply in the case of people with very sensitive consciences who are either unable to believe they are forgiven, or find it hard to distinguish between sin and the daily knocks and bruises of life and so are overscrupulous in defining sin. While secular counselling may be helpful in enabling people to understand and deal with certain problems, there comes a point at which the Church's ministry of reconciliation is vital if people are to be freed from the sense of guilt. Where necessary, like George Herbert, we are to help people to come to peace with God. Richard Hooker, writing at the end of the sixteenth century, observed the devastating effect of being aware of our sin but without assurance of God's mercy:

> For as long as we are in ourselves privy to our own most heinous crimes, but without sense of God's mercy and grace towards us, unless the heart be either brutish for want of knowledge, or altogether hardened by wilful atheism, the remorse of sin is in it as the deadly sting of a serpent.
>
> . . . it hath therefore pleased Almighty God, in tender commiseration over the imbecilities of men, to ordain for their spiritual and ghostly comfort consecrated persons which by sentence of power and authority given from above as it were out of his very mouth ascertain timorous and doubtful minds in their own particular, ease them of their scrupulosities, leave them settled in peace and satisfied touching the mercy of God towards them.[11]

The Church of England has always provided for the need for personal counsel. The first Exhortation in the Order for Holy

Communion in the Book of Common Prayer includes the charge
to examination of life followed by confession, with restitution if
necessary. The minister then adds,

> . . . therefore if there be any of you, who by this means cannot
> quiet his own conscience herein, but requireth further comfort
> or counsel, let him come to me or to some other discreet and
> learned minister of God's Word, and open his grief; that by
> the ministry of God's holy Word he may receive the benefit of
> absolution, together with ghostly counsel and advice, to the
> quieting of his conscience, and avoiding of all scruple and
> doubtfulness.

The thrust of the exhortation is now embedded in Canon B29 'Of
the ministry of absolution'. There is an implicit assumption that
ministers are 'discreet and learned ministers of God's Word',
able to offer 'ghostly counsel and advice'. If we are to be people
of and for reconciliation, part of our formation for this ministry
lies in our being both discreet and learned in God's word, an
aspect of our calling that we have already explored. Other training, particularly training in counselling and listening skills, may
be helpful in our ministry but at root we are to be for God's
word. Chambers dictionary definition of 'discreet' is 'to be careful in one's actions and choice of words; especially able to keep
secrets, tactful, prudent, modest, unpretentious'. Our prudence
comes in large part from our knowledge of God's word, but
knowledge of God's word without discretion can be dangerous.
Reconciliation involves immense care with other people's lives
including utter reliability over confidentiality, which is required
in the case of the confessional.[12] Being learned ministers of God's
word involves knowing what words of comfort and counsel to
offer but also awareness that we are persons in community,
created in the image of the Trinitarian God whose actions are
never harmful, and that some sin has communal implications
which may require putting right or even reporting to the police.
If so, being for reconciliation may require us to stand with the
person as they face the consequences of their actions.

All who are called to the ministry of reconciliation are called to a confidence in the abundance of God's mercy. Charles Wesley sang:

> Love divine, all loves excelling
> Joy of heaven to earth come down,
> Fix in us thy humble dwelling,
> All thy faithful mercies crown.
> Jesus, thou art all compassion
> Pure, unbounded love thou art,
> Visit us with thy salvation,
> Enter every trembling heart.

Samuel Crossman composed the much-loved words,

> My song is love unknown,
> My Saviour's love to me,
> Love to the loveless shown
> That they might lovely be.

To be ministers of reconciliation we need to be more aware of the mercy and love of God than we are of human sin – realistic about the latter, certainly, but still more articulate about the reconciling love of God. Then, in the words of Hamon L'Estrange who wrote in 1659:

> Upon [hearing a humble and sincere] Confession, mixed with a vehement and earnest plying the Throne of God for mercy, it becomes the Minister instantly to interpose, to lay before [the penitent] the inexhaustible treasure of God's infinite mercies, to assure him of his interest therein, and, upon the hypothesis of his contrition to be serious and unfeigned, to give him Absolution.[13]

In our preaching and pastoral care we should be creating an environment of confidence in God's love and mercy in which sin can be owned and the possibility of reconciliation celebrated, other-

wise people have no context of hope in which to face their sinfulness. An anonymous writer in 1657 said:

> And for want of [counsel and comfort to relieve the con-
> science] many have run into very great Mischief, having let the
> Doubt fester so long it hath either plunged them into deep
> Distress of Conscience, or, which is worse, they have, to still
> that Disquiet within them, betaken themselves to all sinful
> Pleasures and so quite cast off all Care of their Souls.[14]

Prison chaplains are particularly likely to encounter situations of
distress born of remorse where human reconciliation is not
possible, with the attendant despair at the possibility of ever
being forgiven. From one high-security prison comes a story of
the chaplain singing to a group of women prisoners who were
separated from other prisoners because they had murdered
children. She sang 'What a friend we have in Jesus' and afterwards wrote, 'As soon as I began to sing the tears started. After
speaking for a while about how they can rely on Jesus to be their
friend, I continued on with singing "Precious Lord, take my
hand". I was so glad they felt safe enough to cry in front of each
other, but talking would be a different thing. I read them the
story of Lazarus being raised from the dead and we had another
prayer before I left.' Another person commented on this, 'I imagined you like a mother singing to soothe a little one who cannot
be reached by words. What a grace-full moment.'[15] In being for
reconciliation, we may have to find such creative and appropriate ways to 'lay before people the inexhaustible treasures of
God's infinite mercies'.

This may or may not involve a rite of reconciliation.
Previously in the Church of England individual confession in
the presence of a priest was included only in ministry to the sick
(assumed to be at the time of death). Now several churches
provide a rite of reconciliation to meet the need for personal
confession in situations where sickness is not a factor. In Great
Britain, the *Methodist Worship Book* (1999) provides such a
rite, and the Church of England's *Common Worship* (2005)

provides two; in the USA the Episcopal Church has provided two forms of this rite since 1979. In both countries the first focuses on the relationship of the individual penitent and God while the second draws in part on the  baptismal liturgy and emphasizes the need for reconciliation to the Church as well as to God.

At ordination, priests are given the responsibility to 'call their hearers to repentance' and 'in Christ's name absolve, and declare forgiveness of sins'[16] – and are to assist the penitent to 'complete' his or her confession with integrity, enabling the penitent 'to recognise the reality of human frailty and God's all-embracing mercy and grace'.[17] This is a very privileged ministry which requires great care on behalf of the priest to whom the penitent has turned for comfort and counsel so that they can be estab- lished in the freedom and forgiveness of Christ.[18] However, we should not lose sight of the fact that even the private celebration of the reconciliation of a penitent remains a corporate action of the Church, because sin affects the unity of the body. For this reason, in the ordination prayer itself the bishop prays that those being ordained will, 'work with their fellow servants in Christ' to 'reconcile what is divided, heal what is wounded and restore what is lost'.[19] This holds the ministry of reconciliation in a much larger frame than just the troubled conscience of the penitent, important as that is. The ministry of reconciliation is also close- ly linked to the charge given to priests to bless God's people and to 'proclaim Christ's victory over the powers of darkness, and absolve in Christ's name all who turn to him in faith',[20] epito- mized in the words of one dismissal, 'May Christ who out of defeat brings new hope and a new future, fill you with his new life . . .'.[21]

If we are asked for this ministry, we do well to take to heart the wisdom that,

Throughout [the] office is not vicarial. [The priest] does not interpose between God and man in such a way that direct com- munion with God is suspended on the one hand or that [the priest's] own mediation becomes indispensable on the other.[22]

When we are asked to hear someone's confession, it is important that we ourselves are prepared. Michael Ramsey talks of being 'calm, serene, and in the true sense "business like"'.[23]

What we have to offer is ourselves, sinners that we are, who know ourselves to be reconciled to God and who have been given the authority to speak the words of God's absolution. The privilege of speaking these words of release and freedom should never elude us: there is joy in heaven at this moment (Luke 15:10). We need to cultivate the art of deliberately forgetting what we have heard, but before we do so there is the opportunity to offer words of counsel and comfort. This is not the time for a sermon, but a time when, with one ear open to God and the other to the penitent, we set what we have heard and what lies behind it in the light of the gospel. It may be appropriate to offer a few words of 'incisive and tender counsel before the absolution'[24] in which case a question to keep before us is 'What is God wanting to say in order to restore and keep this beloved person in a sense of fellowship?' Our own preparation for this ministry is growing wisdom in the ways and mercy of God, coupled with an awareness of our own spiritual depths and our own humanity. For example, we are coming to realize that if we are not to blunder in with mistaken assumptions men have to be open to learn from women's experience, and women from men's.[25] Many versions of the rite end with the priest asking the penitent to 'pray for me, a sinner' as a reminder that we, too, are in need of God's mercy.

Being for reconciliation will make us aware of deliberate actions we never imagined in our worst nightmares and of tender consciences that are so fragile they will break if we are insensitive or hasty. When confronted with the workings of the human heart, the cure of souls demands of us the carefulness and love of souls that blends the compassion of a mother for her child with the wisdom of Solomon. Prayer, prayer and more prayer is essential, along with a deep openness to the gifting of the Holy Spirit. When we are brought face to face with the complexities of human nature and the depth of sin that separates us from God, we may find ourselves drained and for our own well-being we may need to be intentional in finding ways to nurture ourselves as we share in this reconciling work of Christ.

It is easy for people to seek the easing of their own conscience without realizing that the theology of the Church means there is the communal dimension to reconciliation. How can we help people trace this pathway of repentance from individual contrition of heart to reconciliation to the Church? The sixteenth-century Anglican homily on reconciliation sets this out:

> [Repentance is] the conversion or turning again of the whole man unto God, from whom we go away by sin . . . Now there be four parts to repentance . . . the first is the contrition of the heart . . . the second is an unfeigned confession and acknowledging of our sins unto God . . . the third part of repentance is faith whereby we do apprehend and take hold upon the promises of God touching the free pardon and forgiveness of our sins . . . the fourth is an amendment of life, or a new life, in bringing forth fruits worthy of repentance. For they that do truly repent must be clean altered and changed; they must become new creatures . . .
>
> The true meaning of it that the faithful ought to acknowledge their offences, whereby some hatred, rancour, grudge or malice may have risen or grown among them one to another, that a brotherly reconciliation may be had; without which nothing that we do can be acceptable unto God.[26]

We cannot stop at the third stage because forgiveness brings in its trail an ethic of amendment of life and reconciliation, of the healing of the divided body of Christ. Sin is not only a matter between the individual and God, but is a rupture within the Church, a denial of the baptismal and eucharistic community. The early Church took sin and reconciliation seriously, called sinners to repentance, prayed for them, fasted with them, encouraged repentance, held out the hope of reconciliation, and then celebrated the reconciliation with joy. When we treat sin only as a personal thing, we fail to acknowledge the communal effects of sin and the need for communal ways of dealing with it. Pastorally, this can be disastrous, not only for the person who has sinned but for the community that is affected but fails to be reconciled and healed. We know so well the effect of individual sin on the community – the breach of trust that makes further trust impossible; the affair that destroys families and friendships; the gossip that infects a community with half-truths. A quick glance through the minutes of Church Council meetings will reveal the often mundane sources of old division which may be festering still. Since we can offend and take offence so easily, making the trivial into the tumultuous, it is far easier to destroy fellowship than to reconcile and restore fellowship. As ministers we are to be an example, and are asked if we will 'endeavour to fashion our lives and that of our households according to the way of Christ, that we may be a pattern and example to Christ's people'.[27] Richard Baxter frequently exhorted his fellow ministers to 'take heed to yourselves', one of the many reasons he gave being the danger that their example could contradict their doctrine. Being for reconciliation assumes that we do nothing deliberately that creates a need for subsequent reconciliation.

We are called to be peace-makers. Nearly 450 years ago, John Jewel wrote of ministers who, in dealing with those who have offended others and made themselves strangers to the common fellowship, 'after perfect amendment of such persons, doth reconcile them and bring them home again, and restore them to the company and unity of the faithful'.[28] Jewel's phraseology suggests that people can be reconciled to the company, but not actually to the unity, of the faithful. It does not take much imagination to think of situations where an uneasy truce has been established in which people are in the same room but studiously avoiding each other. Being for reconciliation means we must go the extra mile, face the pain of moving beyond this initial stage of uneasy tolerance. This is hard, particularly where wounds are deep, misunderstanding has taken root alongside any deliberate acts that have breached fellowship, or there is fear for people's safety. Particularly where there has been betrayal, we have to acknowledge and work with the accompanying deep pain. Sometimes all we can ask of people, at least initially, is that they are *willing to become willing* to be reconciled. We may need to learn from other colleagues who have faced this situation before, or devote hours to listening, gradually weeding out the deeply established roots of mistrust, while also holding before people their baptismal inheritance of reconciliation with God and one another. After a difficult period for the community in which I lived, I reflected on God's work among us and wrote:

> Unwittingly,
> we cut each other
> with the serrated edges of our pain.
> But you come and,
> like a jigsaw,
> fit the pieces into a
> glorious whole.

This aspect of our ministry, like no other, will humble us and hold before us our own need to be reconciled. We are not immune to falling out with one another. Paul wrote to Euodia and Syntyche who had struggled beside him in the work of the gospel, urging them to be of the same mind in the Lord (Philippians 4:2). They were women of faith and dedicated workers alongside Paul but, even so, Paul knew they could not be reconciled on their own and so he appealed to others to help them. As we saw in Chapter 1, to the Ephesian elders he gave the charge, 'Keep watch over yourselves and over all the flock, of which the Holy Spirit has made you overseers, to shepherd the Church of God that he obtained with the blood of his own Son' (Acts 20:28). Why? Because there would be attempts to divide the flock, to entice some away, to break the communion. We read the second part of Paul's exhortation and miss the first – those sharing any form of team ministry can be so busy keeping watch over others they fail to keep watch over themselves. As a result we model in attitude and action, if not in word, division and lack of reconciliation. If we are to serve others, we must do what it takes to tend to ourselves and our own reconciliation (Matthew 5:23–24). In our version of an ideal world, we may never have chosen our present colleagues, but God has called us together, and learning the skills of being team players with our colleagues and our congregations is the least we can do as people of reconciliation. Being committed to pray for our colleagues is a beginning in maintaining our unity in Christ, while learning to care for one another in practical ways is also vital.

## Reconciliation in God's world

By virtue of our baptism, we are all called to the ministry of reconciliation. The Church is God's agent of reconciliation today. The Church is deeply implicated in life, it is not an isolated holy zone where sinners fear to tread. Joan Chittister has said that 'we have the responsibility to make present in society what we claim is present among us'.[29] In a broken world, reconciliation made tangible among us makes us signs of God's future reign over all creation which, through the ministry of the Holy Spirit, is already beginning to break into our present. It is something we both live into today and also anticipate in its fullness tomorrow; it is one of the blessings for which we, who need to forgive as we have been forgiven, pray in the Lord's Prayer – the coming of God's reign on earth as it is in heaven.

Reconciliation requires us to dream dreams with God, to see beyond what is in front of our eyes, to believe there are other possibilities than the rock and the hard place that trap us in estrangement. Apparently, in Indonesian, to hope is 'to see through the horizon'. Reconciliation and hope are intertwined: if we share the ministry of reconciliation we must learn to see with hope, we have to be able to see through the horizons the world sets. We are called to connect people to hope.[30] But we must keep our feet on the ground. The gospel is always concrete in its application to concrete situations, it applies the other-worldly possibilities of God's way of living to the this-worldly problems of our life today. To be people of reconciliation requires that we be realistic dreamers – people who know our God and know our world – and are prepared to act accordingly. The United Reformed Church describes its ideal for Ministers of Word and Sacrament as people who

. . . have a prophetic detachment, surrendering neither to the cynicism of the world nor to the nostalgia of the Church. [They] should be men and women of God, yet know their way around the world, acting as interpreters between the community and the Church. [They] should have soft hearts and hard heads, they should not have hard hearts and soft heads.[31]

Reconciliation is a pastoral as well as a theological event and, following Christ, the local church is the enfleshment of the good news of God's reconciliation. This may at times be messy, because the situations people mire themselves into are messy and cannot always be cleaned up at once. 'It is a fact of pastoral life that not just the canonically pure come through our doors. Are we ready to live the tension this situation presents?'[32] Being for reconciliation involves being prepared to get our hands messy too as we reach out to others and if necessary walk with them through the tough and troubled times of their lives. A study of how people speak of God in their lives has found that brokenness and healing are significant religious experiences. Several people spoke of an experience of isolation, illness, painful decisions or relationships, rejection or lack of reconciliation, and then told of how they had known God's presence and touch through these experiences. This did not occur easily or quickly, but through a continuous movement, a journey from death to life in which reconciliation was not just a process but a 'mediated process' as others in the community reached out.[33] Our ministry puts us in the forefront of helping to build a reconciling community that can reach out in this way. To do this we need to know our own ways of speaking of God in our lives, our own stories of brokenness and healing, our own stories of reconciliation. Have these personal stories been told in our churches? Have our churches told their corporate stories of brokenness and healing? It may not be possible to move forward in reconciliation until our own brokenness is known and healed.

We are not called to have all the answers, or to be omnicompetent in the face of situations that defy explanation, but we are called to be instruments of God's love. To love someone is to be willing to be alongside them in our poverty, not necessarily to have all the resources that they need. Being comfortable living with mystery is essential in our ministry since we cannot straight-jacket everything into problems to be solved. We trust that God knows the path even through the valley of the shadow of death and so, just as Jesus stayed with the disciples and let the confusion spill out, our ministry as priests may simply be being there offering our presence – sitting on a hospital kerb at 2 a.m., creating the safe silence into which a tortured silence can break, holding someone's hand and staying in the darkness, saying by our presence rather than our words that we are sorry for the suffering. What are we doing? In one sense nothing, in another sense everything, because we are the manifestation of God's love at that moment. Words may follow, but Jesus walked with the disciples on the road to Emmaus, listening to their version of the story, long before he spoke and made sense of the mystery. What people are seeking is the assurance that they are not alone, that God has not abandoned them.

However, there are times when presence is not enough. Reconciliation will, at times, take us into the political and social arenas of life, and will demand that we become articulate about justice. Elsa Tamez, writing of Paul's understanding in Romans of justification by faith, that God by pure grace and without human collaboration justifies and pardons the ungodly and reconciles all humanity in Jesus Christ, goes on to say, 'The abyss between the doctrine and the reality of our poor people allows the doctrine to remain floating in ambiguity, which in turn is conducive to its facile manipulation.'[34] She quotes the South African 'Kairos Document' which refers to the need for reconciliation to include appropriate accountability for injustice and evil actions. In making the removal of present injustices a prerequisite for reconciliation, it goes one stage further than just looking for willingness to become willing to be reconciled,

In our situation in South Africa today it would be totally unchristian to plead for reconciliation and peace before the present injustices have been removed. Any such plea plays into the hands of the oppressor by trying to persuade those of us who are oppressed to accept our oppression and to become reconciled to the intolerable crimes that are committed against us. That is not Christian reconciliation, it is sin.[35]

This is a twentieth-century restatement in an African political context, of the fourth stage of repentance that was outlined 400 years earlier in the Homily on Reconciliation. Where there is not the 'clean change' that the homily refers to, the effects are devastating. Elsa Tamez writes that when people are dehumanized, either by being oppressed or by oppressing others, affection, love and zest for life are lost. Being justified means that we recover by faith the image of God, the dignity of humans created by God for life, and the recreation of that life in justice.[36] She speaks of giving people permission to dream.[37]

Reconciliation is about the recovery of love, the recovery of zest for life, because it is about the restoration of the image of God in humans in opposition to dehumanizing forces. It draws the oppressed and the oppressor, draws strangers, together, giving each as a gift to the other. Very occasionally this may be as dramatic as the story of Bishop Leonard Wilson, who was imprisoned and tortured by his Japanese captors during the Second World War and after the war found himself confirming one of his torturers in a prison chapel,[38] or it may be the gentle welcome extended to, and accepted cautiously by, a small inner-city church to a bag lady.

George Herbert's understanding of the ministry of reconciliation entrusted to the country parson extended to that of seeking to keep his flock from going to law. He encouraged them to resort to him as their judge, supported by other trustworthy people in the parish. To this end he made sure that he was familiar with both the basics and some of the complexities of legal situations. While the situation in seventeenth-century England was very different from today and the approach to ministry was much more paternalistic, the principle at work here holds good – that we should not ignore conflict but seek to defuse disputes between the people entrusted to us wherever possible, before they become matters for the legal processes. But Herbert was realistic about his capabilities and has much to teach us about the ministry of reconciliation in cases that were too complex for him to handle,

> . . . he shows them how to go to law even as brethren and not as enemies, neither avoiding therefore one another's company, much less defaming one another.[39]

Herbert's parson is clearly aware of his different roles – as judge and as parson. In the latter role he never loses sight of his ministry of reconciliation, exhorting people to charity that goes beyond legal requirements of restoration, showing them how to maintain fellowship despite being at odds legally. Justice is not enough: reconciliation and living at peace are our vocation as Christians and it is our vocation to facilitate this way of living.

There is no division between the world-embracing aspect of reconciliation and our reconciliation in the Eucharist. We cannot share bread and wine in the Eucharist if we are unwilling to share bread and wine with a hungry world. A. M. Allchin, writing of Michael Ramsey in 1964, said,

> He turned to one of his favourite quotations from the Fathers . . . to the prophetic words of St Chrysostom, that it is vain to come to the altar in the Eucharist unless we go out to find the altar which is identical with the poor brother: 'This altar thou mayest see everywhere lying both in lands and market places, and thou mayest sacrifice upon it every hour. When thou seest a poor brother reflect that thou beholdest an altar.'[40]

Jesus' ministry of reconciliation frequently involved meals with the poor and the outcast of his society, as well as with the rich and influential. There is something very powerful about eating with one another. It is an offer of hospitality that welcomes strangers and friends to the same table. Inviting people to stay for coffee after a service is a beginning, but reconciling communities are likely to find themselves eating together frequently, either as a whole or in smaller groups. George Herbert's ideals for the country parson included hospitality at his table for all in his parish in turn.[41]

A reconciled community reaches out to draw others in and is not afraid to move beyond its boundaries, seeing them not as barriers but simply as boundaries that define its identity without restricting its mission. Joy is the hallmark of people who know they are at peace with God and one another. The joy may be robust and unavoidable, it may be quiet yet pervasive. We will see it in the sparkle in people's eyes, their body language, the way things are said and done, the way people care for one another. It is our joy and privilege to share in the creation and nurture of communities of reconciliation.

## Being for reconciliation

What does the call to be for reconciliation ask of us as priests? It is not simply an external matter of living peacefully with our neighbours. There is a personal dimension to it as well which has to do with our own reconciliation to our calling and manner of life, to ourselves. Our presence to other people's pain is only possible if we have learned to be present to our own pain, and to let others be present to us in our own vulnerability. If we opt to love others, our own wounds will become evident. Whereas we tend to measure peace by the extent to which we feel good about the way things are going and by the absence of conflict or contradiction, sometimes we have to learn to live into the deeper peace of God that holds us, wounded as we are, through the tempestuous times of life.

Like Paul, if we are to be people of reconciliation we have to learn through our difficult experiences not to lose heart (2 Corinthians 4:1) and to let the love of Christ urge us on (2 Corinthians 5:14). At times we may prefer to despair or to put our feet up, particularly when peace is tantalizingly, even distressingly, absent from our lives. Gerard Manley Hopkins' poem 'Peace' was written just before he was sent by his Order from his beloved Oxford to the industrial town of Bedford Leigh. The poem, with its vivid phrase 'piecemeal peace is poor peace', bears witness to his own struggle with this particular aspect of the calling. However, it is set within the broader and joyful framework of reconciliation with his vocation, and his ongoing robust relationship in prayer and poetry with the God who at times delights and at times seems to abandon him.

When will you ever, Peace, wild wooddove, shy wings shut,
Your round me roaming end, and under be my boughs?
When, when, Peace, will you, Peace? – I'll not play hypocrite
To own my heart: I yield you do come sometimes; but
That piecemeal peace is poor peace. What pure peace allows
Alarms of wars, the daunting wars, the death of it?

O surely, reaving* Peace, my Lord should leave in lieu
Some good! And so he does leave Patience exquisite,
That plumes to Peace hereafter. And when Peace here does
   house
He comes with work to do, he does not come to coo,
      He comes to brood and sit.

Hopkins models to us an honesty in prayer and a way of faithfulness that keeps his strivings with God within the language and
imagery of faith. George Herbert was also familiar with the challenge, and in his poem 'The Collar' he explores some of his own
fighting with God and with himself that resolved, eventually, in
acceptance of his vocation. The title itself is capable of different
interpretations and could refer to his baptismal or his ordained
vocation, while the rhyme structure of the poem – tightly constructed with a concealed rhyme pattern that creates the illusion
of chaos – expresses the poet's inner lack of harmony and reconciliation. But this attempt to break free from the restraint of
Christian commitment is set within a framework, seen in the first
and last lines, of God as the ultimate context within which life is
lived. The numerous alternative readings in this poem reveal the
depth of Herbert's familiarity with the Christian tradition. It is
only in the last four lines that the voice of God is heard above the
chaos and cacophony of the earlier voices. Significantly, too, the
rhyming structure becomes clear:

But as I raved and grew more fierce and wild
   At every word,
Me thoughts I heard one calling, *Child*:
   And I replied, *My Lord*.

* reave: to rob, plunder

The 'one' calling is not capitalized so it need not refer to the divine voice. However, if it is God calling, in seventeenth-century English the implied word 'caller' would sound similar to 'collar' in the title of the poem. If 'calling' is read as a noun, then the one calling is to be a child, with all that suggests about relationship, with the vocation as priest only following from that primary call. Recognition of this primary relationship, which is expressed in baptism rather than ordination, is what brings Herbert to peace and to reconciliation with God and himself.

John Donne was another poet and priest who struggled with God and with himself. In his 'Divine Meditations 14' ('Batter my heart, three-personed God') he balances the imagery of battle for control of his life, pleading with God to use force to free him and make him new with the language of love. 'A Hymn to God the Father' plays with the pun of his name 'Donne' to express his life-long struggle for assurance that God had forgiven his sins and reconciled him,

> When thou hast done, thou hast not done,
> for I have more.

Donne's passion for God is at times expressed in the passionate language of human love, and like Hopkins and Herbert, Donne's poetry reflects a vigorous prayer life that was unashamed to explore the deeper and more difficult reaches of his life. Hopkins, Herbert, Donne, and other poets writing in a similar vein ask us to be honest and no-holds-barred in our own prayer life with God, in order that we may come to peace with God and with our-selves. It is out of this reconciliation that we can be ministers of reconciliation for others.

As we said in Chapter 7, we are accountable for ourselves and our ministry, and need to have appropriate support resources in place. We may find ourselves leading our people into reconcilia-tion by our example. If we are afraid or ashamed to name our own unreconciled and disowned fragments of our lives, sooner or later they will show up in our ministry and draw attention to themselves. Making a fearless review of our life is a brave and demanding thing to do, but is a necessary part of our spiritual discipline if we are to live holy and reconciled lives. We cannot ask our people to do what we will not do ourselves. For many clergy, including those whose tradition is not one of regular use of the rite of reconciliation, making an annual confession in Lent or at some other time, perhaps approaching the anniversary of ordination, is a helpful way of reviewing life and clearing out the debris.[42] Being the season for the reconciliation of penitents, Lent is an appropriate time for self-examination. The Collect for Ash Wednesday is a safe container for this discipline, keeping before us as it does both our sinfulness and God's mercy, and echoing the promise in Ezekiel 36:26 that God will give us new hearts in place of our hearts of stone:

> Almighty and everlasting God,
> You hate nothing that thou hast made
> and forgive the sins of all those who are penitent;
> create and make in us new and contrite hearts
> that we, worthily lamenting our sins
> and acknowledging our wretchedness,
> may receive from you, the God of all mercy,
> perfect remission and forgiveness;
> through Jesus Christ your Son our Lord. Amen.

Obedience may require us to name something as sin that we have tolerated as one of our little ways. It may require us to be honest about whatever we are running from, or whatever we have substituted in our lives for what we know to be the call of God. Alternatively, or additionally, it may require that we learn to accept ourselves as we are and to give up wishing, constantly, to be someone else. Whatever it is that we struggle to accept about ourselves and our poverty may be the point at which our own journey of reconciliation begins, moving us away from 'piecemeal peace' towards the peace that passes understanding, the peace that pervades whether or not our desires are met and our problems solved as we would wish. Jesus, in Gethsemane, knew the struggle that this acceptance can involve and we should not take it lightly. Our ministry depends upon our reconciliation with ourselves. We have nothing to offer to God and to others except ourselves.

Donald Goergen has written,

> Priests and ministers are familiar with crisis. Specialists in
> other people's pain, they recognise how this dynamic of loss
> can be a part of growth. Priests learn again and again in their
> pastoral ministry that a crisis is not an abandonment by God
> but an avenue for God's intervention.[43]

In the course of our ministry we will be entrusted with many
people's pain. This is an immense privilege and responsibility.
We can be so careless or so careful with the lives of others. People
will want us to wave a wand and make things better, they will
project onto us their guilt, their anger, their despair. But we never
assume the responsibility that rightly belongs to others, since to
deny appropriate responsibility is to deny personhood and also
to deprive a person of the experience of healing and reconciliation. On the other hand, we share and bear the pain of those who
risk opening their hearts to us. We may be shocked, we may feel
overwhelming sorrow, we may feel afraid. These are our reactions and it is our responsibility to handle them appropriately
with the necessary help from others. We are not to burden the
person who has sought our counsel with the weight of our own
reactions. People need us to become familiar with the pathways
of redemption that run, somewhere, through the valley of the
shadow of death, through the fog of confusion. They need us to
know that, while the path may not be clear, there is indeed one
there and God has not abandoned us to wander alone in the
wilderness of suffering.

There will be times when people are too hurt to allow us to
reach out to them in their pain; times when we can dream dreams
of healing and reconciliation but cannot effect them because to
do so would be to violate another person's integrity. At times like
that, all we can do is be there, pray and love, creating a world
where love extends to all a welcome: a place of gentle warmth
where thawing can occur, an open space into which people can
move at their own pace. There will also be times when to be for
reconciliation means grasping the call to be peace-makers, refusing to let our hearts be dull to suffering, risking the unpopularity

of the establishment because we insist on God's justice and mercy. These are different sides of the same coin of being God's dreamers, people who are passionate for a world made whole.

The tendrils of reconciliation run widely and intricately throughout God's world, the tap root is the reconciliation of God in Christ who is our peace. We who are reconciled to God ourselves are entrusted with the ministry of reconciliation:

> Come Prince of Peace, our fading hope rekindle.
> 'Your kingdom come!' we pray, let peace be made.[44]

# BEING FOR BLESSING

Ring the bells and sing the story,
peal God's praise from shore to shore,
join the song the angels started:
alleluia evermore.
Hear that song begun in Bethl'em
echo through two thousand years,
swell the chorus, all God's people,
sing, so all creation hears.

Glorious God of our salvation
we bring grateful thanks today;
you created and redeemed us,
turned our hearts to seek your way;
through the years you led your people,
nurtured, tested, loved, restored;
guide us as we face the future,
light the path before us, Lord.

In your sight a thousand ages
like an evening pass away,
yet these years of human history
yield the song we bring today:
praise for blessings richly given,
tears wrung from the times of pain,
hope and suffering blended closely
weave a world-wide, bold refrain.

Gracious God, once born among us,
holy God on heaven's throne,
yours the power and yours the glory,
yours the love in Christ made known.
Alleluia! sing the angels,
alleluia! we reply,
for two thousand years of blessing
glory be to God on high.[1]

## The blessing of God

The Christian life rests on God's goodness and abundant loving-kindness showered upon us in blessing. Whether we are visiting a sick person, dealing with the church heating system, helping asylum seekers settle in a strange land, singing with the toddlers group or facing the challenge of leading a church community through a period of renewal of its life and ministry, at the heart of all our work – large or small – is the blessing of God on all creation (Matthew 5:45).

Our ministry is to make known God's blessing, to share in the Church's vocation to be a blessing. We have been drawn into the communion of the three Persons of the Trinity and experience the blessing of fellowship with God (1 John 1:3). God has blessed us in Christ with every spiritual blessing in the heavenly places (Ephesians 1:3). Indeed God's first act after creating human beings was to bless them (Genesis 1:28), as it was when calling Abram to a life of discipleship (Genesis 12:2). The hymn at the beginning of this chapter dwells on God's blessing in Christ, since it was written for the millennium, but we can never forget that the Old Testament is full of God's blessing and desire to bless the people: so much so that the Jewish people developed a form of prayer, the *berakah* or blessing, in response to the blessing of God. Typically, the *berakah* begins with the blessing, adds a descriptive phrase, and ends with the particular grounds for the blessing. We find this blessing of God breaking out throughout the Bible, from the psalmist to the monarch (for example, Psalm 72:18–19; 1 Kings 8:56), from Job's blessing of God in adversity

(Job 1:21) to the outpouring of joy and praise in the greeting at the beginning of some of the epistles (2 Corinthians 1:3; 1 Peter 1:3). This is the other side of the coin to God's blessing of the people who worship God (Psalm 67:1; Matthew 5:2–11; Revelation 19:9) expressed in the well-known blessing from the Pentateuch, 'The Lord bless you and keep you; the Lord make his face to shine upon you, and be gracious to you; the Lord lift up his countenance upon you and give you peace' (Numbers 6:24–26).

Blessing flows from relationship within God and God with us. At the heart of blessing is communion with God, three Persons in one God, a communion of love into which we are invited in Christ. God's inclination to bless knows no bounds: God's blessing of us and of all creation transcends any boundaries we might draw between sacred and secular. God simply will not be restrained into safe holy places, but is prodigal with blessing that – as the poet Francis Thompson wrote in his poem 'In no Strange Land' – rests as much on Charing Cross as on anywhere else in creation. Lest even this poem seem too distant, we might try inserting the name of places familiar to us in the last verses to see what impact that has on our perception of God's passion to bless:

> O world invisible, we view thee,
> O world intangible, we touch thee,
> O world unknowable, we know thee,
> Inapprehensible, we clutch thee! . . .
>
> The angels keep their ancient places; –
> Turn but a stone, and start a wing!
> 'Tis ye, 'tis your estranged faces,
> That miss the many-splendoured thing,
>
> But (when so sad thou canst not sadder)
> Cry; – and upon thy so sore loss
> Shall shine the traffic of Jacob's ladder
> Pitched betwixt heaven and Charing Cross.

Yea, in the night, my Soul, my daughter,
Cry; – clinging heaven by the hems;
And lo, Christ walking on the water,
Not of Gennesareth, but Thames!

## Living into blessing

Augustine's famous prayer, 'You made us for yourself and our hearts are restless until they find their rest in you' is a cry that millions have echoed down the centuries. Restlessness for God is often a stage on the journey to blessing as we are allured by joy. Blessing is not primarily about what God does for us, or what we do for God, but about who God is for us, who we are for God. Four hundred years ago, Teresa of Avila encouraged her nuns to seek the God of consolations, not the consolations of God. Yet it is easy to confuse blessing with getting what we want or what we have previously experienced as good. Teresa's friend, who became known as John of the Cross, was a man who knew much suffering when he was imprisoned by the Church for his witness to his faith in sixteenth-century Spain. He wrote of the blessing of the heart when it is filled with the love of God, using language, like that of many mystics, of the lover for the beloved,

How gently and how lovingly
you wake in my heart
where in your secret you dwell alone,
and in your sweet breathing
filled with good and glory,
how tenderly you swell my heart with love.[2]

There is an intimacy to blessing. At the heart of our vocation is a call to be beloved. God yearns to bless us as a lover, wakening our heart and swelling it with love. As John of the Cross knew, God's blessing is not dependent upon comfortable circumstances and if we ourselves are people of fair-weather blessing we will be ill-equipped to help people mine the depths of troubled times. The fourth Gospel tells us that Simon Peter had one of the most intimate, yet difficult, encounters with Jesus to be recorded in the Bible. By the Sea of Galilee, close to the same smell of charcoal that was associated with his memory of betraying Jesus, he was asked about his love for Jesus and was not allowed to be distracted by concern for, or curiosity about, the other disciples (John 21:15–19, 21). Taken back to the smell of failure and there assured of Jesus' love, his experience tells us that we may hear God's words of love and life even in the most unexpected places, including places we will do anything to avoid. It is as we face them that we discover the possibility that not only the places of joy, but also the places of disappointment and failure, can become holy ground. It is only as we take the risk of letting our places of poverty come to the light of God's word that we will be given the treasures of darkness, the riches hidden in secret places of which Isaiah spoke (Isaiah 45:3), the riches that, like diamonds or gold, lie buried.

So often, darkness carries negative connotations and yet Isaiah reminds us of the truth a hurting world needs to know so desperately, that darkness can be the place of hidden beauty and treasure, and that darkness is a prerequisite for much growth: indeed, our very life begins in darkness. Having the courage to plumb our own depths of darkness will make us gentle and wise believers in the truth that there are riches to be uncovered in all people's lives. In Isaiah we read that God's banquet of blessing is to be found in even the seemingly unfruitful places, 'They shall feed along the way and on bare heights shall be their pasture, he who has pity on them will lead them and by springs of water he will guide them' (Isaiah 49:9–10). Blessings abound everywhere if we are willing to receive them and to release our grip on our lives, living with the lightness of touch and openness to the presence of God that portend blessing. This blessing is most likely to occur in the midst of the commonplace events of life, if for no other reason than the fact that most of life is commonplace. Through the course of our ministry we will become specialists in the ordinary. Gary Dorsey's study of a United Church of Christ congregation in New England describes 'a simple community reeling in the full erotic mystery of an innocently ordinary,

intentionally purposeful life' where 'wonder was familiar' among
the realm of familiar faces in a familiar place. The minister there,
Van Parker, said, 'We don't have anything profound to say.
What we do here is just the steady, undramatic task of ordinary
days.'[3] The dramatic is not a prerequisite for blessing, all our
ordinary world is etched with God and with God's blessing.

Jesus calls us to give for alms the things that are within (Luke
11:41), to offer not only the parts of our lives that feel holy, but
also the mundane parts and the parts we would rather hide from
ourselves, from others and from God. When we risk exposing to
God those places that tend to make us close in on ourselves as we
try to protect ourselves from further encounter with whatever is
shaming or distressing us, we will discover that they become holy
ground, places of blessing because God was there, even though at
the time we did not know it (Genesis 28:16).

When I was ordained priest, I was given a card with Irenaeus
of Lyons' famous words that we quoted in Chapter 2, 'The glory
of God is the human person fully alive'. Now framed, it serves as
a reminder that our calling is concerned with life, life in its fullness manifest in human beings. Jesus said, 'I came that they may
have life, and have it abundantly' (John 10:10) and in God's
presence there is fullness of joy (Psalm 16:11). Paul wrote to the
Romans in a phrase we can pray to be true of our own ministry,
'I know when I come to you, I will come in the fullness of the
blessing of Christ' (Romans 15:29).

God has long been bringing abundant life and fullness of
blessing. If we only see this in the 'spiritual' aspects of life, we
diminish God's blessing. The TV pictures of the exuberance and
exhilaration as crowds celebrated the fall of the Iron Curtain
and of various communist dictators, as women in Afghanistan
experienced the sun on their faces for the first time in years, are
vivid illustrations of God's blessing of human freedom. Anyone
who has had the joy of seeing another person gradually come to
life before our eyes, as they have been released from whatever has
bound them and have grown into freedom in God, has had a
glimpse of the blessing of God in action. This need not be a rare
event, as Macrina Wiedekehr puts it so vividly when she writes,

There is a table to which we are invited each day. It is a table
that Love prepares for us each moment. It is the table of daily
life. Freely we are invited to come and eat. We do not have to
be worthy to be present at this table. We only have to be willing to taste life and let God serve us. Can we accept the heresy
of God's extravagant love?[4]

Loving extravagance is God's hallmark. Joy will suffuse our
ministry as we live lives that are brushed regularly by blessing. As
we live into God's extravagant love and life we will discover
again and again that this is the root of our ministry of blessing.
At his enthronement service in Durham in 1952, Michael
Ramsey charged his clergy to be people rooted in joy:

> Let me therefore charge you, it is my first counsel, to serve
> Christ in his church above all else with *joyfulness*. Members of
> the clergy, rejoice that you are privileged to teach His truth, to
> care for His people, to celebrate the mystery of His body and
> blood, and to know perhaps His patience and His suffering as
> you serve Him. Let the source and the spring of your joy come
> – not from your environment, not from the way things go – but
> from Him.[5]

In the difficult times of the mid-fourteenth century, Julian of
Norwich's revelations of divine love opened her to the blessings
of God at the table of daily life. She wrote of being filled with
heartfelt joy by the Trinity, the Trinity who 'is our Maker and
keeper, our eternal lover, joy and bliss'. Her response to this?

> 'Benedicite Domine!' I said, and I meant it in all reverence even
> though I said it at the top of my voice. I was so overwhelmed
> that he, so holy and aweful, could be so friendly to a creature
> at once so sinful and carnal.[6]

God gave her another revelation of the foundation of blessing in
the love of God,

It was at this time that our Lord showed me spiritually how intimately he loves us. I saw that he is everything that we know to be good and helpful. In his love he clothes us, enfolds and embraces us; that tender love completely surrounds us, never to leave us. As I saw it he is everything that is good.

And he showed me more, a little thing, the size of a hazelnut, on the palm of my hand, round like a ball. I looked at it thoughtfully and wondered, 'What is this?' And the answer came, 'It is all that is made.' I marvelled that it continued to exist and did not suddenly disintegrate; it was so small. And again my mind supplied the answer, 'It exists, both now and for ever, because God loves it.' In short, everything owes its existence to the love of God.

In this little thing I saw three truths. The first is that God made it; the second is that God loves it; and the third is that God sustains it. But what he is who is in truth Maker, Keeper and Lover I cannot tell, for until I am essentially united with him I can never have full rest or happiness; in other words until I am so joined to him that there is absolutely nothing between my God and me.[7]

If we took Julian's truths to heart we would live with a peace and a joy that radiate blessing to ourselves and to others. We promise at ordination to endeavour to fashion our own life and that of our household according to the way of Christ. Is this just about ethics? What happens if we fashion our lives according to the way of Christ who was so secure in his Father's blessing that he could see in the lilies of the field an assurance that God would provide for him, and who would rise before dawn to share uninterrupted communion with his Father? When was our prayer life last overrun with the gratitude and blessing expressed by Martin Rinkart, the hymn writer and pastor, who in the midst of the suffering and endless conduct of funerals associated with the Thirty Years War and its famines, could lead others in singing,

Now thank we all our God
With hearts and hands and voices,

Who wondrous things hath done,
In whom his world rejoices.
Who from our mother's arms
Has blessed us on our way
With countless gifts of love
And still is ours today?

When did we take time to mull over God's blessing, reliving the joy, the waiting, the laughter, the tears? Sometimes we may be in so much of a hurry to say 'thank you' that we pass over the gift we are thankful for. It is one thing to say we are thankful for our family or friends, it is another thing to live thankfully, spending time with them, nurturing the relationships, experiencing the blessing that we say they are and, in turn, sharing with them the blessing that we are. Nearly a millennium ago, Bernard of Clairvaux observed that we find rest in those we love, and provide a resting place for those who love us. So often, it seems, we are so busy that we deny ourselves the blessing of this rest.

How do we nourish our lives with everyday blessings that can so easily pass us by? Jesus must have sat down and considered the lilies carefully, but do we similarly enjoy our garden or the public park? The old caricature of vicars as fanatics about cricket and trains has a healthy streak behind it and we may need to consider if we give enough time to a hobby that recreates and stimulates us. When did we last do something for the sheer joy and fun of doing it? When did we give priority to seeing our children's school play or to an evening out with our spouse? Or when did we, as a single person, last pamper ourselves because there is no one else to make sure that we are treated as special? We will find rest, relaxation and blessing in nourishing our own lives, and will be more whole as a result. This need not take extra time, it may simply mean being more intentional about nourishing ourselves amid the normal events of life. For example, how do we read the letters and cards we receive from friends – do we read functionally and display Christmas cards without a second thought, or do we savour the friendship behind the words, with gratitude and engaged memory of the writer? Do we take time to write a letter that will be a blessing to someone else? Or to give a gift 'just because'? Attentiveness to whatever is life-giving for us is essential. Mary Coelho, writing on removing obstacles to prayer, says,

> We need to sing more if we sing, or dance more if we dance, in order to sustain our celebration of life. We need the ability to be carefree, to disregard appearances, to relax and laugh at the world and at ourselves. These are all ways of being grateful and saying 'yes' to life.[8]

We can do worse than take to heart the blessing of Richard Rolle, the fourteenth-century English mystic, who prayed in his wonderfully named 'Ghostly Gladness',

> May you lead your life in light-heartedness,
> Keep loneliness far away;
> May gloom not remain with you,
> But may God's cheerfulness
> Forever sing out merrily in your life.[9]

Light-heartedness is not the same as flippancy but is the opposite of being heavy laden or overburdened. We have a responsibility to ourselves and to others to ensure that we deal with our burdens in an appropriate way, not dumping them in inappropriate places on people who cannot cope with our burdens or with our being weighed down. Clergy need somewhere safe to unburden themselves, perhaps with a spiritual director or a support group, and should give priority to ensuring that such a safe place exists. Otherwise, whether we intend to or not, we will burden others. Gloom is more than just concern or reasonable worry, definitions include murkiness, obscurity, dreariness: all are the very opposite of being for blessing. Rolle's prayer that God's cheerfulness will forever sing out merrily in our lives gives a new slant on blessing – there is a lightness of heart and of touch here, not just happiness but the much richer merriness is singing out.

Rolle's imagery and words find an echo in Hopkins' poem, 'As Kingfishers Catch Fire', where he not only catches the exuberance of God's cheerfulness singing out merrily, but also the uniqueness of each person's expression of God's life. Hopkins himself adapted Duns Scotus' concept of the 'thisness', the uniqueness of being of each individual, and called it 'inscape'. Inscape is how each part of God's creation reflects its creator in its unique way simply by being true to itself. For Hopkins, the awareness of the inscape of a person or thing led him to praise of the creator. In this poem he revels in the loveliness, the blessing, as each person is herself or himself before God and thus 'Christ plays in ten thousand places':

> As kingfishers catch fire, dragonflies draw flame;
> As tumbled over rim in roundy well
> Stones ring; like each tucked string tells, each hung bell's
> Bow swung finds tongue to fling our broad its name;
> Each mortal thing does one thing and the same:
> Deals out that being indoors each one dwells;
> Selves – goes its self; *myself* it speaks and spells,
> Crying *What I do is me: for that I came.*
>
> I say more: the just man justices;
> Keeps grace: that keeps all his goings graces;
> Acts in God's eye what in God's eye he is –
> Christ. For Christ plays in ten thousand places,
> Lovely in limbs, and lovely in eyes not his
> To the Father through the features of men's faces.

Each one of us is unique and thus each one of us is unique in our expression of the ministry to which God has called us. What shines out through our faces as we share in the ministry of blessing? Is it the loveliness of Christ as he plays through us in our particular place?

From the Orthodox tradition we are given a slightly different perspective on Irenaeus' words, 'the glory to which humanity is called is that we should grow more and more God-like by

becoming more and more human'.[10] Our responsibility is to offer
this redeemed humanity to God in praise:

> In the immense cathedral which is the universe of God, each
> man, whether scholar or manual labourer, is called to act as
> the priest of his whole life – to take all that is human, and to
> turn it into an offering and a hymn of glory.[11]

Oh for the exuberance of God's blessing to be known through
our uniqueness in our humanity! 'The glory of God is a human
being fully alive.'

## Look up and see

We begin this section, as the last, with Augustine. The call he
heard to 'take up and read'[12] has been taken to heart by the
western Church: we are people of the word. We would do well to
balance that with Jesus' call to 'come and see' (John 1:46) and
the Orthodox Church's emphasis 'look up and see the glory of
God'. Six centuries after Julian of Norwich looked at a small
thing like a hazelnut and saw through it something of the ways of
God, R. S. Thomas looked at his beloved Welsh countryside and
people with the eyes that saw traces of God, as he describes in
'The Bright Field'.

> I have seen the sun break through
> to illuminate a small field
> for a while, and gone my way
> and forgotten it. But that was the pearl
> of great price, the one field that had
> the treasure in it. I realise now
> that I must give all that I have
> to possess it. Life is not hurrying
>
> on to a receding future, nor hankering after
> an imagined past. It is the turning
> aside like Moses to the miracle

of the lit bush, to a brightness
that seemed as transitory as your youth
once, but is the eternity that awaits you.

Ever since shepherds listened to angels, turned aside to see what
was going on and then set off for Bethlehem, God has been
taking people by surprise, wrapping the blessings of heaven in
unexpected containers. Hence shepherds exulted in the verse
from the seventeenth-century 'The Shepherd's Hymn', written by
Richard Crashaw, on which Wesley later drew for a hymn:

> Welcome, all wonders in one sight!
> Eternity shut in a span,
> Summer in winter, day in night,
> Heaven in earth and God in man;
> Great little one! Whose all embracing birth
> Lifts earth to heaven, stoops heaven to earth.

At about the same time, Thomas Traherne was describing his
experience of growing in understanding of God's blessing experienced in the world in which the all-embracing birth occurred,

> Little did I imagine that while I was thinking these things
> [about God and the world] I was conversing with God . . . as I
> read the Bible I . . . found by degrees that these things had been
> written of before, not only in the Scriptures but in many of the
> fathers, and that this was the way of communion with God in
> all saints . . . By which I evidently saw that the way to become
> rich and blessed was not by heaping accidental and devised
> riches to make ourselves great in the vulgar manner; but to
> approach more near, and to see more clearly with the eye of
> our understanding, the beauties and glories of the whole
> world; and to have communion with the Deity in the riches of
> God and nature.[13]

Traherne's ecstasy may be easier to share in beautiful parts of the
world or with people we love, but a walk down a grim inner-city
street with our eyes and hearts open may reveal astounding

concealed beauty. A drawing of the numerous cracks in the pavement of a former steel town became the outline of a crucifixion painting that hung in a small community's chapel overlooking the noisy main road, a reminder that Christ is alongside us even in the despair of an urban wasteland. Isaiah caught the vision of the ruins of Jerusalem breaking out in singing when God comforted the people (Isaiah 52:9) and the psalmist loved even the rubble and dust of the city (Psalm 102:14). What singing have we heard from wastelands? What rubble is precious to us because God has blessed us in its desolate ruins?

Sometimes God's blessing comes not as a complete solution to our needs or an infusion of unspeakable joy, but as the beginning of new life, the sense that we have turned the corner and that movement is possible where previously we were boxed in, that hope is budding. As we noted in Chapter 4, the root meaning of the word 'ecstasy' is 'to be led out of a state or place of standstill'. In the last two lines of the first verse of Gerard Manley Hopkins' poem, 'The Wreck of the Deutschland' which is as much about his conversion as it is about the shipwreck in 1875, we see the ecstasy, the leading out of standstill, in God's touch of blessing. Hopkins expresses in words a similar moment to that which Michelangelo painted on the ceiling of the Sistine Chapel, when God and Adam reach out to touch fingers:

> Thou mastering me
> God! giver of breath and bread;
> World's strand, sway of the sea;
> Lord of living and dead;
> Thou hast bound bones and veins in me, fastened me with
>   flesh,
> And after it almost unmade, what with dread,
> Thy doing: and dost thou touch me afresh?
> Over again I feel thy finger and find thee.

Our priestly ministry involves helping people to reach out, to feel God's finger and to find themselves found. Eugene Peterson describes his ministry as helping people to see grace operating in their lives, as speaking 'God' in a situation where God has not been named before so that joy – the 'capacity to hear the name and recognise that God is here' – can break out.[14] That, in itself, is a blessing we deny ourselves and others when we fail to pay attention to the movement of God, fail to see that God, who never plays by our rules, is gloriously rampant in our world. It asks of us a basic humility that acknowledges that we are not in control of what God is doing among us. Peterson, again, has a vivid way of describing this,

> The cure of souls is a cultivated awareness that God has already seized the initiative . . . the cure of souls takes time to read the minutes of the previous meeting, a meeting more likely than not at which I was not present . . . The biblical conviction is that God is 'long beforehand with my soul'.[15]

The cure of souls, an old-fashioned but very rich description of our ministry, suggests long-term engagement with people rather than rushing in with a quick spiritual fix. The ministry of spiritual direction may be a part of that long-term engagement. Spiritual direction, with its focus on growth rather than problem-solving, has been described in various ways. One that is particularly appealing in the context of being for blessing is Margaret Guenther's description of the spiritual director serving as midwife, helping to bring new life to birth.[16]

God's blessing embraces all of life. When we pronounce God's blessing at the end of the Eucharist, it is immediately followed by the dismissal. This is no accident but a deeply theological juxtaposition: it is in the world that we live into God's blessing. The raw materials for blessing lie in everyday life, in its ordinary commonplaceness, where we live in anticipation of wonder breaking out among us. Secular employment, child care, the inactivity of sickness or old age: all can be the stuff of blessing. The ordinary is a gift to us. Teresa of Avila's description of the seventh mansion of the interior castle includes the picture of godly contentment and the blessing of a grateful life that has been described as, 'a mellow rootedness in being where one now

is. Our pilgrim is living fully into the present with a jovial enthusiasm and a great capacity for work. He or she experiences a
deep gratitude for all that has been and all that is and will be.'[17]
The ideas of living with deep gratitude, being fully present, are
behind Gerard Manley Hopkins' passion that we pursue the
blessing that comes from glorifying God in daily life,

> It is not only prayer that gives God glory, but work. Smiting on
> an anvil, sawing a beam, white-washing a wall, driving horses,
> sweeping, scouring, everything gives God some glory if being
> in His grace you do it as your duty. To go to communion
> worthily gives God great glory, but to take food in thankful-
> ness and temperance gives him glory too. To lift up the hands
> in prayer gives God glory, but a man with a dungfork in his
> hand, a woman with a slop pail, give him glory too. He is so
> great that all things give Him glory if you mean that they
> should. So then, my brethren, live.[18]

Hands are among the most important work tools of the priest.
We use our hands in many aspects of our ministry, particularly in
blessing. Our hands hold the bread and wine, our manual acts
are part of the liturgy, our hands are what people see when we
place the bread in their hands and give the cup to their lips. Our
hands touch people, tenderly at times, firmly at others – the
weight of our touch can be so significant in communicating to
others that we should be very sensitive to the pressure we exert
with our hands and to all the dangers of manipulation or subtle
abuse. We hold hands with children, with the elderly, with the
lonely, with friends and lovers, we wipe away tears with our
hands, we lift our hands in worship, we hold our hands open to
welcome, we use our hands when praying for and anointing the
sick. We make the sign of the cross on ourselves and others with
our hands. There is a close link between what we do with our
bodies, especially with our hands, and what we do in our hearts.
That is why some bishops anoint the hands of newly ordained
priests: they are the tools of our trade, God's gift to us and to
others through our ministry.

*Living out of blessing*

'The purer the heart becomes, the larger it becomes'[19] is the succinct reminder from John of Krondstadt, a nineteenth-century Russian Orthodox priest, that purity and blessing go hand in hand since blessing flows from a heart that God has enlarged, that God has swelled with love. Given the magnitude of God's love and blessing, priests are called to bless people, participating in the joy of the blessing that is already ours in Christ. We are called to holiness of life but do not offer a blessing of our own making, instead we draw people further into the blessing of God in Christ. At our ordinations we are reminded that we are called by God to work as servant and shepherd among the people to whom we are sent and to bless them in the name of the Lord. We bless the people because it is God's nature to bless; we are caught up in a circle of blessing. The words Ellen Davis writes of the preacher's task apply here, too:

> I propose that the preacher's first and most important responsibility is to educate the imagination of her hearers so that they have the linguistic skills to enter into the world which Scripture discloses, and may thus make a genuine choice whether to live there. The biblical preacher is a sort of elementary language teacher, not a translator, as we most frequently (if unconsciously) assume.[20]

In speaking God's blessing, we educate the imagination of our hearers so that they can enter a world in which God's blessing is experienced, and can make a genuine choice to live there. Part of this blessing may be to refuse the headlong rush into instant gratification, but to wait with eager longing for God's time, to linger with and welcome the incompleteness of yearning. Barbara Brown Taylor writes of her experience of this,

> I stood in the presence of something holy, something that knew more about me than I knew about it. Worship offered me a way of staying with it, not of clarifying the mystery but of harnessing it, so that I was carried along in its numinous wake.[21]

The inability to stay with things and to enter into God's time is often born of the desire to grasp at what we, perhaps mistakenly, perceive to be the blessing. This is starkly evident at Christmas. In its wisdom the Church has given us the season of Advent as a season of waiting and preparation, yet we rush into Christmas without allowing Advent its true span. Waiting and hoping, learning to live with the incompleteness that comes with being a people of eschatological hope, are integral to joy and blessing.

Some of the richest blessings are experienced in adversity. From a Soviet prison camp we have the following letter,

> On Easter Day all of us who were imprisoned for religious convictions were united in the one joy of Christ . . . there was no solemn Paschal service with the ringing of church bells, no possibility in our camp to gather for worship, to dress up for the festival, to prepare Easter dishes. On the contrary, there was even more work and more interference than usual. All the prisoners here for religious conviction, whatever their denomination, were surrounded by more spying, by more threats from the secret police.
>
> Yet Easter was there: great, holy, spiritual, unforgettable. It was blessed by the presence of our risen God among us – blessed by the silent Siberian stars and by our sorrows. How our hearts beat joyfully with the great Resurrection! Death is conquered, fear no more, an eternal Easter is given to us! Full of this marvellous Easter, we send you from our prison camp the victorious and joyful tiding: Christ is risen![22]

This profound and painfully experienced blessing comes from a deep understanding of the resurrection as:

> . . . the explosion of cosmic joy at the triumph of life, after the overwhelming sorrow over death – death which even the Lord of life had to suffer when he became man. 'Let the heavens rejoice and the earth exult, and let all the world invisible and visible keep holiday, for Christ our eternal joy is risen.' All things are now filled with the certainty of life, whereas before all had been moving steadily towards death.[23]

To be for blessing is to live in the power of the resurrection, filled with the certainty of life, and to draw others to so live. Then, together, we cannot help but exult, 'Come, let us give vent to our happiness for the saviour of our souls, having in his compassion transfigured human nature, has made it blaze on Tabor.'[24]

In Christ human nature is transfigured. This changes everything. It means that we do not translate God's blessing into the experience of our people, but live it and speak it as a fact of life in God's economy, inviting people to live in Christ at the intersection of heaven and earth. That is one reason it is so important to encourage people to worship, because in worship we become more and more at home in the reality of God's presence and the Church becomes more and more who it truly is. It has been said that in the West we have a history of being concerned with what happens to the elements in the Eucharist, whereas the East is far more concerned with what happens to the Church. In worship the Church expresses and lives into its identity as the body of Christ, sharing in every spiritual blessing in the heavenly places that God has poured out on us in Christ (Ephesians 1:3).

## People of blessing

Being for blessing is the vocation of the Church. This is effected very often simply by just being there, being present in the midst of the life of the world. The parochial system is a tangible expression of this vocation. The psalmist knew (Psalm 133:1) how very good and pleasant it is when kindred live together in unity, a blessing that is all too scarce in many parts of society. As those who are called to promote unity, peace and love among all Christian people, especially among those whom we serve, we bless both by our lives and our words. Earlier, I referred to the community chapel on the main street of a former steel town. That same community had, years earlier, planted hanging baskets and been ridiculed by a neighbour for wasting money since the flowers were bound to be vandalized. In fact they were not touched. Over the succeeding years nearby residents started to care for their gardens and to hang baskets, then to renovate their own homes, as had the community. A study of the town noted that the community's presence in a few houses, and the resulting stability leading to property improvements by neighbours, had halted the spread of urban decline and drug dealing from the nearby, semi-derelict town centre. Each Advent the community put a candle light in every window, creating a block of light in an otherwise fairly dark street. These lights shining in the literal and metaphorical darkness led a former resident of the town, who had not been able to go to the town centre for years because the memories were so painful, to rediscover hope when she eventually saw them shining in the darkness. In a chance meeting with a member of the community she recounted how 'they said to me, "Welcome home, God has not abandoned this place."' God's blessing can come through hanging baskets in summer and electric candles in winter. We must not despise the day of small things if we are to be people of blessing (Zechariah 4:10).

Rogation and harvest are two of our annual opportunities to celebrate the blessings of God through nature. It can be a challenge to celebrate these days in a meaningful way now that supermarkets have dulled us to the seasonality and freshness of God's varied blessings with which earlier generations were familiar. Farming parishes have much to share with urban congregations about the rhythm and seasonality of some of God's blessing, about working with nature and learning to wait for the blessing to come to its fullness. Seasonality brings with it waiting. Waiting is so hard in a generation used to instant everything. We are called to be people of hope, people who model hope as a way of life. This priestly modelling of hope can be an immense pastoral gift to those whose hope is fragile.

The Celtic idea of thin places may be helpful. Thin places are those places where the boundaries are particularly permeable between this world and what the Celts called the other world. In Christian ministry the paradox is that some of the thinnest, most liminal places, are to be found alongside suffering when presence rather than words is called for, when tears wrung from the time of pain are somehow holy and blessed because God is there. Dietrich Bonhoeffer wrote that listening can be a greater service than speaking. He observed, sadly, that many people who are looking for a listening ear 'do not find it among Christians because these Christians are talking when they should be listening . . . in the end there is nothing left but spiritual chatter and clerical condescension arrayed in pious words'.[25] If we are uncomfortable with keeping silence with another person, perhaps because no one (ourself included) has ever kept silence with us in our pain, we will rush to fill it with well-intentioned chatter that drowns out the blessing of presence. Job's friends began well when they sat for seven days in silence with Job and thus enabled him to break his silence and speak his grief, but then they spoiled it by rushing in with explanation (Job 2:11–13). Shared silence is a precious and powerful blessing. Apparently in Russia it was traditional for a whole household to gather to bless a person going on a trip. They stood in silence for several minutes, then the oldest person present made the sign of the cross. At that point everyone faced the household icon and signed themselves with the sign of the cross while offering a silent prayer for the traveller. Silence and blessing go hand in hand – both the silent gasp of awe at a sunset and the silent sharing of pain in a time of difficulty. Then as we say with the Psalmist, 'For God alone my soul in silence waits' (Psalm 62:1) we are drawn into the mystery that Isaac the Syrian understood, 'Speech is the organ of this present world. Silence is a mystery of the world to come.'[26]

Blessing is not mediated only by silent presence. Sometimes words are, indeed, called for but perhaps not as frequently as we might think. In worship we regularly speak God's blessing. This is most obvious at the end of the service when, using words which it is a great privilege to speak, we do not pray for God's blessing but say 'The blessing of God almighty, the Father, the Son and the Holy Spirit be among you and remain with you always.' This blessing is one of the most familiar yet underheard parts of the liturgy and is an open invitation to healing and wholeness. If we all took God's blessing to heart our churches might be transformed with hope and healing. But it is not only at the end of the service that we bless or are blessed: the president and the people greet one another with a blessing; we bless God in the Gloria; we bless one another with peace, and in the eucharistic prayer we amplify the reasons for our blessing and join with the song of heaven, 'blessing and honour and glory and power be yours for ever and ever'.

The rich tapestry of blessing woven in the Eucharist through the multi-layered relationship between presider and people, is given further texture and colour by our gender. With the ordination of women all members of the Church now have the blessing, previously only available to men, of seeing a person of their own gender lead the sacramental worship and in that way mediating God to others. All can also share the blessing, previously only available to women, of receiving the ministry of a person of the opposite gender who therefore brings complementary attributes to their ministry. The same is true of pastoral ministry where it sometimes helps a person if they can turn to a person of their own gender; equally sometimes talking with a person of the opposite gender is helpful. Both likeness and unlikeness can be channels of blessing.

As we noted in Chapter 6, prayer is a means of blessing in itself, and it is our prayer life that will shape our ministry. Our personal prayer for others can be a way of blessing them as we hold people tenderly before God. There are also times when people will ask us, as priests, to bless them. Urban Holmes writes of puzzling over what was in people's minds when they asked him for a blessing, and of finding help from a chaplain at a Baptist Hospital in New Orleans who said, 'The request for a blessing is related to a person's desire for change, for healing, for wholeness. The priest is perceived as one who has power to change people.'[27] When we are ordained we take on a representative role and have to respond sensitively to such perceptions of our calling, as well as to the desire that lies behind them. There is a trap here for the unwary; to avoid falling into it by creating a misplaced dependency upon us and our gifts or trying to fulfil unrealistic expectations, we need to be clear from whom the blessing comes and of our own role as people entrusted with the privilege of blessing others in the name of the Lord, of being used by God to enable change and, like midwives, to bring life to birth.

Over the centuries God has brought blessing and new life to birth in multitudes of people, each one of whom is unique. In our worship we remember, and in our lives we take for an example, the saints who have gone before us. Saints are a reminder of the many blessings that God can pour out through one life lived faithfully and in holiness. But not all saints are comfortable: some perturb, even disturb, us with their stories and we might not even be sure that we would want to meet them day by day. They give us hope that the people we *do* meet day by day are saints in the making, that the people with whom we worship day by day, week by week, *are* the blessing of God in and to the world.

Each church has its own unique history of saints who have blessed others in their lifetime, many are commemorated within the building. In one church of which I was a member, an eighteenth-century wooden board told us of the good works of former saints in that village. One who had given money for the relief of the poor rejoiced in the name of Epaphroditus Christmas. Ever since I read it, I have wanted to meet someone with that name. One January afternoon we gathered for the funeral of a member of the church. Thanks to storms the day before, there was no power for light, heat or the organ, a stained-glass window was boarded up and we had to walk round a massive uprooted yew tree to enter the church. We worshipped by candlelight and sang to the accompaniment of a hastily assembled string quartet, 'Holy, holy, holy . . . all the saints adore thee . . .'. As we sang in the cold, dimly lit church there was a palpable sense of the communion of saints who had gathered under similar conditions over the centuries: perhaps the principal difference, apart from our clothing, was the dim late afternoon light coming through the south transept window which for the first time in centuries was not blocked by the yew tree. It could have been Thomas Hardy's Mellstock, and Epaphroditus Christmas could have been in the congregation.

A burst of glory shatters silent space,
a thousand years compress into this one;
the saints cry out, 'this is, this is the place
to kneel, adore, embraced by praise begun
before we ever knew the grounded grace
of heaven's Word, this world's incarnate Son'.[28]

The Liturgy of St James includes a list of saints within the
eucharistic prayer, most of whom are unknown to us today. This
unknowing has the effect of distancing us, so it can be an interesting exercise to reflect on who we might include were we to be
writing the list of saints. Which saints, in their various ways,
have been or are now a blessing to us? For whom are we a blessing? Whom are we enabling to be for blessing in the world? Do
we see signs of the answer to the prayer at our ordination, 'Give
them wisdom and discipline to work faithfully with their fellow-
servants in Christ, that the world may come to know your glory'?
We are to be for blessing so that the Church, this mixed bag of
saints-in-the-refining, can fulfil the calling to bless God, be
blessed by God, and be for blessing in the world. Truly, 'the Lord
is glorious in his saints'. We are called to serve the saints of God
and our greatest joy is to bring others into the blessing of Christ.

# 10

# Being Sent

God's call rings out across the years:
disciples heard by Galilee
the call to life, the call to serve,
the call of Jesus, 'Follow me.'

Sent to proclaim good news for all,
they lived and breathed the gospel's grace;
since then the church from age to age
embodies hope in every place.

Sent by the God whose name is love,
so, when the world cries out in pain,
amidst the rampant fear, God's life
astounds and heals us once again.

Come, Holy Spirit, breathe new life,
the world yearns for your holy way;
disturb, empower and send your church
to live with lively joy each day.

Still your call rings from age to age,
untamed, unequalled, 'Follow me.'
With your disciples through the years
we turn to you wholeheartedly.[1]

## Jesus sends his disciples in the Spirit

'[Jesus] went up the mountain and called to him those whom he
wanted, and they came to him. And he appointed twelve, whom
he also named apostles, to be with him, and to be sent out to

proclaim the message, and to have authority to cast out demons' (Mark 3:13–15). Jesus calls and chooses people to be *with* him and to be *sent out* by him. This is the fundamental pattern of Christian life which is rehearsed every time we celebrate the Eucharist, as the ancient Emmaus journey into the life and work of Christ is travelled again and again. We gather together as Christ's followers and he draws close. We listen to the scriptures and our hearts burn as Jesus speaks his word. We meet around his table and our eyes are opened to the wonder of his risen reality in the taking, blessing, breaking and giving of the bread. And then we go to tell the world that God truly has done what he promised of old. He has come to his people and set them free. The new creation has begun and is breaking in upon us. 'The Lord has risen indeed!' (Luke 24:34). *Hoc est corpus meum* – 'This is my body' – was a pivotal moment in the medieval Eucharist. 'Here I am for you' declares the risen Christ. 'I have called you, spoken to you, now come to me, receive me, live in me – *be with me*.' But even this was not the culmination of the Eucharist. That came right at the end. *Ite, missa est* – 'Go, you are sent.' This is where the Mass, quite literally found its meaning. The Mass is the *missio*, the mission. The sacrifice of praise is proved in the sacrifice of lips that confess Christ's name (Hebrews 13:15). The communion in the body and blood of Christ is consecrated in lives that drink deeply from the same cup of witness (*martyrion*, in Greek) to the justice and mercy of God from which Jesus drank. The Lord's Supper is for the Lord's work.

The fundamental ordering of Christian life in terms of *being with* Christ and *sent by* Christ was first embodied in the original apostles. They were called to be both disciples, those who spent time with their Rabbi, and apostles (*apostoloi*), literally messengers, those who are sent on a mission (*apostole*) by their Rabbi to proclaim his teaching and extend his work. This was their original commission in Jesus' earthly ministry (Matthew 10:1) and their continuing commission in his risen ministry:

When they saw him, they worshipped him . . . And Jesus came and said to them, 'All authority . . . has been given to me. Go

therefore and make disciples of all nations, baptizing them in
the name of the Father and of the Son and of the Holy Spirit,
and teaching them to obey everything I have commanded you.
And remember that I am with you always, to the end of the
age.                                      (Matthew 28:17–20)

As they obeyed *everything* that Christ commanded his apostles,
their lives would become structured in the same sort of way as
Jesus' first and most intimate followers. They were to be with
him and sent by him. 'One shall not divide discipleship from
apostolate, gathering from sending, community with Christ from
witnessing to Christ.'[2]

On the other side of Pentecost, when the Spirit is poured out
on all the followers of the Messiah, the apostles' mandate is to
order the Church into the messianic pattern of faithfulness and
fruitfulness, of life *with* Christ, and life *for* Christ. This is the reason why apostolic derivation has always been a critical criterion
of Christian ministry. The apostles of the New Testament period
– a group which extended beyond the original twelve and certainly included Paul and other apostolic figures – embody the
essence of Christian life. They move with the beat of friendship
with Christ and faithful service to him. They are worshippers
and witnesses. They are disciples mentored by him and missionaries representing him. They are called to create churches that
love Christ and love his work. And from their commission all the
ministries of the Church flow. Deacon, priest and bishop are to
personify this pattern. Through their different ministries in the
power of God's Spirit, they are to work with the Spirit so that
this order of Christian existence can be reproduced in the genetic
constitution of the churches and all their members. This is why
the ordination rite for all three orders in the Church of England
concludes with 'The Sending Out' and may include the giving of
the Bible as, in the case of priests, 'a sign of the authority which
God has given you this day to preach the gospel of Christ and to
minister his holy sacraments'.[3]

## The Father sends the Son in the Spirit

The Bible confirms our authority both to speak of the grace of Christ's call and commission, and to shape people and churches for life *with* Christ and life *for* Christ. It does so because it tells us that this pattern of being *with* and *for* others is not only the way we live out our lives in Christ, it is the way God lives out his life for us. God chooses the world to be with him. God does not need the world. God – Father, Son and Holy Spirit – is perfectly complete and completely fulfilled in the triune life of love. But God chooses, freely and graciously, to create: to be *with the world*. Moreover, although God is with the world, the world does not always choose to be with God, and so God sends his Son into the world 'to redeem those under the law' (Galatians 4.5), and sends his Spirit into the world that we may cry '"Abba! Father"' (Galatians 4:6). This is the mission of God. The sending of God by God. The sending of the self-sending God. The sending of the Son and the Spirit by the Father so that the world, created by the Father through the Son and the Spirit, might be brought to the perfection originally intended, and God would dwell with the people made in his image. This mission of God, which involves the sending of the Son in the power of the Spirit's presence, includes the sending of the apostles by the Son and their infilling with the Holy Spirit, and extends to every baptism of each new believer who is immersed in the divine life of Christ and anointed with the messianic Spirit of Christ. 'Jesus said to them again, "Peace be with you. As the Father has sent me, so I send you." When he had said this, he breathed on them and said to them, "Receive the Holy Spirit."' (John 20:21–22)

The nineteenth century is often described as the missionary century. With the founding of missionary societies and countless stories of heroic evangelistic endeavours into unchartered places of the world, it was a time of unprecedented missionary *activity*. But the twentieth century was the century of unprecedented missionary *thinking*. It was at the International Missionary Council Conference at Willingen in Germany in the middle of the century (1952), that the full grounding of the Church's mission in the triune life and love of God came to particularly clear expression: 'The missionary movement of which we are part has its source in the triune God Himself. Out of the depths of His love for us, the Father has sent forth His beloved Son to reconcile all things to Himself, that we and all people might, through the Spirit, be made one in Him with the Father, in that perfect love which is the very nature of God.'[4] The Church's mission, there-fore, is the mission of God – the *missio Dei* – the missionary movement of the trinitarian God which creates and recreates the world through the divine Word and the divine Spirit, so that the world may share in the divine life of love. As Jürgen Moltmann was to say in the latter part of the century, 'It is not the Church that has a mission of salvation to fulfil in the world; it is the mission of the Son and the Spirit through the Father that includes the Church, creating a Church as it goes on its way.'[5] The Church is the recipient of the mission of God. We have been caught up into the life of God's kingdom by the sending of the Son and the gathering of God's Spirit. And the life of the kingdom – because it is life lived *with* Christ – is a life orientated towards the world to which Christ came and for which he died and to which he will come at the appointed time to bring salvation (Hebrews 9:28). 'Christian life', as Bonhoeffer said, 'is participation in the encounter of Christ with the world.'[6] Therefore, by virtue of being the recipient and beneficiary of God's mission, the Church is the agent and instrument of God's mission. We are saved and sent, called and commissioned, reconciled to God and ministers of reconciliation to him.

'The life of the Church depends upon its being missionary,'[7] declared the delegates to the the first International Missionary Conference – a remarkable event held in Edinburgh in 1910 that drew together for the first time people and organizations com-mitted to the task of world mission. Although most of them were members of missionary societies, they had the grace to see that mission should never be simply an activity of the Church, even less one which is franchised to organizations that do it on behalf of the Church. Mission belongs to the identity of the Church. 'The Church of the living God must arise as the great Missionary

Society', as one speaker said. It must adopt the 'Moravian ideal', exhorted another, in which the life of the whole Church is dedicated towards mission as it is in the Moravian Church.[8] The Conference was in no doubt that this would require a major reorientation of the Church's self-understanding and a thorough restructuring of its life – a work that 'amounts to nothing short of the re-creation of the Church',[9] a work that only God could do.

But it warned, prophetically perhaps at the beginning of the twentieth century, that 'The only thing which will save the Church from the imminent perils of growing luxury and materialism, is the putting forth of all its powers on behalf of the world without Christ. Times of material prosperity have ever been the times of greatest danger to Christianity.' Their diagnosis was that the incipient forces of materialism and eroding effects of secularism would prove the impotence of the Church's own capacities. Their prescription was that the Church needed to recover a recognition of its own weakness, its own *incapacity*, its own *insufficiency*. It needed something to 'throw the Church back upon God Himself'.[10] This is what mission does for the Church. Mission is a divine, mysterious work. Farmers know that while they can 'plough the fields, and scatter the good seed on the land', 'it is fed and watered by God's almighty hand'. Likewise, the Church instinctively knows that people only come to faith because the Father draws them (John 17:6) and the Son reaches out to them (John 17:25–26) and the Spirit convicts and changes them (John 15:8–11; 17:17). This is true even when the culture is hospitable towards the gospel. In an age like ours it is incontrovertible. There is so much in our culture that is contrary to the gospel and cynical of the Church. So many of society's intellectual assumptions are as inimical to the 'word of truth' (Colossians 1:5) as the predilections of popular culture are antithetical to the 'more excellent way' of love (1 Corinthians 12:31). Unless God builds the house of faith in people's hearts and minds, all our evangelistic labours are in vain (Psalm 127:1). In the early years of the twentieth century the Edinburgh Conference 'resolved that the problem of missions is the problem of the Church's faith in God: that the only solution to the problem of missions is the Sufficiency of God'.[11] The challenge for us in the twenty-first century is the same, just as it was for Paul in the first century of the Christian era – to believe that God's 'grace is sufficient for us' and that 'God's power is made perfect in weakness' (2 Corinthians 12:9).

## Missionary pastors

'Tend the flock of God that is in your charge . . . *be examples to the flock.*' This exhortation to the presbyters in 1 Peter 5 has been an underlying theme throughout this book. The ordained are signs of the deepest identity of the people of God. As priests we are paradigms of the Church, personifying and summing up the character of the Church. By virtue of our calling by the 'chief shepherd' and our commission to lead and serve in his way (1 Peter 5:3–4), we are *missionary ministers*, leaders in the messianic community. We are to embody and to demonstrate the Church's *sentness*. We are invited to share Jesus' desire for others, his longing to be in community with others and for others to be in community with him – a desire that expresses the desire of God not only for his own people but for the stranger, the unseen other, the alien other. We are called to the sort of longing in the Spirit experienced by St Siloam, a simple Russian monk who lived in the first part of the twentieth century. 'My soul grieves,' he confessed, 'weeping in sorrow for people who do not know the sweetness of a holy and softened heart. My soul burns with longing for the mercy of the Lord to be with all people, for the whole wide universe and all humanity to know how deeply the Lord loves us, like beloved children.'[12]

Much of the Church's traditional theology and imagery of the ordained ministry is rightly drawn from the pastoral epistles. It is here that we can see the pattern of the Church's common life emerge, and here that the regulative and organizing principles of Church life become clear. The predominant emphasis is on the pastor caring for the people, teaching them, building them up in the truth, overseeing their growth, leading them towards maturity in Christ. In days when the life of the Church is settled, when membership of the community is virtually coterminous with membership of the Church, and when the fundamental values and priorities of the nation coincide with those of the kingdom, it is easy to miss the missionary orientation of pastoral ministry. Not so in our own age, when the distance between the ways of the world and the ways of the kingdom are so marked, and where so many 'love not the Lord Jesus'[13] because they have not even heard of his love. In our times, the calling of the ordained to serve a missional community, tending, shaping, forming them into the messianic community into which they have been baptized, is a practical necessity.

We can be helped by the more obviously missionary imagery of the Gospels. Here the shepherd cares for the sheep – yearning for the absent and searching for the lost. As in the pastoral epistles, Jesus is always the model. But in the Gospels – no doubt because of the way they preserve and present the words of Jesus – there is a rawness and power, an energy and a passion in the example of Christ as the supreme missionary pastor. Like the totally focused figure of Christ in Passolini's film of Matthew's Gospel, who strides out to confront the world, leading his troops into battle, the Good Shepherd '*goes ahead*' (John 10:4) of his sheep, reaching out to claim those who deny him yet belong to him. He calls them into the one flock, one fellowship. 'I have other sheep', says Jesus; 'I must bring them also' (John 10:16). Like the very best shepherd he is ready 'to bring them' by 'laying down his life for them' (John 10:17). Sacrifice is never far from one who is sent. This is the shepherd who is even ready 'to leave the ninety-nine . . . and go after the lost until he finds it' (Luke 15:4) – not in order to abandon some in favour of others, but so that the lost can be found and brought home, and so that all can celebrate. 'Rejoice with me . . .' (Luke 15:6), says the missionary pastor. 'Rejoice with me' and with 'the angels of God' that the sinner has been reconciled and the Church is being completed, for what was lost is found, what is missing is now here, the absent are present, the body is restored.

Whether the weight is put on the tending of the congregation or on searching for the lost, the interweaving of the themes in both the pastoral epistles and the Gospels themselves warn us against rending asunder what God has joined together. The priest who loves to lead the Church in worship is not different in kind from the priest who longs to pioneer new ways of mission into the world. The seminal images of the priestly people of God in 1 Peter 2 hold together worship and witness, Church life and missionary activity, in one nexus of priestly existence. In verse 5 the people of God are described as 'a spiritual house . . . a holy priesthood' offering 'spiritual sacrifices acceptable to God through Jesus Christ' (1 Peter 2:5). In verse 9 the spiritual sacrifices of this 'royal priesthood' are defined as 'proclaiming the mighty acts of him who called you out of darkness into his marvellous light'. This is a proclamation by the Church before God and before the world. It includes praise of the Lord and communication to the world, song and service, prayer and action, Eucharist and evangelism. Mission begins in worship because 'it is the first demonstration before the world of our *sentness*, as we respond to God's grace in the good news of Jesus Christ'.[14] Mission extends into the world as we demonstrate before God *to his world* that we believe and trust in the baptismal faith we have proclaimed in our worship – that Jesus Christ is Lord, and that we are ready to work with all the power of the Spirit who enables us to say those words, for the establishing of Christ's Lordship over the whole of the creation to which Christ was sent. And the high calling of the ordained is to serve the people of God so that they can be truly 'built into a spiritual house', to see that the ministries are in place for the shaping and building of these 'living stones' into the worshipping and witnessing communities that the missionary purposes of God desire them to be.

Lesslie Newbigin, one of the most significant and strategic of the twentieth century's missionary thinkers and do-ers, whose influence is continuing to grow as the twenty-first century proceeds, described the 'task of the ministry' as leading:

. . . the congregation as a whole in a mission to the community as a whole, to claim its own public life, as well as the personal lives of all its people, for God's rule. It means equipping all the members of the congregation to understand and fulfil their several roles in this mission through their faithfulness in their daily work. It means training and equipping them to be active followers of Jesus in his assault on the principalities and powers which he has disarmed on the cross. And it means sustaining them in bearing the cost of that warfare.[15]

'The Local Church, the Hope of the World' is the title of a course one of my colleagues has designed and teaches to our ordinands. It is a course that has grown out of nearly forty years of ordained ministry. As well as being a tutor in a theological college, he is also rector of a large and thriving church in the south of England which seeks to be 'devoted to God, to each other and to a broken world'.[16] The vision of a renewed Church that effectively communicates the gospel by the authenticity of its life and integrity of its witness is very much what Newbigin meant in his famous description of the local congregation as the 'hermeneutic of the gospel':

> And yet I confess that I have come to feel that the primary reality of which we have to take account in seeking for a Christian impact on public life is the Christian congregation. How is it possible that the gospel should be credible, that people should come to believe that the power which has the last word in human affairs is represented by a man hanging on a cross? I am suggesting that the only answer, the only hermeneutic of the gospel, is a congregation of men and women who believe it and live by it.[17]

One of my favourite figures from the life of the Church is Aidan, the seventh-century missionary bishop. He was sent by the monks of Iona after Oswald, the Christian King of Northumbria, begged them for someone to evangelize the hard-bitten tribes of his kingdom. The godly Aidan proved to be an effective evangelist. Word and deed, a lifestyle that spoke of the gospel and a way of communicating that grew out of relationship with people were combined in this holy monk fired with the love of God. As he travelled the exposed moors of Northumberland and its windswept North Sea coastline, he always went on foot, shunning the ease and prestige of the horse, even though the king would have gladly supplied him with every aid to effective ministry that money could buy. The people he met liked that. They saw Aidan as one of them – poor. They saw something of the Christ of whom he spoke in him – one who had nowhere to lay his head, who took the form of a slave (Philippians 2:7). 'Do you love God?' he would ask the simple pagan poor that he met on his travels. If they answered 'Yes, we love God', he would say, 'Then let me tell you more about the love of God in Jesus Christ'. If they said, 'No, we do not love God,' he would respond, 'Then let me tell you about Jesus Christ and you will hear how much God loves you.'[18]

Many discovered the love of God in Christ through the Spirit-inspired ministry of Aidan. But he did not do it alone, neither did he leave people to fend for themselves in the faith. The first thing he did was to establish a community of prayer and worship, fellowship and study on the island of Lindisfarne. I used to wonder why Columba, Aidan and Cuthbert and the other Celtic monks had such a fascination with remote islands. Surely these places on the edge of civilization were in exactly the wrong places for strategic missionary advance? While on my first visit to Lindisfarne I waited in a long queue of cars for the tide to turn and reconnect the island with the mainland, I was even more bemused. But when I got up early on the next day to pray the office on Cuthbert's little inner island (which in turn gets cut off from Lindisfarne itself), I began to understand at least one reason why they chose these places so much on the edge. I had an amazing panorama of Northumberland. What better place in which to pray for the conversion of the land than here? What better place in which to contend with the principalities that grip us with fear as soon as we think about heading into inhospitable places with the story of salvation? The monastery was to be a power-house of prayer, a front line of spiritual warfare to support the missionaries it sent out 'to proclaim the mighty acts of God who called [the world] out of darkness into his marvellous light' (1 Peter 2:9).

Not only did Aidan evangelize from a community, he built communities of believers throughout Northumberland. In apostolic fashion he planted churches, grew them into communities and established their ministries so that they likewise would be self-perpetuating missional communities that would draw others into Christ's body. The missionary leadership of a priest involves much more than evangelizing individuals, and more even than equipping others to evangelize in their homes and workplaces. It involves building missional communities that 'prefigure and embody the reconciliation of the world'[19]: counter-cultural collectives of resident aliens. These colonies of heaven hold before the world a different way of living, invite individuals, households, networks of people into an alternative order of human life based not on the survival of the fittest but the raising of the weakest. These outposts of the kingdom of God mirror the risk-taking, self-sacrificing, cross-bearing obedience to the one who laid down his life as a ransom for many (Mark 10:45).

## The Rule of the Church

This sort of missionary leadership of the priest requires a deep understanding of the 'inner nature' (as the Second Vatican Council called it)[20] of the Church. In order to steer the sort of 're-creation of the Church' that the Edinburgh Conference so clearly saw as necessary at the beginning of the last century, we need to know what Dan Hardy, an architect of contemporary Anglican ecclesiology, calls the 'logic of the Church'[21] – its primary features, characteristics and dynamics. We might call it the fundamental Rule of the Church – the underlying reality which makes the Church what it is and without which the Church would lose essential marks of its identity.

The Rule of the Church is different from the *rules* of the Church. Anglicanism, like the Orthodox and Roman Catholic churches, organizes itself through a complex system of canon law. Any social body needs a way of ordering its common life. Canon law, sometimes indeed called common law, is simply how the Church at any one point in time organizes itself. For nearly five hundred years the Roman Catholic Church, wisely, has allowed its common law to be adapted for missionary purposes by the *Apostolic Faculties* – a set of permissions which freed the local bishop to change the rules to suit particular missionary situations. Even the pre-Second Vatican Council Roman Catholic Church – not exactly renowned for its flexibility and versatility – 'realised that missionaries have to be furnished with special faculties in order to be able to establish the Church and to exercise their holy calling among newly converted Christians'.[22] Here was a recognition that the fundamental Rule of the Church is deeper, richer and more dynamic than particular rules which try to express it at one point in any one place. The deepest Rule of the Church is the gospel of grace which generates communities that are *organized* around 'the apostolic teaching and fellowship' and 'the breaking of the bread and prayers' (Acts 2:42). They are *ordered* towards mutual responsibility expressed through a network of interrelated and interdependent gifts and ministries which promote its growth in love (Philippians 2:4; Ephesians 4:7–16). And they are *orientated* towards those who do not confess Christ as the Messiah, by proclaiming him as Lord and by baptizing those who 'welcome the message' with the result that 'the Lord adds to their number' (Acts 2:36–47).

Both the *Apostolic Faculties*, first promulgated by Leo X in 1521, and the visionary hopes of the Edinburgh Conference in 1910, saw mission as something that happens overseas, beyond Europe, in places where the gospel was being taken for the first time. Today, after centuries of missionary expansion and the growth of healthy life-generating churches throughout the world, and after the unrelenting erosion of Christian faith in the West, we recognize not only that mission is *from everywhere to everywhere*, but that the missionary task here in our land, on our own patch, is serious and urgent. This is leading to a new and exciting apostolic release in many churches. People are being called and sent. New positions in ministry are being constructed and financed. Systems and structures are being redesigned to begin to allow the sort of space that the Spirit needs to renew the Church's mission in our day. As Steven Croft has said, 'It's a wonderful thing to be aware of God moving in people's lives and in communities. As the apostles found in Acts 15, it can also be a wonderful thing to be aware of God moving through the committee rooms and policies of our Church in order to resource the mission in which we are called to share.'[23]

All this creates exciting opportunities and challenges for being a priest today. Whether ministering in a relatively established church situation, or in a more pioneering church-establishing situation or, as will be increasingly true for many of us, in a combination of the two, it is vital to be what Henry De Lubac calls an *ecclesiastical person*.[24] Being ecclesiastical is not about the way you dress or speak. It is not about being absorbed with the affairs of the Church. It is not about an obsession with the surface of the Church and still less a defence of the *status quo* of the Church. It is about *loving* the *ecclesia* – the people God has called and gathered, 'delighting in its beauty and rejoicing in its well-being' as the Church of England ordination service has it. It is about *knowing* the *ecclesia*, realizing that it is the 'Body of Christ, the people of God, a dwelling place of the Holy Spirit'. It is about *understanding the purposes* of the *ecclesia*, that it is 'summoned to witness to God's love and to work for the coming of the kingdom'. Priestly identity requires a deep immersion into the fundamental realities of the Church – into its 'life-principles'[25] as the Second Vatican Council puts it; into its *logic* or *code*, as the Anglican ecclesiologist Dan Hardy calls it; into its *DNA*, as the North American protestant Howard Snyder pictures it;[26] or into the *Rule of Church* as I have described it. Only then will we be able properly to improvise on the theme of the Church and to develop the sort of 'faithful flexibility' that allows us to reshape the Church for today's mission in ways which preserve its integrity and work with, not against, its *life-giving principles*. Only then, like the accomplished jazz musician, who through persistent practice and hard training has acquired the skills and understanding to work with and around the tune, will we be able to respond to the theme of God's ways with the Church:

> In the beginning the jazz. An uncontainable theme
> Spills out its tunes. Both whole and spendthrift
>
> As though full grows fuller. O insatiable Madam
> Of variations, self-fulfilling in your self-gift.
>
> Immensity of a theme just for a while unwombed
> In me. And small wonder our spoilt bodies bend
>
> Under its weight. Variations unique and subsumed;
> A music sustains us and brings us to our end.
>
> Chaos in order, order at the heart of chaos.
> Theme and overflow and all that sweeps between them.
>
> Spilling of contingency shape the ends of a theme.
> Nourish me, my jazz. Play this tune to its close.[27]

'They will know we are Christians by our Regulated Improvisation,'[28] says one writer about the Church. Improvisation involves imagination. But the imagination to perceive the shape the Church is called to be in our age, requires an understanding of the fundamental features of the form of the Church in every age.

In 1959, C. Wright Mills wrote an influential book called *The Sociological Imagination*.[29] Essentially it was a study of the intersection of individuals with society, of individuals in social setting. That is the heart of sociology. It is also the centre of ecclesiology. Wright Mills was critical of any sort of 'Grand Theory' of sociology that tries to cover and account for everything in one complete system of thought. He was equally critical of 'Abstracted Empiricism', an absorption with the particular and personal, the local and limited, which avoids the wider social context. He claimed that there is a set of 'simple viewpoints' that work for different individuals and societies, and can be imaginatively applied to different settings. A 'Grand Theory', with its tendency to pin everything down into an invariable pattern is, perhaps, the classic temptation of catholic ecclesiology. 'Abstracted Empiricism', with its tendency to focus on the problems and solutions of local situations in isolation from their wider implications is, perhaps, the classic temptation of evangelical ecclesiology. Before I took up the reigns of being a principal of a theological college, a retired priest told me that his memory of my new college was of playing and losing a game of football against it when he was training at another college – 'Our tight Anglo-Catholic formation', he said, 'was no match for their free flowing Evangelical play!' Actually, we need the best of both. We need the discipline to see what lies at the heart of the Church's form in Christ, and the discernment to work with the Spirit to help the Church move and play with the sort of speed and style, confidence and creativity, faithfulness and freedom that will enable us to 'bend it like Beckham'! We need *ecclesiological imagination.*

This priestly ministry of improvisation and imagination cannot be exercised alone. To attempt to do so is to miss the interrelationality and interdependence, the apostolicity and accountability that belong to the Rule of the Church. 'To serve this royal priesthood, God has given particular ministries' and 'Christ has given his gifts abundantly to equip God's holy people for the work of ministry,' as the Church of England's ordination service says. Presbyteral ministry is only one ministry among others and its calling to 'discern and foster the gifts of all God's people' is exercised 'with the Bishop and their fellow presbyters'. Working with the bishop, sharing together in the cure of souls, being a person under authority is not a constraint that binds us, it is a relationship that should liberate us – liberate us from the loneliness of leadership, free us from the crippling effects of discouragement, enable us to take risks for the gospel and to imagine what the Church might be in our time and place.

I once said to a bishop that some ordinands tend to think that they should keep their good ideas from their bishops, especially those that appear to sit rather loosely with some of the *rules* of the Church. His response was immediate and passionate. 'I don't see enough life. I long to see more creativity and more imagination. I want to see what is good and help it to grow and to flourish.' Bishops are called to be apostolic figures. They are *senders*. They *send* priests into the mission field and support them by helping to create the conditions for the harvest to be brought in. They want to be able to exercise their *apostolic ministry* of sending and supporting, creating space for the Church to grow, blessing and nurturing new life as it emerges. And, of course, they send us to work with the other ministries we find (and are called to nurture) in the places to which we are sent.

'Will you work with your fellow servants of the Gospel for the sake of the kingdom of God?'[30] asks the bishop to those about to be ordained. Every priest is called to be a missionary, to be what the Edinburgh Conference called a 'finely disciplined traveller'[31] for the gospel. A person who knows how to find one's way around, and who can speak the language; a person who is quick to pick up cultural variation and feel the pulse of a new place; a person who is confident enough to communicate with others who are very different, and interested enough to learn and to grow in that conversation. 'By the help of God, I will', is the reply to the bishop. We can only be that sort of person if like Stephen, the first Christian witness (*martys* in Greek) who *witnessed unto death*, we are 'full of wisdom and the Holy Spirit'. With the wisdom that is God's gift to us in Christ, we will be able to follow in his missionary footsteps, and discern the *theological history* of a community (the story of God's work among them) and announce the good news of Jesus for them now. Full of the Holy Spirit, our lives, like Stephen's, will begin to reflect the one of whom we speak. 'The missionary must be a sacramental personality, one through whom the presence of God comes to others,' wrote Oswald Chambers in his spiritual treasure, *So I Send You.*[32]

Although there may be moments when we are unusually empowered and anointed by God's Spirit, we do not instantly become 'sacramental personalities'. It happens disconcertingly slowly, almost imperceptibly, as we take successive steps in what Eugene Peterson calls 'the long road in the same direction'. It happens as we inhabit the fundamental callings to be *for God* and *for the other* that we explored in Part 1, which lie at the root of priestly life. It happens as we faithfully attend to all of those disciplines of spiritual life which, as we saw in Part 2, 'shape the priestly life' – worship, word and prayer. As we do so, the fundamental virtues of priesthood are sustained in us. We are equipped to resist the temptations of the world, the flesh and the devil, and to pastor our churches to do the same. We are strengthened to withstand the temptations of the abuse of money, sex and power, and to lead our people to stand with the poor, to seek to be pure and to be obedient to the radical demands of the gospel. This is how, by the help of God, we begin to 'fashion our own lives . . . according to the way of Christ, that we may be a pattern and example to Christ's people'.[33]

Mary, the mother of Christ, is sometimes called the first Christian evangelist: she 'set out and went with haste' (Luke 1:39) to tell Elizabeth and Zechariah the amazing news about the coming of Jesus, 'the son of the most High' (Luke 1:32). Mary can also be seen as the mother of evangelists. 'They have no wine' (John 2:3), she says at the wedding in Cana of Galilee. Her analysis of the failing wedding feast tells of the emptiness of the world – and the Church – without the presence and power of God. Her command to the servants, 'Do whatever he tells you' (John 2:5) echoes across the centuries to all who are called to serve in God's kingdom as they call to heed Jesus' parting words to his disciples at the conclusion of his earthly ministry: 'Go therefore and make disciples of all nations, baptizing them in the name of the Father and of the Son and of the Holy Spirit, and teaching them to obey everything I have commanded you' (Matthew 28:19–20).

If in John 2 Mary is presented as the mother of missionaries, calling us to see the world's need and to do as her Son instructs us, in John 21 Peter is the model missionary, the 'picture of apostolic leadership in the Church'. This first-century evangelist is

222  *The Fruit of Priestly Life*

described by the twentieth-century evangelist Lesslie Newbigin in this way:

> He is a fisherman who, however, catches nothing until he submits to the Master's instruction. When he does so, there is a mighty catch which he brings, with the net intact and as the fruit of his work, one undivided harvest, to the feet of Jesus. Then the image changes and Peter is a pastor to whom Jesus entrusts his flock. He can so entrust it because Peter loves him more than all. But then, finally, the image changes again. Peter is a disciple who must go the way the Master went, the way of the cross. He is not to look around to see who else is following. He is to look one way only – to the Master who goes before him. Ministerial leadership is, first and finally, discipleship.[34]

May we, like Peter and the first disciples, be ready to be *sent* (Mark 3:14).

# SOME CONCLUDING WORDS

Being a priest today is an immense privilege. It is a life-changing vocation that is *lived out and lived into* for the rest of our lives. In this book we have tried to explore some of the implications of this particular calling by God to be *with and for* others so that the priestly people of God can together minister the grace of God to a world in need.

As we said at the beginning, there is no one way to be a priest. The way we live our priestly vocation is unique for each of us as, with God, we shape the dance, the picture, the story, the garden that is our own expression of the fully alive human person who is the glory of God. And yet we are also inheritors of and participants in a long tradition that spans not only centuries and continents, but also the denominations into which the Church has divided over the years. It is into this tradition that we are woven, and into this tradition that we bring the unique gift of our own lives and ministry. We hope that this book has helped to set the living of this calling in a wider context of God's calling of people over the centuries, drawing together some of their wisdom and sparking off new insights for our own generation, so that we who live today can contribute to the living and lively tradition of the Church's ministry.

Our own experiences of being a priest have been very different. Although spanning two continents and several different communities, as well as our different personal stories, our experience of being ordained is united by the joy of this vocation. It is the sort of deep joy that arises from our frail attempts to follow the one who has proved beyond all measure the enduring power of love. To Christ our great high priest, and shepherd of the Church, be glory and praise for ever!

# NOTES

*Chapter 1*

1 Rosalind Brown. Copyright © 1989 Rosalind Brown. Tune: Diademata. Published in Rosalind Brown, Jeremy Davies and Ron Green, *Sing! New Words for Worship*, Salisbury: Sarum College Press 2004.

2 Rowan Williams, *A Ray of Darkness*, Cambridge MA: Cowley 1995, p. 157.

3 See, for example, Dallas Willard, *The Divine Conspiracy*, London: Fount 1998.

4 R. C. Moberly, *Ministerial Priesthood*, London: John Murray 1919, p. 256.

5 See David Ford, *Self and Salvation: Being Transformed*, Cambridge: Cambridge University Press 1999.

6 Ford, *Self and Salvation*, p. 159.

7 The Council for Christian Unity, *The Porvoo Common Statement*, London: CCU 1994.

8 *Anglican–Orthodox Dialogue: The Moscow Statement* (eds, Kallistos Ware and Colin Davey) London: SPCK 1977, p. 91.

9 Although the Anglican Ordinal is bound into the covers of the 1662 Book of Common Prayer, it is strictly speaking a separate document, which was first published in 1550 and then later revised. For these reasons we will refer to it as '1550/1662'.

10 Charles Gore, *The Christian Ministry*, London: Rivingtons 1889, p. 94.

11 Early ordination liturgies can be found in Paul Bradshaw, *Ordination Rites of the Ancient Churches of East and West*, New York: Pueblo Publishing Company 1990.

12 See Bradshaw, *Ordination Rites of the Ancient Churches*, p. 108.

13 See Bradshaw, *Ordination Rites of the Ancient Churches*, p. 115.

14 *St Chrysostom on the Priesthood* (ed. Allen Moxon), London: SPCK 1907, p. 111.

15 *On the Priesthood*, p. 150 and pp. 40–2.

16 From the Armenian Ordination Prayer, see Bradshaw, *Ordination Rites of the Ancient Churches*, p. 131.

17 *On the Priesthood*, p. 63.
18 This is from the English translation of the 'Second Typical Edition' of the Roman Catholic Rite of Ordination of a Priest.


Chapter 2

1 Rosalind Brown. Copyright © 1992 Celebration. Tune: Intercessor. Published in Rosalind Brown, Jeremy Davies and Ron Green, *Sing! New Words for Worship*, Salisbury: Sarum College Press 2004
2 See Paul Bradshaw, *Ordination Rites of the Ancient Churches of East and West*, New York: Pueblo Publishing Company 1990, p. 132.
3 J. B. Lightfoot, *The Christian Ministry*, London: Chas. J. Thynne and Jarvis Ltd 1927, p. 119.
4 R. C. Moberly, *Ministerial Priesthood*, London: John Murray 1919, pp. 258, 260.
5 House of Bishops of the General Synod, *Eucharistic Presidency: A Theological Statement*, London: Church House Publishing 1997.
6 From the Preface to *Against the Heresies, V*.
7 This is a useful expression from the Roman Catholic Ordinal that we will be quoting on a number of occasions in the rest of the book.
8 *On the Priesthood*, p. 52.
9 *On the Priesthood*, p. 54.
10 From the Church of England Ordinal, 1550/1662.
11 From the Roman Catholic Rite of the Ordination of Priests.
12 Lightfoot, *The Christian Ministry*, p. 119.
13 Richard Baxter, *The Reformed Pastor* (ed. J. T. Wilkinson) London: Epworth Press 1939, p. 82.
14 Baxter, *The Reformed Pastor*, p. 73.
15 *On the Priesthood*, p.77.
16 Alastair Redfern, *Ministry and Priesthood*, London: Darton, Longman and Todd 1999, pp. 68–9.
17 Gregory the Great, *On the Pastoral Charge* (trans. H. R. Bramley) Oxford and London: James Parker 1874, p. 87.
18 From the poem, 'Walking Away – for Sean', by Cecil Day Lewis.
19 *On the Pastoral Charge*, p. 129.
20 *On the Pastoral Charge*, p.237.
21 See, for example, Christian A. Schwarz, *Natural Church Development: A Guide to Eight Essential Qualities of Healthy Churches*, Carol Stream, Illinois: ChurchSmart Resources 1996.
22 *On the Pastoral Charge*, p. 35.
23 Sue Walrond-Skinner, quoted in Redfern, *Ministry and Priesthood*, p. 37.
24 *On the Pastoral Charge*, p. 7.
25 *On the Pastoral Charge*, p. 18.

## Chapter 3

1 Rosalind Brown. Copyright © 1996 Rosalind Brown. Tune: Gerontius.
2 From the poem, 'The Windows'. See George Herbert, *The Complete English Poems*, (ed. J. Tobin) London: Penguin 1991, p. 61.
3 Dietrich Bonhoeffer, *Discipleship*, Dietrich Bonhoeffer Works, Vol. 4, Minneapolis: Fortress Press, 2001.
4 Aelred of Rievaulx, *Treatises and the Pastoral Prayer*, Kalamazoo, Michigan: Cistercian Publications 1971, p. 105.
5 *Treatises and the Pastoral Prayer*, p. 107.
6 Moberly, *Ministerial Priesthood*, p. 285.
7 These very complementary quotations are from the Church of England and Roman Catholic Ordination liturgies.
8 Baxter, *The Reformed Pastor*, pp. 155, 158.
9 Baxter, *The Reformed Pastor*, p. 157.
10 Steven Croft, *Ministry in Three Divisions: Ordination and Leadership in the Local Church*, London: Darton, Longman and Todd 1999, pp. 112–13.
11 Croft, *Ministry in Three Dimensions*, p. 187.
12 Eugene H. Peterson, *Working the Angles: The Shape of Pastoral Integrity*, Grand Rapids, Michigan: William B. Eerdmans Publishing Company 1987, p. 48.
13 Peterson, *Working the Angles*, p. 50.
14 *Pseudo-Macarius: The Fifty Homilies and the Great Letter* (trans. and ed. George Maloney), New York: Paulist Press 1992, p. 115.
15 'A Passion for Reconciliation: A Profile of Professor Miroslav Volf', *Berkeley at Yale*, Winter 2001, No. 18, pp. 14–15.
16 From Wesley's sermon, 'The Catholic Spirit'. See John Wesley, *Forty-Four Sermons*, London: Epworth Press 1944, pp. 442–56.
17 The last verse of the Easter hymn attributed to John of Damascus, 'The Day of Resurrection'.
18 Cited by John Baggley, 'Orthodox Icons for the Easter Season' in Christopher Irvine, *Celebrating the Easter Story*, London: Mowbray 1996, pp. 72–89 (p. 82).

## Chapter 4

1 Rosalind Brown. Copyright © 1997 Rosalind Brown. Written for Mississippi; alternative tune, Blaenwern.
2 From Isaac Watts' hymn, 'When I survey the wondrous cross'.
3 Alexander Schmemann, 'Liturgical Theology: Remarks on Method' in Thomas Fisch (ed), *Liturgy and Tradition: Theological Reflections of Alexander Schmemann*, Crestwood: St Vladimir's Seminary Press 1990, pp. 142, 147.

4 George Herbert's poem, 'Love (3)', in *The Complete English Poems and The Country Parson*, p. 178.

5 Daniel Hardy and David Ford, *Jubilate: Theology in Praise*, London: Darton, Longman and Todd 1984, p. 8.

6 Hardy and Ford, *Jubilate*, p. 22.

7 *Common Worship: The Ordination of Priests, also called Presbyters*.

8 See Gordon Lathrop, *Holy Things: A Liturgical Theology*, Minneapolis: Fortress Press 1993, p. 89.

9 *On the Priesthood*, p. 148.

10 Robert Barron, 'The Priest as Bearer of the Mystery' in K.S. Smith (ed.), *Priesthood in the Modern World*, Franklin: Sheed and Ward 1999, pp. 94–5.

11 Robert Hovda, *Strong, Loving and Wise: Presiding in Liturgy*, Collegeville: The Liturgical Press 1976, p. 19.

12 Hovda, *Strong, Loving and Wise*, p. 34.

13 Hovda, *Strong, Loving and Wise*, p. 60.

14 Hovda, *Strong, Loving and Wise*, p. 31.

15 From the Church of England Ordinal 1550/1662.

16 *Common Worship: The Ordination of Priests, also called Presbyters*, copyright © The Archbishops' Council 2005. Used by permission.

17 See Paul Bradshaw, *Ordination Rites of the Ancient Churches of East and West*, New York: Pueblo Publishing Company 1990, p. 170.

18 From Luther's *The Blessed Sacrament of the Holy and True Body and Blood of Christ, and the Brotherhoods*.

## Chapter 5

1 Rosalind Brown. Copyright © 2000, Rosalind Brown. Tune: Abbots Leigh.

2 *Common Worship: The Ordination of Priests, also called Presbyters*, copyright © The Archbishops' Council 2005. Used by permission.

3 *William of St Thierry, The Golden Epistle: A Letter to the Brethren at Mont Dieu*, Kalamazoo, MI and Spencer, MA: Cistercian Publications, 1971, p. 92.

4 There are many editions of the Rule of Benedict, some with commentaries. A helpful one is Joan Chittister's *Wisdom Distilled from the Daily: Living the Rule of St Benedict Today*, San Francisco: Harper San Francisco 1991.

5 Barbara Brown Taylor, *The Preaching Life*, Cambridge, MA: Cowley 1993, p. 52.

6 Maria Boulding, *The Coming of God*, London: SPCK 1982, p. 75.

7 From *Common Worship: The Ordination of Priests, also called Presbyters*.

8 John Myrc, *How thou schalt thy paresche preche*, (trans. Geoffrey

Bryant and Vivien Hunter), Barton on Humber: Workers' Educational Association 2000, p. 52.

9 From 'The Ordination of Priests', *The Alternative Service Book 1980*, copyright © 1980 the Central Board of Finance of the Church of England.

10 Ellen Davis, *Imagination Shaped*, Valley Forge: Trinity Press International 1995, p. 125.

11 Mary Grey, *The Outrageous Pursuit of Hope*, London: Darton, Longman and Todd 2000, p. 77.

12 Walter Brueggemann, *Finally Comes the Poet*, Minneapolis: Fortress Press 1989, p. 75.

13 Gregory the Great, *On the Pastoral Charge*, p. 99.

14 George Herbert, *The Complete English Poems and The Country Parson*, p. 222.

15 John Donne, 'Upon the Annunciation and the Passion Falling Upon One Day' in John Donne, *The Complete English Poems* (ed. A.J. Smith), London: Penguin Books 1986, p. 452.

16 R.S. Thomas, *Collected Poems 1945–1990*, London: Phoenix 1993.

17 *John Donne: Poetry and Prose* (ed. F. J. Warnke), New York: Random House Press 1967, p. 300.

18 P. Collinson, *The Religion of Protestants*, Oxford: Clarendon Press 1982, p. 244.

19 Herbert, *The Complete English Poems*, p. 209.

20 Herbert, *The Complete English Poems*, p 295.

21 *John Donne: Poetry and Prose*, p. 360.

22 Richard Baxter, *The Reformed Pastor* (ed. J. T. Wilkinson), London: Epworth Press 1939, pp. 136–37.

23 Baxter, *The Reformed Pastor*, p. 151.

24 Herbert, *The Complete English Poems*, p. 209.

25 Davis, *Imagination Shaped*, p. 170.

## Chapter 6

1 Rosalind Brown, copyright © 1997 Rosalind Brown. Written for St Helena, alternative tunes: In Babilone, Nettleton. Published in Rosalind Brown, Jeremy Davies and Ron Green, *Sing! New Words for Worship*, Salisbury: Sarum College Press 2004.

2 A survey by the Crusade for World Revival and the Evangelical Alliance (published in 1996 as *Leaders Under Pressure* by Colin Buckland and John Earwicker) found that 88% of pastors surveyed said that they wanted to be a person of prayer. This was second only to being a preacher, which 90% said they wanted to be. 86% of congregations surveyed said that they wanted their pastor to be a person of prayer

(following 94% answering 'pastor' and 90% answering 'preacher').
When asked what they do, only 40% of pastors answered 'pray', and
when the priorities that pastors set for themselves were set alongside
what they actually report doing, prayer was the aspect of ministry where
practice fell furthest from aspiration. The authors of the survey note
'these figures highlight the problem of prayer within Christian ministry.
For many the vocation to ministry is shaped by prayer and by a
commitment to deepen their life of prayer. The pressures of pastoral
ministry, however, often make it very difficult to live out the life of
prayer.' This survey was conducted among churches of several denominations that are affiliated to these two organizations, and therefore
reflects a particular type of church. While the results might be slightly
different if a wider cross section of Anglican churches was to be surveyed, they are a barometer of the hopes of both clergy and churches.

3  Theophan the Recluse, in Igumen Chariton of Valamo (compiler), *The
   Art of Prayer: An Orthodox Anthology*, London: Faber and Faber
   1966, p. 51.
4  Rowan Williams, *A Ray of Darkness*, p. 82.
5  Kenneth Leech, *True Prayer*, London: Sheldon Press 1980, p. 10.
6  Michel Quoist, *Prayers of Life*, Dublin and Melbourne: Gill and Sons
   1963, p. 22.
7  The full form of his self-examination can be found in *A Scheme of Self-
   Examination Used by the First Methodists in Oxford*.
8  R. Somerset Ward, *To Jerusalem*, Harrisburg: Morehouse Publishing
   1994, p. 111.
9  Ward, *To Jerusalem*, p. 127.
10 St Seraphim of Sarov (1759–1833), a Russian Orthodox priest, spent
   twenty years in seclusion before opening his cell door to those who came
   to him for counsel.
11 R. Gill and L. Kendall (eds), *Michael Ramsey as Theologian*, London:
   Darton, Longman and Todd 1995, p. 139.
12 John Donne: *Selections from Divine Poems, Sermons, Devotions and
   Prayer* (ed. John Booty), New York: Paulist Press 1990, p. 188.
13 Gill and Kendall, *Michael Ramsey as Theologian*, p. 136.
14 *Common Worship: The Ordination of Priests, also called Presbyters*,
   copyright © The Archbishops' Council 2005. Used by permission. See
   also Habakkuk 2: 1–3.
15 Theophan, *Letter* 47. Theophan (1815–94) was a Russian Orthodox
   bishop known for his translation of the Philokalia.
16 For example, Mark 6:46; Luke 11:1 which implies that Jesus had
   'certain places' to pray, as does the account of his prayer and arrest in
   the Garden of Gethsemane since Judas knew where to find him.
17 Psalm 55:17; 92:2; Daniel 6:10; Acts 3:1; 10:30.

18 Alexander Carmichael, *Carmina Gadelica* (ed. C. J. Moore), Edinburgh: Floris Books 1992, p. 53.

19 Bonaventure (1217–74) was a Franciscan and professor at the University of Paris.

20 John Calvin, *The Institutes of the Christian Religion* (ed. J. McNeill) Westminster: John Knox Press 2001, Book 1 Chapter V.

21 Thomas Traherne, *Selected Poems and Prose* (ed. A. Bradford), London: Penguin 1991, pp. 196–8.

22 W.H. Gardner (ed.), *Gerard Manley Hopkins: Poems and Prose*, London: Penguin 1985, p. 208.

23 Benedicta Ward, *The Sayings of the Desert Fathers*, London and Oxford: Mowbray 1981, p. 103.

24 Gill and Kendall, *Michael Ramsey as Theologian*, p. 130.

25 Gill and Kendall, *Michael Ramsey as Theologian*, p. 135

26 George Herbert, *The Complete English Poems and The Country Parson*, pp. 303–4.

27 The names and some details have been changed in this, and other stories of pastoral encounters, to protect the privacy of those involved.

28 That is not to say that there has to be praise in the midst of lament: the time for praise may not come until much later. In this instance, the decision had been made to follow this psalmist's lead.

## Chapter 7

1 Rosalind Brown. Copyright © 2001 Rosalind Brown. Tune: Jerusalem. Published in Rosalind Brown, Jeremy Davies and Ron Green, *Sing! New Words for Worship*, Salisbury: Sarum College Press 2004.

2 See *Common Worship: The Ordination of Priests, also called Presbyters*.

3 Charles Spurgeon, *Lectures to My Students*, Edinburgh: Marshall, Morgan and Scott, 1954, p. 17.

4 See Moberly, *Ministerial Priesthood*, p. 300.

5 Richard Baxter, *The Reformed Pastor*, p. 94.

6 *William of St Thierry, The Golden Epistle*, p. 9.

7 From Eucharistic Prayer B ('Order 1: Holy Communion') in the Church of England's *Common Worship*.

8 Spurgeon, *Lectures to My Students*, p. 194.

9 A. W. T. Perowne, 'Foreword' in F.W.B. Bullock, *The History of Ridley Hall Cambridge: Volume 1*, Cambridge: Cambridge University Press 1941, p. xi.

10 Baxter, *The Reformed Pastor*, 1939, p. 79.

11 Alasdair MacIntyre, *After Virtue: A Study in Moral Theory*, London: Duckworth 1992, 2nd edition.

12 Rowan Williams, *A Ray of Darkness*, pp. 114–15.

13 Gregory of Nazianzus, *Catechism of the Christian Church*.

14 Macrina Wiederkehr, *A Tree Full of Angels*, San Francisco: Harper-Collins 1988, p. 88.

15 Henri Nouwen, *The Wounded Healer*, London: Darton, Longman and Todd 1979, p. 89.

16 Society of Saint John the Evangelist (SSJE), *The Rule of the Society of Saint John the Evangelist*, Cambridge MA: Cowley 1997, p. 69.

17 *Common Worship: The Ordination of Priests, also called Presbyters*.

18 Ibid.

19 Donald J. Goergen (ed), *Being a Priest Today*, Collegeville: Liturgical Press 1992, p. 134.

20 World Council of Churches, *Baptism, Eucharist and Ministry*, Geneva: World Council of Churches 1982, pp. 21–22.

21 Jon Sobrino, *Spirituality of Liberation*, Maryknoll: Orbis Books 1990, p. 84.

22 Eugene Peterson, *The Contemplative Pastor*, Grand Rapids: Wm B. Eerdmans 1993, p. 49.

23 Thomas Morgan, 'Taking Responsibility for Hope' in K.S. Smith (ed.), *Priesthood in the Modern World*, Franklin: Sheed and Ward 1999, p. 88.

24 Nouwen, *The Wounded Healer*, p. 38.

25 *John Donne: Selections from Divine Poems, Sermons, Devotions and Prayer* (ed. John Booty), New York: Paulist Press 1990, pp. 178–179.

26 Nouwen, *The Wounded Healer*, pp. 135, 137.

27 *Common Worship: The Ordination of Priests, also called Presbyters*.

28 Catherine M. Wallace, 'Storytelling, Doctrine and Spiritual Formation' in *Anglican Theological Review*, volume 81.1 (1999), pp. 49–50.

29 Baxter, *The Reformed Pastor*, 1939, p.135.

30 Baxter, *The Reformed Pastor*, 1939, p. 133.

31 Baxter, *The Reformed Pastor*, 1939, pp. 157–8.

32 Moberly, *Ministerial Priesthood*, p. 255.

33 See 'The Form of Prayers and Ministration of the Sacraments, 1556' in R.C.D. Jasper and G.J. Cuming (eds), *Prayers of the Eucharist: Early and Reformed*, Collegeville: The Liturgical Press 1987, p. 256.

34 Baxter, *The Reformed Pastor*, 1939, p. 79.

*Chapter 8*

1 Rosalind Brown. Copyright © 2000 Rosalind Brown. Tune: Finlandia. Published in Rosalind Brown, Jeremy Davies and Ron Green, *Sing! New Words for Worship*, Salisbury: Sarum College Press 2004.

2 See 2 Corinthians 5:17–21; Romans 5:10–11; Ephesians 2:13–16; Colossians 1:19–22 for some of the New Testament understanding of

God's reconciliation.

3 Miroslav Volf, *Exclusion and Embrace*, Nashville: Abingdon 1996, p. 129.

4 Volf, *Exclusion and Embrace*, p. 126.

5 Paul Fiddes, *Participating in God: A Pastoral Doctrine of the Trinity*, London: Darton, Longman and Todd 2000, p. 193.

6 Benedicta Ward, *The Sayings of the Desert Fathers*, London and Oxford: Mowbray 1981, p. 150.

7 See Gabe Huck (ed), *A Sourcebook About Liturgy*, Chicago: Liturgy Training Publications 1995, p. 166.

8 Volf, *Exclusion and Embrace*, p. 130.

9 *Common Worship: The Ordination of Priests, also called Presbyters.*

10 George Herbert, *The Complete English Poems and The Country Parson*, p. 225.

11 Richard Hooker, *Of the Laws of Ecclesiastial Polity, Book VI*, (1648) in J. Robert Wright, *Prayer Book Spirituality*, New York: Church Hymnal Corporation 1989, pp. 394, 396.

12 For a fuller discussion of confidentiality issues, see The Church of England, *Common Worship: Christian Initiation*, London: Church House Publishing 2006, p. 270.

13 Hamon L'Estrange, *The Alliance of Divine Offices* (1659) in *Prayer Book Spirituality*, pp. 399–400.

14 Anonymous, *The Whole Duty of Man* (1657) in *Prayer Book Spirituality*, p. 399.

15 Personal communications.

16 *Common Worship: The Ordination of Priests, also called Presbyters.*

17 *Common Worship: Christian Initiation*, p. 267.

18 *Common Worship: Christian Initiation*, p. 266.

19 *Common Worship: The Ordination of Priests, also called Presbyters.*

20 *Common Worship: The Ordination of Priests, also called Presbyters.*

21 *Christian Initiation*, The Reconciliation of a Penitent.

22 Lightfoot, *The Christian Ministry*, p. 135.

23 Michael Ramsey, *The Christian Priest Today*, London: SPCK 1972, p. 52.

24 Ramsey, *The Christian Priest Today*, p. 51.

25 Carol Gilligan's writing about the differences between men and women has stimulated others to apply her insights in the context of the Christian faith. In relation to sin, it has been noted that whilst men are likely to name pride as a besetting sin, for women it may not be pride but the refusal or inability to assert themselves appropriately that is the greater (often unnamed) sin. See C. Gilligan, *In a Different Voice*, Cambridge MA: Harvard University Press 1993.

26 From the 'Second Book of Homilies', quoted in *Prayer Book Spirituality*, pp. 378ff.

27 From *Common Worship: The Ordination of Priests, also called Presbyters.*
28 John Jewel, 'An Apology of the Church of England', quoted in *Prayer Book Spirituality*, p. 386.
29 Joan Chittister at Aliquippa, PA, December 1993.
30 Phoebe Griswold, 'Living the Theology of a Bishop's Spouse: Experience, Experiment and Adventure', *Anglican Theological Review* vol. 81 (1999), p. 83.
31 The United Reformed Church Moderator's Report to the General Assembly of the United Reformed Church 2000, paragraphs 2.4.8–2.4.10.
32 J. Dallen and J. Favazza, *Removing the Barriers: The Practice of Reconciliation*, Chicago: Liturgy Training Publications 1991, p. 69.
33 Kathleen Hughes, 'Reconciliation – Cultural and Christian Perspectives' in R. J. Kennedy (ed), *Reconciliation: The Continuing Agenda*, Collegeville: The Liturgical Press 1987, pp. 125–6.
34 Elsa Tamez, *The Amnesty of Grace: Justification by Faith from a Latin American Perspective*, Nashville: Abingdon Press 1993, p. 20.
35 *The Kairos Document,* CIIR/BCC, 1985, p. 9. Later these theologians concluded that, in the context of the new South Africa, reconciliation and healing required the approach that became enshrined in the Truth and Reconciliation Commission.
36 Tamez, *The Amnesty of Grace*, pp. 131, 133.
37 Elsa Tamez at Sarum College. May 2001.
38 The story was told by his daughter, Susan Cole King, in her sermon at the Lambeth Conference Eucharist, organised by the Japanese Bishops, on the Feast of the Transfiguration (Hiroshima Day) 1998.
39 Herbert, *The Complete English Poems*, p. 235.
40 Gill and Kendall, *Michael Ramsey as Theologian*, p. 58.
41 Herbert, *The Complete English Poems*, p. 219.
42 Helpful advice for those preparing to make their confession can be found in Martin Smith's book, *Reconciliation: Preparing for Confession in the Episcopal Church,* Cambridge: Cowley 1985.
43 Donald J. Goergen (ed), *Being a Priest Today*, Collegeville: Liturgical Press 1992, p. 17.
44 Rosalind Brown, Copyright © 2000 Rosalind Brown.

*Chapter 9*

1 Rosalind Brown. Copyright © 1998 Celebration. Tune: written for Hyfrydol, published with Helvellyn. Published in Rosalind Brown, Jeremy Davies and Ron Green, *Sing! New Words for Worship*, Salisbury: Sarum College Press 2004.
2 John of the Cross, *The Living Flame of Love*, London: Fount Paperbacks 1995, p. 163.

3 Gary Dorsey, *Congregation*, London: Penguin 1995, pp. 9, 195, 25.

4 Macrina Wiederkehr, *A Tree Full of Angels*, San Francisco: HarperCollins 1988, p. 135.

5 Gill and Kendall, *Michael Ramsey as Theologian*, p. 129.

6 Julian of Norwich, *Revelations of Divine Love*, London: Penguin 1966, p. 67.

7 *Revelations of Divine Love*, pp. 67, 68.

8 Mary Coelho, 'When You Can't Pray' in D. L. Fleming (ed), *The Christian Ministry of Spiritual Direction*, St Louis: Review for the Religious 1988, p. 308.

9 Jenny Roberston (ed), *Praying with the English Mystics*, London: Triangle 1990, p. 126.

10 Fr Dimitru Staniloae, *Orthodoxy, Life in the Resurrection*, London: Eastern Churches Review 1969, p. 374.

11 P. Evdokimov, 'La sacerdoce universel des laics dans la tradition orientale' in L.A. Elchinger, *L'Eglise en Dialogue*, Paris, 1962, pp. 39–40.

12 Augustine, *Confessions*, Book VIII.

13 Thomas Traherne, *Selected Poems and Prose* (ed. A. Bradford), London: Penguin 1991, pp. 260–1.

14 Eugene Peterson, *The Contemplative Pastor*, pp. 5–6.

15 Peterson, *The Contemplative Pastor*, p. 60.

16 Margaret Guenther, *Holy Listening*, London: Darton, Longman and Todd 1992

17 Carolyn Humphreys, *From Ash to Fire*, New Rochelle: New City Press 1992, p. 154.

18 W.H. Gardner (ed.), *Gerard Manley Hopkins: Poems and Prose*, London: Penguin 1985, p. 144.

19 W. J. Grisbrooke (ed), *The Spiritual Counsels of Fr John of Kronstadt*, London: James Clarke 1967, p. 183.

20 Ellen Davis, *Imagination Shaped*, Valley Forge: Trinity Press International 1995, p. 250.

21 Barbara Brown Taylor, *The Preaching Life*, Cambridge MA: Cowley 1993, p. 18.

22 Kallistos Ware, *The Orthodox Way*, Crestwood: St Vladimir's Seminary Press 1998, p. 87.

23 Staniloae, *Orthodoxy, Life in the Resurrection*, p. 371.

24 Lesser Vespers, Tone 4 on the Transfiguration.

25 Dietrich Bonhoeffer, *Life Together*, London: SCM Press 1954, p. 75.

26 *Ascetical Homilies*, 65.

27 Urban T. Holmes, *The Priest in Community*, New York: Seabury Press 1978, p. 88.

28 The experience at the funeral is behind this extract from a poem about the church which was written some years later.

## Chapter 10

1 Rosalind Brown. Copyright © 2003, tune: Fulda. Published in Rosalind Brown, Jeremy Davies and Ron Green, *Sing! New Words for Worship*, Salisbury: Sarum College Press 2004.

2 Darrell L. Guder, *The Continuing Conversion of the Church*, Grand Rapids, Michigan / and Cambridge, England: Eerdmans 2000, p. 207.

3 From *Common Worship: The Ordination of Priests, also called Presbyters*.

4 Quoted in Tormod Engelsviken, *Missio Dei*: 'The Understanding and Misunderstanding of a Theological Concept in European Churches and Missiology', *International Review of Mission* 92 (2003), pp. 481–97, 482.

5 *The Church in the Power of the Spirit: A Contribution to Messianic Ecclesiology*, London: SCM Press 1977, p. 64.

6 Dietrich Bonhoeffer, *Ethics*, London: SCM Press 1963, p. 110.

7 W. H. T. Gairdner, *'Edinburgh 1910': An Account and Interpretation of the World Missionary Conference*, Edinburgh and London: Oliphant, Anderson and Ferrier 1910, p. 90.

8 Gairdner, *'Edinburgh 1910'*, pp. 240–41.

9 Gairdner, *'Edinburgh 1910'*, p. 241.

10 Gairdner, *'Edinburgh 1910'*, p. 89.

11 Gairdner, *'Edinburgh 1910'*, p. 264.

12 Archimandrite Sophrony, *Saint Silouan the Athonite*, Maldon, Essex: Stavropegic Monastery of St John the Baptist 1991, p. 385.

13 From the Introduction to the traditional Nine Lessons and Carols Service.

14 Guder, *Continuing Conversion of the Church*, p. 155.

15 Lesslie Newbigin, *The Gospel in a Pluralist Society*, London: SPCK 1989, p. 238.

16 The strapline of St Saviour's Guildford, Diocese of Guildford, Church of England.

17 Newbigin, *Gospel in a Pluralist Society*, p. 227.

18 For an account of Aidan's ministry see Bede, *Ecclesiastical History of the English People*, London: Penguin 1990.

19 Richard Hayes, quoted in Guder, *Continuing Conversion of the Church*, p. 58.

20 'Dogmatic Constitution on the Church (*Lumen Gentium*)' in W. M. Abbott (ed.), *The Documents of Vatican II*, London: Geoffrey Chapman 1967.

21 See Daniel W. Hardy, *Finding the Church*, London: SCM Press 2001.

22 See J. de Reeper, *A Missionary Companion: A Commentary on the Apostolic Faculties*, Dublin: Browne and Nolan 1952, p. 1.

23 Steven Croft, 'The Pioneers are Coming', *Church of England Newspaper*, 3 February 2006, p. 11.

24 Henri De Lubac, *The Splendour of the Church*, London: Sheed and

Ward 1956. De Lubac takes as his inspiration the words of the third-century theologian, Origen: 'For myself, I desire to be truly ecclesiastic', quoted on p. 76.

25 See Abbott (ed.), 'Dogmatic Constitution on the Church (*Lumen Gentium*)'.

26 Howard A. Snyder, *Decoding the Church: Mapping the DNA of Christ's Body*, Grand Rapids, Michigan: Baker Books 2002.

27 Micheal O'Siadhail, 'Madam', in *Our Double Time*, Newcastle upon Tyne: Bloodaxe Books 1998, p. 93.

28 Mary McClintock Fulkerson, '"They will know we are Christians by our Regulated Improvisation": Ecclesial Hybridity' in Graham Ward (ed.), *The Blackwell Companion to Post-Modern Theology*, Oxford: Blackwell 2001, pp. 265–9.

29 C. Wright Mills, *The Sociological Imagination*, Oxford: Oxford University Press 1959.

30 From *Common Worship: The Ordination of Priests, also called Presbyters*.

31 From the Commission Report in Gairdner, '*Edinburgh 1910*', p. 230.

32 Oswald Chambers, *So I Send You: A Series of Missionary Studies*, London: Simpkin, Marshall 1934, second edition, p. 165.

33 From *Common Worship: The Ordination of Priests, also called Presbyters*.

34 Newbigin, *Gospel in a Pluralist Society*, p. 241.